A RHETORIC OF

BOURGEOIS REVOLUTION

D1478189

A BOOK IN THE SERIES

BICENTENNIAL REFLECTIONS ON THE FRENCH REVOLUTION

General Editors: Keith Michael Baker, Stanford University
Steven Laurence Kaplan, Cornell University

A RHETORIC OF
BOURGEOIS REVOLUTION
The Abbé Sieyes and *What Is the Third Estate?*

William H. Sewell, Jr.

DUKE UNIVERSITY PRESS

Durham and London

1994

© 1994 Duke University Press
All rights reserved
Printed in the United States of America on acid-free paper ∞
Typeset in Garamond No. 3 by Keystone Typesetting, Inc.
Library of Congress Cataloging-in-Publication Data
appear on the last printed page of this book.

To my mother,
Elizabeth Shogren Sewell

CONTENTS

EDITORS' INTRODUCTION

N PARIS, IN THIS SYMBOLIC NIGHT OF 14 JULY, NIGHT OF fervor and of joy, at the foot of the timeless obelisk, in this Place de la Concorde that has never been more worthy of the name, [a] great and immense voice . . . will cast to the four winds of history the song expressing the ideal of the five hundred Marseillais of 1792." The words, so redolent in language and tone of the instructions for the great public festivals of the French Revolution, are those of Jack Lang, French Minister of Culture, Communications, Great Public Works, and the Bicentennial. The text is that of the program for the grandiose opera-parade presenting "a Marseillaise for the World," the internationally televised spectacle from Paris crowning the official celebration of the bicentennial of the French Revolution.

The minister's language was aptly fashioned to the occasion. It was well chosen to celebrate Paris as world-historical city—joyous birthplace of the modern principles of democracy and human rights—and the Revolution of 1789 as the momentous assertion of those universal human aspirations to freedom and dignity that have transformed, and are still transforming, an entire world. It was no less well chosen to leap over the events of the Revolution from its beginning to its end, affirming that the political passions engendered by its momentous struggles had finally ceased to divide the French one from another.

The spectacle on the Place de la Concorde exemplified the un-avowed motto of the official bicentennial celebration: "The Revolution is over." Opting for a celebration consonant with the predominantly centrist, consensualist mood of the French in the late 1980s, the presidential mission charged with the organization of the bicentennial celebrations focused on the values which the vast majority of French citizens of all political persuasions underwrite—the ideals exalted in the Declaration of the Rights of Man. It offered the nation—and the world—the image of a France finally at peace with itself: a people secure in the tranquil enjoyment of the human rights that constitute France's true revolutionary patrimony, confident in the maturity of French institutions and their readiness to meet the challenges and opportunities of a new European order, firm in the country's dedication to securing universal respect for the democratic creed it claims as its most fundamental contribution to the world of nations. No hint of subsequent radicalization, no echo of social conflict, no shadow of the Terror could mar this season of commemoration. It followed that the traditional protagonists and proxies in the great debate over the Revolution's character and purposes, Danton and Robespierre, were to be set aside. The hero for 1989 was Condorcet: savant, philosopher, reformer, "moderate" revolutionary, victim of the Revolution he failed to perfect and control.

But the Revolution—ambiguous, complex, subversive as it remains, even after two hundred years—still proved refractory to domestication. Not even the solemn bicentennial spectacle on the night of 14 July was sheltered from certain treacherous counterpoints. Spectators watching the stirring parade unfold down the Champs-Élysées toward the Place de la Concorde already knew that this same route would shortly be followed by participants in a counterrevolutionary commemoration returning a simulacrum of the guillotine to its most notorious revolutionary site. These spectators were moved by the poignant march of Chinese youths pushing their bicycles in evocation of the recent massacre in Tienanmen Square, even as this brutal silencing of demands for human rights was being justified in Beijing as reluctant defense of the Revolution against dangerous counterrevolutionary elements. The spectators were stirred by Jessye Norman's heroic rendition of the *Marseillaise,* even as it reminded all who cared to attend to its words that this now universal chant of liberation was also a ferocious war song calling for the letting of the "impure blood" of the enemy. On the very day of the parade a politely exasperated Margaret Thatcher, publicly contesting the French claim to the paternity of the Rights of Man and insisting on the identity of Revolution with Terror, reminded the world of the jolting equation, $1789 = 1793$. For their part, the performers sent by the USSR to march in the parade, garbed in dress more Russian than Soviet, raised questions about the socialist axiom that the Russian Revolution was the necessary conclusion to the French. As men and women throughout the communist world rallied for human rights, was it any longer possible to see 1917 as the authentic future of 1789?

The tensions and contradictions of commemoration have their own political and cultural dynamic, but they are nourished by the tensions and contradictions of historical interpretation. If the Revolution has been declared over in France, its history is far from terminated—either there or elsewhere. Indeed, the bicentennial of the French Revolution has reopened passionate historiographical debates over its meaning that began with the Revolution itself. As early as September 1789, readers of the *Révolutions de Paris*—one of the earliest and most widely read of the newspapers that were to play so powerful a role in shaping the revolutionary consciousness—were demanding "a historical and political picture of everything that has happened in France since the first Assembly of Notables," to be offered as a means of explaining the nature of "the astonishing revolution that has just taken place." Observers and participants alike sought from the outset to grasp the causes, nature, and effects of these remarkable events. And if they concurred on the momentous character of the Revolution, they differed vehemently on its necessity, its means, its fundamental mission. Burke and Paine, Barnave and de Maistre, Condorcet and Hegel were only among the first in a dazzling succession of thinkers who have responded to the need to plumb the historical identity and significance of a phenomenon that has seemed from its very beginning to demand, yet defy, historical comprehension.

This rich tradition of political-philosophical history of the Revolution, which resounded throughout the nineteenth century, was muted and profoundly modified in the wake of the centennial celebrations. In France, 1889 inaugurated a new age in revolutionary historiography dedicated to that marriage between republicanism and positivism that underlay the very creation of the Third Republic.

This marriage gave birth, within the university, to the new Chair in the History of the French Revolution at the Sorbonne to which Alphonse Aulard was elected in 1891. From this position, occupied for more than thirty years, Aulard directed the first scholarly journal devoted to the study of the Revolution, presided over the preparation and publication of the great official collections of revolutionary documents, and formed students to spread the republican-positivist gospel. He established and institutionalized within the university system an official, putatively scientific history: a history dedicated to discovering and justifying, in the history of the Revolution, the creation of those republican, parliamentary institutions whose promise was now finally being secured in more felicitous circumstances. Danton, the patriot determined in 1793 to institute the emergency government of the Terror to save the Republic in danger, but opposed in 1794 to continuing it once that danger had eased, became the hero of Aulard's French Revolution.

Given his institutional authority, his posture as scientific historian, and his engaged republicanism, Aulard was able to marginalize conservative interpretations of the Revolution, ridiculing the amateurism of Hippolyte Taine's frightened account of its origins in the philosophic spirit and culmination in the horrors of mass violence, and dismissing, as little more than reactionary ideology, Augustin Cochin's analysis of the genesis and implications of Jacobin sociability. Within the university, the revolutionary heritage became a patrimony to be managed, rather than merely a creed to be inculcated. But this did not preclude bitter divisions over the manner in which that patrimony was to be managed, or its now sacred resources deployed. Aulard's most talented student, Albert Mathiez, became his most virulent critic. The rift was more than an oedipal conflict over the republican mother, Marianne. Mathiez questioned Aulard's scientific methods; but above all, he detested his mentor's Dantonist moderation. As an alternative to an opportunistic, demagogic, and traitorous Danton, he offered an Incorruptible, Robespierre, around whom he crafted a popular, socialist, and Leninist reading of the Revolution. The Bolshevik experience reinforced his Robespierrism, investing it with a millennial hue, and stimulated him to undertake his most original work on the "social movement" of the Terror. Thereafter the relationship between the Russian Revolution and the French Revolution, between 1917 and 1793, haunted the Marx-ianized republican interpretation to which Mathiez devoted his career.

Although Mathiez was denied Aulard's coveted chair, he taught in the same university until his early death. His exact contemporary, Georges Lefebvre, shared much of his political sensibility and his interest in history from below, and succeeded him as president of the Society for Robespierrist Studies. Lefebvre's election to the Sorbonne chair in 1937 proved decisive for the consolidation, and indeed the triumph, of a social interpretation of the French Revolution based on the principles of historical materialism. More sociological than Mathiez in his approach, and more nuanced in his judgments, he broke fresh ground with his monumental work on the peasants (whose autonomy and individuality he restituted) and his subsequent studies of social structure; and he rescued important issues from vain polemics. His rigor, his pedagogical talent, and the muted quality of his Marxism—most effectively embodied in the celebrated study of 1789 he published for the sesquicentennial of the French Revolution in 1939—earned him, his chair, and the interpretation he promoted worldwide prestige. After 1945, and until his death in 1959, he presided over international research in the field as director of his Institute for the History of the French Revolution at the Sorbonne. Under Lefebvre's aegis, the Marxianized republican interpretation of the French Revolution became the dominant paradigm of revolution-ary historiography in France following the Second World War; and it was largely adopted, from the French leaders in the field, by the growing number of historians specializing in the subject who became so striking a feature of postwar academic expansion, particularly in English-speaking countries.

Lefebvre conveyed his mantle of leadership to his student, Albert Soboul, who succeeded to the Sorbonne chair in 1967. Soboul owed his scholarly fame above all to his pioneering thesis on the Parisian sansculottes, a work recently subjected to severe criticism of its sociological and ideological analyses, its understanding of the world of work, and its often teleological and tautological methods. But his influence far transcended this acclaimed monograph. A highly placed member of the French Communist party as well as director of the In-stitute for the History of the French Revolution, Soboul saw himself as both a "scientific" and a "communist-revolutionary" historian. Tireless, ubiquitous, and prolific, he tenaciously rehearsed the Marxist account of the French Revolution as a bourgeois revolution inscribed in the logic of the necessary transition from feudalism to capitalism. But his relish for confrontation, and his assertive defense of an increasingly rigid orthodoxy, eventually invited—and made him the chief target of—the revisionist assault on the dominant interpretation of the Revolution as mechanistic, reductive, and erroneous.

Challenges to the hegemony of the Sorbonne version of the history of the French Revolution were offered in the late 1950s and early 1960s by Robert Palmer's attempt to shift attention toward the democratic politics of an Atlantic Revolution and, more fundamentally, by Alfred Cobban's frontal assault on the methodological and political assumptions of the Marxist interpretation. But such was the power of the scholarly consensus that, condemned more or less blithely in Paris, these works drew relatively little immediate support. Not until the late 1960s and early 1970s did the revisionist current acquire an indigenous French base, both intellectual and institutional. The charge was led by François Furet, who left the Communist party in 1956 and has subsequently gravitated toward the liberal political center. One of the first French historians to become intimately familiar with Anglo-American scholarship (and with American life more generally), Furet served as the third president of the École des Hautes Études en Sciences Sociales, accelerating its development into one of Europe's leading centers for research in the social sciences and humanities—and a formidable institutional rival to the Sorbonne. Disenchanted with Marxism, he also turned away from the *Annales* tradition of quantitative social and cultural history vigorously espoused in his earlier work. For the past fifteen years he has sustained a devastating critique of the Jacobin-Leninist "catechism," redirecting scholarly attention to the dynamics of the Revolution as an essentially political and cultural phenomenon; to the logic, contradictions, and pathos of its invention of democratic sociability; to its fecundity as a problem for the political and philosophical inquiries of the nineteenth century upon whose inspiration he insists historians must draw.

It is one of the great ironies of revolutionary historiography, then, that whereas the centennial of the Revolution inaugurated the consolidation of the official republican exegesis, so the bicentennial has marked the disintegration of its Marxist descendant. The field of inquiry is now more open, more fluid, more exciting than it has been for many decades. By the same token, it is also shaped by concerns and sensibilities deriving from recent changes and experiences. These latter are many and varied. Any comprehensive list would have to include the eclipse of Marxism as an intellectual and political force; the dramatic decline in the fortunes of communism, especially in France; the resurgence of liberalism in the West, with its rehabilitation of the market as model and morality, asserting the intrinsic connection between political liberty and laissez-faire; the dramatic shifts in the East from Gulag to glasnost and perestroika, from Maoism to Westernization, with their oblique and overt avowals of communist failure and ignominy extending from Warsaw to Moscow to Beijing. But such a list could not omit the memory of the Holocaust and the traumas of decolonization among colonized and colonizers alike, from the Algerian War to the sanguinary horrors of Polpotism. It would have to include the stunning triumph and the subsequent exhaustion of the *Annales* paradigm, with its metaphor of levels of determination privileging a long-run perspective and quantitative techniques; the emergence of a new cultural history, pluralistic and aggressive, fueled by diverse disciplinary and counter-disciplinary energies; the striking development of the École des Hautes Études en Sciences Sociales as counterweight to the traditional French university; and the efflorescence of a tradition of French historical studies outside France whose challenge to Parisian hegemony in the field can no longer be ignored. Neither could it neglect the dramatic eruption of the revolutionary imagination in the events of 1968, and the new radical politics of race, sex, and gender that have become so profound a preoccupation in subsequent decades.

The implications of this new situation for the study of the French Revolution are profound. Many fundamental assumptions, not only about the Revolution itself but about how to study it, have been called into question. Though the Revolution is better known today than ever before, the collapse of the hegemonic structure of learning and interpretation has revealed egregious blind spots in what has hitherto counted for knowledge and understanding. While the republican-Marxist view innovated in certain areas, it sterilized research in many others. Today it is no longer possible to evoke complaisantly the bourgeois character of the Revolution, either in terms of causes or effects; the roles, indeed the very definition, of other social actors need to be reexamined. A rehabilitated political approach is avidly reoccupying the ground of a social interpretation in serious need of reformulation. Questions of ideology, discourse, gender, and cultural practices have surged to the forefront in fresh ways. Fewer and fewer historians are willing to accept or reject the Revolution "en bloc," while more and more are concerned with the need to fathom and connect its multiple and contradictory components. The Terror has lost the benefit of its relative immunity and isolation. And despite extravagant and often pathetic hyperbole, the Right has won its point that the Vendée in particular—and the counterrevolutionary experience in general—require more probing and balanced treatment, as do the post-Thermidorian terrors. Finally, there is a widespread sense that the narrow periodization of Revolutionary studies must be substantially broadened.

When the bicentennial dust settles, there will therefore be much for historians of the French Revolution to do. Many questions will require genuinely critical research and discussion, searching reassessment, vigorous and original synthesis. Our ambition in editing these Bicentennial Reflections on the French Revolution is to contribute to this endeavor. In organizing the series, which will comprise twelve volumes, we have sought to identify fundamental issues and problems—problems that have hitherto been treated in fragmentary fashion; issues around which conventional wisdom has disintegrated in the course of current debates—which will be crucial to any new account of the French Revolution. And we have turned to some of the finest historians in what has become an increasingly international field of study, asking them to reassess their own understanding of these matters in the light of their personal research and that of others, and to present the results of their reflections to a wider audience in relatively short, synthetic works that will also offer a critical point of departure for further work in the field. The authors share with us the belief that the time is ripe for a fundamental rethinking. They will of course proceed with this rethinking in their own particular fashion.

The events that began to unfold in France in 1789 have, for two hundred years, occupied a privileged historical site. The bicentennial has served as a dramatic reminder that not only our modern notions of revolution and human rights, but the entire range of our political discourse derives from them. The French Revolution has been to the modern world what Greece and Rome were to the Renaissance and its heirs: a condensed world of acts and events, passions and struggles, meanings and symbols, constantly reconsidered and reimagined in the attempt to frame—and implement—an understanding of the nature, conditions, and possibilities of human action in their relation to politics, culture, and social process. To those who would change the world, the Revolution still offers a script continuously elaborated and extended—in parliaments and prisons; in newspapers and manifestoes; in revolutions and repressions; in families, armies, and encounter groups. . . . To those who would interpret the world, it still presents the inexhaustible challenge of comprehending the nature of the extraordinary mutation that gave birth to the modern world.

"Great year! You will be the *regenerating year,* and you will be known by that name. History will extol your great deeds," wrote Louis-Sébastien Mercier, literary anatomist of eighteenth-century Paris, in a rhapsodic *Farewell to the Year 1789.* "You have changed *my Paris,* it is true. It is completely different today. . . . For thirty years I have had a secret presentiment that I would not die without witnessing a great political event. I nourished my spirit on it: there is *something new* for my pen. If *my Tableau* must be *redone,* at least it will be said one day: In this year Parisians . . . stirred, and this impulse has been communicated to France and the rest of Europe." Historians of the French Revolution may not bid farewell to the bicentennial year in Mercier's rapturous tones. But they will echo at least one of his sentiments. Our tableau must be redone; there is something new for our pens.

Keith Michael Baker and Steven Laurence Kaplan
26 August 1989

PREFACE

I FIRST ENCOUNTERED *WHAT IS THE THIRD ESTATE?* IN 1969, when I taught the History of Western Civilization course at the University of Chicago. There, as at many other colleges and universities, we read selections from this famous pamphlet by the abbé Sieyes in the section of the course devoted to the French Revolution. I found the pamphlet exceptionally easy to teach: Sieyes's political passions touched a responsive chord among undergraduates in that now remote revolutionary age. But even as undergraduate sympathy for revolution began to flag in the 1970s, *What Is the Third Estate?* lost little of its appeal, for either the students or their teacher. It seemed that a new dimension of Sieyes's argument unfolded each time I reread the text or discussed it in class. With the help of my students, I slowly excavated the pamphlet's many-layered rhetorical structure. I began to feel that even my fellow historians of the French Revolution did not fully understand the significance of this extraordinary work of political propaganda. They usually read *What Is the Third Estate?* as a typical and readily understandable response to the burdensome inequalities of Old Regime society, as representing the common sense of the unprivileged classes of French society. I was beginning to see the pamphlet less as a passive reflection of an already existing common sense than as an astoundingly successful attempt to transform common sense, to make its readers see a familiar social and political order with new eyes. I began to see *What Is the Third Estate?* not as an illustration of the ideas and feelings that made the French

Revolution possible, but as a powerful political intervention that
helped determine the revolution's shape.

My first public discussion of the pamphlet came in my book *Work
and Revolution in France,* where I spent some six pages on its arguments in a chapter on the French Revolution's abolition of privilege. [1]
But I knew that much more remained to be said. In 1984, I was
invited to give a keynote address to the Consortium for Revolutionary History, a gathering of historians of the revolutionary era that
takes place every year in the southeastern United States. This seemed
the perfect occasion to spell out my ideas about *What Is the Third
Estate?* to a sympathetic, knowledgeable, and critical audience. My
lecture attempted to anatomize in some detail the pamphlet's master-
ful rhetoric and to show how Sieyes used it to mobilize the elite of the
Third Estate to support his political program. The scholars assembled at Duke University listened to the talk attentively and engaged
me in a stimulating postlecture discussion, making me feel that I had
at last said my piece on the abbé Sieyes. [2]

But after the session Linda Orr, a professor of French at Duke and
an expert on nineteenth-century historical writing on the French
Revolution, punctured my self-satisfaction. [3] After telling me how
much she appreciated my talk, she remarked that I had made it seem
as if Sieyes had succeeded in the impossible: consciously inventing a
political rhetoric that actually mastered the French Revolution. She
expressed some polite poststructuralist literary-critical doubts: Was
it really possible for anyone to master fully the language of any text,
let alone to prescribe the rhetoric of a revolution? Was *What Is the
Third Estate?* really as seamless as I had portrayed it? Wasn't the text
replete with gaps, fissures, and contradictions that subtly subverted
Sieyes's arguments?

Linda Orr's suggestions launched me on the project that has
become this book. I found that her questions made me look at the

1. William H. Sewell, Jr., *Work and Revolution in France: The Language of Labor from
the Old Regime to 1848* (Cambridge: Cambridge University Press, 1980), pp. 78–84.
2. This lecture was published as William H. Sewell, Jr., "The Abbé Sieyès and the
Rhetoric of Revolution," *The Consortium on Revolutionary Europe, Proceedings, 1984*
(Athens, Ga., 1986), pp. 1–14.
3. Linda Orr, *Jules Michelet: Nature, History, Language* (Ithaca: Cornell University
Press, 1976); and Orr, *Headless History: Nineteenth-Century French Historiography of the
Revolution* (Ithaca: Cornell University Press, 1990).

text in a very different way. I began to think back to quandaries that had arisen in class discussions of *What Is the Third Estate?* and especially to passages that raised doubts about two central propositions of Sieyes's argument: his apparently total opposition to privilege and his seeming espousal of political equality among all members of the Third Estate. Sieyes had equivocated about the question of the privileges of the clergy in one of his footnotes, and in one brief passage he had seemed to imply that the nation should be governed by precisely those members of the Third Estate who most closely resembled the hated nobility. Rereading the text, I began to see that these passages were more than mere slips of the pen, that they were only the most blatant signs of deep ambivalences that also emerged at other scattered points in the pamphlet. Orr's questions and my consequently deepening reading of *What Is the Third Estate?* pushed me toward a more sustained encounter with literary theory and techniques. I eventually decided to write a new and far more critical article that would simultaneously anatomize Sieyes's remarkable rhetorical achievements and ferret out the multiple contradictions that laced even this exceptionally well-made text.

By 1986 I had completed a draft of my article, but it was already dangerously long. I began to read some of Sieyes's other speeches and pamphlets, and I encountered Roberto Zapperi's newly published transcriptions of Sieyes's intriguing manuscript notes on political economy.[4] My article was growing into a book. In 1988, I taught at the Ecole des Hautes Etudes en Sciences Sociales in Paris and took advantage of this opportunity by giving a seminar on the abbé Sieyes and *What Is the Third Estate?* The bulk of the archival and library research on which this book is based was completed in the gaps between my biweekly lectures, which I wrote up longhand in my rather sorry approximation of French academic style. In the years since, I have tried to wrest enough time from a busy university schedule of teaching, research, and administration to turn the awkward French into acceptable English and to revise, refine, and extend the sometimes hurried arguments of my lectures. It is a comment on the deliberate pace of academic research that in five years, the same

4. Emmanuel-Joseph Sieyès, *Ecrits politiques,* ed. Roberto Zapperi (Paris: Editions des Archives Contemporaines, 1985).

period of time that has elapsed between the preparation of my lectures and the completion of this book, the French Revolution accomplished an entire political cycle, from the liberal revolution of the summer of 1789, through the Terror of 1792 and 1793, to the thermidorian reaction in 1794.

No scholarly work is possible without the assistance of many other people and institutions. I carried out much of the research in the magnificent collections of the Bibliothèque Nationale and the Archives Nationales in Paris. I would like to thank the Ecole des Hautes Etudes en Sciences Sociales and the University of Michigan, under whose joint auspices I accomplished much of my research and writing in 1988. I devoted several months to this study during the academic year 1990–91, which I spent at the Center for Advanced Study in the Behavioral Sciences in Stanford, California. There I was supported by a fellowship from the John Simon Guggenheim Memorial Foundation, by National Science Foundation grant BNS-870064, and by the University of Chicago. My research has also been aided by the University of Chicago's Social Science Divisional Research Fund. I have had the privilege of discussing portions of the argument of this book with audiences at the Ecole des Hautes Etudes en Sciences Sociales, at history department seminars at the universities of Michigan and Virginia, at an interdisciplinary seminar of the History and Society Program at the University of Minnesota, at seminars of the Workshop on the History of Political Theory and the Committee on Critical Practice at the University of Chicago, and at meetings of the Consortium for Revolutionary History, the Society for French Historical Studies, and the Bay Area French Historians' Group. I have received valuable comments on various drafts of the book by David Bien, Jim Chandler, Matt Ismail, Bernard Manin, Mary Ong, Ellen Sewell, John Shovlin, and Dror Wahrman.

I owe a particular debt to Linda Orr, whose interdisciplinary provocation pushed me in the right direction at the right time and who gave me a wonderfully detailed reading of the manuscript once it was finished. Carlos Forment "pretested" this book by assigning the penultimate draft to an undergraduate seminar at Princeton University and sending me copies of the brief papers that the students prepared in response to the book. I am grateful both to Carlos and to his students for this unusual and enlightening practical application of reader response theory. Steve Kaplan read the manuscript with characteristic thoroughness, speed, and zest, saving me from various errors of fact and interpretation and relentlessly pushing me to greater clarity. François Furet encouraged me to prepare the lectures that eventuated in this book for a seminar under his auspices and responded to my presentations with astute and helpful suggestions. Keith Baker read the manuscript carefully and offered valuable comments. He and I have been comparing notes and arguing about the French Revolution since we jointly taught a course on that subject at the University of Chicago in 1974. He knows how much I owe to his suggestions, critiques, and comradeship over the intervening years. In this book I take issue with some of the ideas of both Furet and Baker. I hope they will recognize that my critique is the sincerest form of homage to their pathbreaking and field-shaping work.

This book is dedicated to my mother. Through the years, her example has taught me the value of sympathetic listening, craftsmanship, and patience. I hope that some of these qualities come through in the pages that follow.

What is a bourgeois *next to a privileged person? The latter always has his eyes on the noble time* past. *There he sees all his titles, all his strength, he sees his ancestors. The bourgeois, by contrast, his eyes always fixed on the ignoble* present, *on the indifferent* future, *prepares for the second and sustains the first by the resources of his industry. He is, instead of having been; he endures hard work and, even worse, the shame of employing his entire intelligence and all his strength for our present service, and lives from work which is essential for us all. Ah! Why can't the privileged go into the* past *to enjoy their titles, their grandeur, and leave to a stupid nation the* present *with all its ignobility?*—Emmanuel-Joseph Sieyes, *Essai sur les privilèges*

1

INTRODUCTION

WHAT IS THE THIRD ESTATE? IS AN EXTRAORDINARY text.[1] It was, by all accounts, the most influential pamphlet of the thousands published in the months leading up to the French Revolution. Appearing in January 1789, *What Is the Third Estate?* was longer than most at 127 pages, and it contained some difficult philosophical arguments as well. But its scintillating style, its exceptionally clear posing of the issues, and its radical conclusions won it immediate acclaim. It probably did more than any other work to chart out the radically democratic path that the revolution was to follow in its first year. Its blistering antiaristocratic rhetoric did much to turn the commoners—known in France as the Third Estate—against the nobility. Moreover, it set forth a radical theory of national sovereignty and elaborated a revolutionary political strategy that was followed by the National Assembly when it seized sovereignty from the king in the summer of 1789.

The author of *What Is the Third Estate?* was an obscure ecclesiastic named Emmanuel-Joseph Sieyes, a canon of the cathedral of

---

1. I have used Emmanuel-Joseph Sieyes, *Qu'est-ce que le Tiers état?*, critical ed. Roberto Zapperi (Geneva: Librairie Droz, 1970), which discusses the publication history of the pamphlet and indicates all the changes introduced by Sieyes in his three editions of 1789. A facsimile of the 127-page first edition has been reprinted in Emmanuel-Joseph Sieyes, *Oeuvres de Sieyès,* ed. Marcel Dorigny, 3 vols. (Paris: EDHIS, 1989). An English translation is Emmanuel-Joseph Sieyès, *What Is the Third Estate?* trans. M. Blondel, ed. S. E. Finer, introd. Peter Campbell (London: Pall Mall Press, 1963).

Chartres.[2] The pamphlet launched him on a remarkable political career; it is commonly said that he not only opened the French Revolution by publishing *What Is the Third Estate?* and authoring the National Assembly's declaration of sovereignty in June 1789 but closed it by helping to engineer Napoleon Bonaparte's coup d'état a decade later in 1799. The pamphlet's combination of philosophical depth, rhetorical cunning, and practical importance—combined with its author's fascinating political itinerary—makes *What Is the Third Estate?* an enticing subject for historical analysis and an unsurpassable point of entry into the political culture of the French Revolution.

The Political Crisis of the Pre-Revolution

What Is the Third Estate? appeared in the midst of the long political controversy that led to the French Revolution, and it bore the marks of its time. Understanding the pamphlet requires some knowledge of the political conjuncture from which it sprang. When *What Is the Third Estate?* appeared, France had been embroiled in a deep political crisis for over two years, since the summer of 1786, when the controller general informed the king that the state was on the verge of bankruptcy. The intervening months of intense political maneuvering had failed to rescue the state budget and had succeeded only in raising the stakes. To balance the budget, the crown needed desper-

---

2. The spelling and pronunciation of Sieyes's name is a matter of some controversy. The great revolutionary scholar Albert Mathiez devoted three brief notes to the question: "Sieys ou Sieyes," *Annales révolutionnaire* 1 (1908): 346–47, and "L'Orthographe du nom Sieys," *Annales historiques de la Révolution française* 2 (1925): 487, 583. Sieyes himself spelled the name in three different ways during the course of his lifetime: Sieys, Siéyes, and Sieyes. It was spelled Sieyes, without an accent, in most of his published writings. For reasons unclear to me, the spelling Sieyès was adopted in the nineteenth century and is the most common spelling today. I am using the unaccented form Sieyes, which was the most common during his lifetime. Although current pronunciations vary considerably in practice, there is less controversy about this matter among scholars. Mathiez affirms that in the family the name has always been pronounced "Siès;" Camille Desmoulins wrote in a letter to his father on 3 June 1789 that "one pronounces Syess" (Mathiez, "L'Orthographe," and Henri Calvet, "Sieys ou Sieyes," *Annales historiques de la Révolution française* 10 (1933): 538). Although the spellings differ, the French pronunciations of "Siès" and "Syess" are identical; the English equivalent would be "See-ess."

ately to tap the revenues of the nobility, a wealthy class that was nevertheless exempt from most taxation. But the state was so weakened by the fiscal crisis that the king was unable to impose his will without obtaining some form of legal consent from the aristocracy. Many nobles were willing to pay, but not without extracting major political concessions from the crown, which over the past century had largely stripped them of autonomous power in the increasingly centralized and absolutist state.

According to traditional constitutional theory, all new taxation was supposed to be approved by the Estates-General, a body made up of representatives of the three estates of the realm: the clergy, the nobility, and the commoners or Third Estate. In fact the Estates-General had not met since 1614, and the crown had in the meantime imposed all sorts of taxes without its consent. Calling the Estates-General threatened to unleash an avalanche of stored-up grievances, as well as demands that the Estates be granted the right to meet regularly, which might transform them into something like the British Parliament. This the crown wished to avoid. A second alternative would be to submit plans for tax reforms to the Parlement of Paris, the kingdom's highest court. But the Parlement had for decades been the major locus of a liberal resistance to royal absolutism, and the crown feared a protracted battle in which the aristocratic Parlement might rally the populace to its support by championing limitations on royal power and guarantees of personal freedoms and legal rights.

Faced with these unpalatable alternatives, the crown eventually decided to convoke another institution that had not met since the seventeenth century—an Assembly of Notables. The calculation was that this body, composed of some of the most distinguished nobles and prelates in the land, would be more amenable than the Parlement or the Estates-General. But the crown's strategy backfired disastrously. The Assembly of Notables proved recalcitrant: after debating at great length, it refused to assent to new levies and asserted the authority of the Estates-General in all matters of taxation. As the crisis deepened, the Parlement openly defied the king and campaigned for the rights of individuals and the rule of law. In May of 1788 the crown attempted to push through its fiscal reforms by dismissing the Parlement and promulgating edicts unilaterally, but this provoked revolts in several of the provinces and rendered the country ungovernable. Finally, in September 1788, Louis XVI capitulated and called the Estates-General after all.

The calling of the Estates-General was a great victory for the "patriots," who wished to limit the power of the crown and establish a constitutional government. The initial beneficiary seemed to be the Parlement of Paris. Exiled to the provinces in May of 1788, the Parlementaires returned to Paris in triumph in September. But within a few days of their return they ruled that the Estates should be convoked in exactly the same form as at their last meeting in 1614. This meant that each estate or order would meet separately, each with the same number of delegates, and each with a single vote; consequently the clergy and nobility, the two orders with extensive fiscal and other privileges, would always be able to outvote the Third Estate. This ruling turned public opinion sharply against the Parlement, which was accused of trying to turn the common victory to the sole advantage of the aristocracy.

In the fall and winter of 1788–89, an unending succession of publicists, men of letters, journalists, and intellectuals wrote pamphlets denouncing the royal administration and the aristocracy and extolling the Third Estate—which, as they endlessly pointed out, accounted not only for 95 percent of the population but for most of the nation's wealth as well. The common demand of these pamphlets was what was known as the "doubling of the Third"—granting the Third Estate as many representatives as the other two orders combined—and the taking of votes by head instead of by estate.[3] Together these would assure the commoners a voice at least equal to that of the privileged orders.

The Pamphlet and the Revolution

This was the context in which *What Is the Third Estate?* was published. The pamphlet was an immediate and spectacular success; it

3. On the pamphlet literature of the pre-Revolution, the best account remains Mitchell B. Garrett, *The Estates General of 1789: The Problems of Composition and Organization* (New York: Appleton-Century, 1935).

went through three editions in the winter and spring of 1789.[4] *What Is the Third Estate?* electrified public opinion. It was distributed and debated by various political clubs and committees that had sprung up in the heated atmosphere of the winter and spring of 1789. Its author was catapulted from obscurity to fame and became a leading figure in the Society of Thirty, which constituted itself as a kind of organizing committee for the emerging patriot party and included such luminaries as the Duc de La Rochefoucauld-Liancourt, the Marquis de Lafayette, and the philosophe Condorcet. Although he was a cleric, the abbé Sieyes was elected as a representative of the Third Estate of Paris and became one of the guiding spirits of the Revolution during the crucial summer of 1789.

The triumph of *What Is the Third Estate?* was not just personal. It also succeeded in focusing the political and constitutional debate that was raging in the spring of 1789 on the question of aristocratic privilege. Hostility to the nobles and their privileges was widespread in the political discourse of these months, but attacks on the nobility made up only one of many themes in the debate. Sieyes's pamphlet differed from most by identifying noble privileges not as one of many defects of the current political regime but as the essential source of all other disorders in the kingdom. He argued, in fact, that nobles were not really members of the French nation, but enemies. Because their privileges made them idle consumers of wealth instead of active producers, because they insisted on special privileges and exceptions to the laws that governed the rest of the nation, and because they defended these distinctions from other Frenchmen by deliberating in a separate body in the Estates-General, their interests were utterly removed from those of the nation at large. His answer to the question *What Is the Third Estate?* was that the Third Estate alone actually constituted the entire French nation, because the nobles had in effect seceded from the nation by clinging to their privileges.

Sieyes not only attacked the nobility with uncommon bitterness and acerbity; he also suggested a radical but practicable means for eliminating the nobles' privileges and restoring political power to the

---

4. The publication history is from Zapperi's introduction to his critical edition of Sieyes, *Qu'est-ce que le Tiers état?*, pp. 90–93.

real French nation. He argued that in cases like the present one, when the very constitution of the nation was at issue, the Estates-General was incompetent to act because it embodied the constitution's most blatant flaw, a division of the kingdom into a privileged aristocracy and an oppressed Third Estate. Instead, the king should have called a constituent assembly, representing equally all members of the nation, which could meet and discuss fundamental questions of political organization outside the current constitutional framework. But the Estates-General had already been called and would soon be meeting in Versailles. What might the Third Estate do under these circumstances to establish a just and proper constitution for France? Here the logic of Sieyes's argument was compelling: if the Third Estate was actually the entire nation, then its representatives to the Estates-General had the authority to declare themselves the country's legitimate national assembly in the absence of representatives of the other two orders and proceed to elaborate a constitution on their own.

Astonishingly, the representatives of the Third Estate actually took this course of action. On 17 June they voted overwhelmingly for a declaration, authored by Sieyes, in which they designated themselves the National Assembly, thus arrogating to themselves the power to determine the nation's constitution and make binding laws. This seizure of constitutive and legislative power by the Third Estate was, from a juridical perspective, the crucial event of the Revolution of 1789. It transferred sovereignty from the king to the nation and placed a National Assembly of the people's representatives at the head of the state. Although the National Assembly had seized the initiative, it was hardly secure in its exercise of power until the crown was further weakened over the summer and fall of 1789 by a series of popular uprisings—the storming of the Bastille on 14 July, a massive revolt of the peasants in July and August, and the "October days," in which the king was forced to move from Versailles to Paris, becoming a virtual hostage of the Parisian National Guard. But beginning in June 1789, the National Assembly carried out a radical juridical and political revolution and elaborated a written constitution based on the rights of man and citizen. The crucial step of the juridical revolution was taken on 4 August, when the National

Assembly abolished all legal privileges, thereby eliminating the nobility as a separate order in state and society.

Through the summer of 1789, the French Revolution would appear to have followed the script written by the abbé Sieyes in *What Is the Third Estate?* His pamphlet not only set forth the essential principles adopted by the new state—the destruction of all privileges and the establishment of national sovereignty and equality before the law—but elaborated the political strategy by which the political revolution was accomplished. We seem to be faced with a case of textual determinism, in which the arguments set forth by a political intellectual structured the course of political events.

But is such a thing possible? How could a single pamphlet have charted the course of an event so massive and chaotic as the French Revolution? It could not have done so, of course, unless it spoke to sentiments, opinions, and political visions already in circulation in the body social. In fact, virtually all of the themes and ideas expressed in *What Is the Third Estate?* were also present in other pamphlets published in the months before the meeting of the Estates-General. The abbé Sieyes certainly did not singlehandedly invent the discourse and politics of the summer of 1789. Rather, what might be claimed is that *What Is the Third Estate?* focused the chaotic debate of the pre-Revolution on certain issues and provided a coherent strategy and program for political change. Alternatively, it could be argued that *What Is the Third Estate?* did not shape the Revolution, but that the close fit between its themes and the actuality of political developments was more a sign of Sieyes's exceptionally clear understanding of the revolution's political dynamics than of his persuasive power. But this alternative interpretation seems even less plausible. I find it easier to imagine that in *What Is the Third Estate?* Sieyes managed to catch up the emotions and thoughts that were swirling around him, crystallize them into a powerful and coherent text, and then capitalize on the fame that his pamphlet brought him to push his program through the National Assembly. This would be an astounding accomplishment for a political text, but not as improbable as correctly predicting in December of 1788 how so unimaginable an event as the French Revolution might unfold.

The argument of this book is predicated on the assumption that

What Is the Third Estate? was a significant determinant of the course of the Revolution at least through 4 August 1789. It is the pamphlet's extraordinary power to shape the revolution that makes it an irresistible object of historical and literary reflection. One of the major tasks of my investigation is to determine how it was possible for the pamphlet to have had so powerful an influence. How did Sieyes deploy his arguments, and why was this deployment so successful? How much of the persuasive power of *What Is the Third Estate?* was due to the sheer logical force of his arguments? How did he appeal to his readers' emotions—their hopes, fears, resentments, and passions? To what audience did Sieyes especially address his appeals? What figurative or literary devices did Sieyes employ to harness his readers' enthusiasms? Chapter two of this book will attempt to reconstruct the rhetorical armature of this remarkable political text.

But my reflection will not end with a demonstration of how Sieyes solved the seemingly unsolvable problem of harnessing the French Revolution to his own political and ideological purposes. For although I am convinced that *What Is the Third Estate?* is a truly extraordinary work of political rhetoric and that its effects on the course of the French Revolution were profound, there are good reasons to doubt that any text, however brilliant, could become an unambiguous instrument of its author's intentions and then serve as an authoritative recipe for putting them into practice. After establishing the pamphlet's sources of rhetorical power, I will go on to examine some of the ambiguities and contradictions of the pamphlet and its sometimes paradoxical relation to what we can reconstruct of its author's political intentions. A closer examination of the polished surface of *What Is the Third Estate?* reveals some small but extremely deep fissures, whose exploration I believe will illuminate not only the political and ideological dynamics of the French Revolution but the powers and limitations of political language more generally.

Who Was the Abbé Sieyes?

This book is by no means a biographical study, but it must say something of the life and career of the abbé Sieyes. Sieyes figured centrally in revolutionary history; his most recent biographer, Jean-

Denis Bredin, dubs him "the key to the French Revolution."[5] Although the implication that Sieyes's career can unlock the Revolution's mysteries is surely hyperbolic, there is no question that he was a crucial actor in both opening and closing the political drama that unfolded in France between 1789 and 1799. He helped open it by publishing his great pamphlet in January 1789 and by authoring the resolution that transformed the deputies of the Third Estate into the National Assembly on 17 June. By a stunning irony of history, he also helped close it by engineering the coup d'état that brought Napoleon Bonaparte to power ten years later, in 1799.

All of this was quite an accomplishment for a man of modest origins who in January of 1789 was a little-known canon of the cathedral of Chartres. Emmanuel-Joseph Sieyes, who was forty-one at the outset of the French Revolution, was a native of Fréjus, a town of some three thousand inhabitants in Provence, on the French Mediterranean coast. His father was a minor royal official, a *receveur de droits royaux* and *directeur de postes.* Born in 1748, Sieyes was a frail boy with a precocious intellect who came from a large and far from wealthy family; he accepted a career in the church in spite of his utter lack of religious vocation because it seemed the only practical means of getting ahead. In 1765, at the age of eighteen, he entered the Seminary of Saint-Sulpice in Paris; while at the seminary, he studied theology at the Sorbonne. He was at best an indifferent student: after five years he received his first diploma in theology but was ranked at the bottom of the list of passing candidates. In 1772, at the age of twenty-four, he was ordained as a priest, and in 1774 he obtained his *licence* in theology, ranked fifty-fourth in a class of eighty-eight.[6]

Sieyes made up for his lack of zeal in theological studies by becoming an insatiable reader of the philosophes. While still a seminarian he began to fill innumerable pages with his notes and commentaries on Condillac, Bonnet, Helvétius, Grotius, Locke, Mercier de la Rivière, Quesnay, Mirabeau, and Turgot, as well as on works of mathematics, music, and natural history.[7] By the time he

5. Jean-Denis Bredin, *Sieyès, La clé de la révolution française* (Paris: Editions de Fallois, 1988).
6. Bredin, *Sieyès,* pp. 29–30.
7. These notes are available in the Archives Nationales (henceforth abbreviated AN), especially 284 AP 1 and 2. For an inventory and discussion of the Sieyes archives, see Robert Marquant, *Les Archives Sieyès* (Paris: S.E.V.P.E.N., 1970).

completed his formal ecclesiastical education, Sieyes had become a brilliant and sophisticated student of the philosophes, as is attested by the highly original *Letters to the Economists on Their Political and Moral System,* which he wrote in 1774. Sieyes went to the trouble of having this work transcribed in preparation for publication, but the fall of the reforming Turgot ministry in 1776 altered the political climate and ended his hopes of seeing it in print. The manuscript languished in his papers until 1985, when it was published in a collection of Sieyes's writings.[8]

In fact, Sieyes published nothing until he was roused to action by the political crisis of 1788, but his reading, reflection, annotation, and commentaries continued through the intervening years. A biographical note published in 1794, thought to be largely the work of Sieyes himself, explained his lack of publications:

> The dominant quality of his mind is the passion for truth, and the search for it absorbs him almost involuntarily: he is not content, once having taken up a subject, until he has deepened it, analyzed it into all its parts, and then reconstructed it into a whole. But the need for knowledge once satisfied, he remains with his notes and his analytical tables, which are intended only for himself. He finds insupportable the tidying up, the filling up of holes, and that sort of toilette, which even the authors least concerned for literary recognition [*fumée litéraire*] cannot refuse to writings destined to see the light; he has already passed on to other meditations.[9]

It was only under the pressure of immediate political struggles that Sieyes was ever moved to publish; as he put it in his biographical note, he only abandoned his usual "laziness" about publication when he was "led on by the sentiment of a great public interest and in moments when he had a reasonable hope of being useful."[10] Virtually every word he published was either a political pamphlet, a legislative report, or the text of a speech delivered in his capacity as a legislator

8. Sieyes, *Ecrits politiques,* pp. 25–43. The manuscript is in AN, 284 AP 2, dossier 10.
9. *Notice sur la vie de Sieyes, membre de la première Assemblée Nationale et de la Convention* (Paris, 1795), p. 10.
10. Ibid.

or official. Sieyes seems not to have been driven by a desire for literary fame.

In any case, his long period of reading, meditation, and writing personal notes was not wasted. As his pamphlets and speeches of the revolutionary period attest, Sieyes was a political philosopher of remarkable ability. All his works were written to influence the political events of his day; yet they are characterized by a consistency, a precision of argument, and a philosophical depth that would be remarkable for a scholar musing in his study, let alone for a harried politician reacting to the endless twists and turns of contemporary struggles. Murray Forsythe, who has written the most systematic recent study of Sieyes's political thought, claims that his "system of political ideas is superior in originality, breadth and depth to that of any of his contemporaries, not excluding such well-known figures as Thomas Paine or Condorcet. He is, more than any other, the man who articulates the political theory of the French Revolution."[11] His methodical and assiduous private meditations in the two de- cades before the revolution prepared him for a remarkable role as a philosopher-politician.

But during the 1770s and most of the 1780s, philosophical spec- ulation was a passionate hobby for Sieyes, not a career. Lacking both the private income and connections that allowed a Condorcet to pursue a philosophical career and a taste for the rough-and-tumble world of Grub Street journalism that formed such future revolution- aries as Gorsas, Desmoulins, Collot d'Herbois, Fabre d'Eglantine, and Brissot, Sieyes had to make his way in the Old Regime church.[12] This was no easy task for an ill-connected commoner, even one with the extraordinary talents of Emmanuel-Joseph Sieyes. No commoner could nourish hopes of rising to the dignity of bishop; the episcopal order was essentially reserved to men born into the nobility. As was true elsewhere in Old Regime society, advancement depended above all on the patronage of the powerful.

11. Murray Forsythe, *Reason and Revolution: The Political Thought of the Abbé Sieyes* (Leicester: Leicester University Press, 1987), p. 3.
12. On Condorcet, see Keith Michael Baker, *Condorcet: From Natural Philosophy to Social Mathematics* (Chicago: University of Chicago Press, 1975). On Grub Street, see Robert Darnton, *The Literary Underground of the Old Regime* (Cambridge: Harvard University Press, 1982).

Thanks to the untiring efforts of his father, who made the most of his local ties, Sieyes became a protégé of the abbé de Césarge. Césarge, who began his ecclesiastical career as the vicar general of Fréjus and became almoner of the king's oratory in Versailles in 1769, was the younger son of a marquis. Césarge eventually arranged for Sieyes to become the secretary of de Lubersac, a fellow royal almoner, also of noble parentage, who in 1775 was named bishop of Tréguier in Brittany. That same year, de Lubersac obtained for Sieyes the expectative of a position as canon of Tréguier—meaning that he would only assume the benefice when its current occupant died. In 1779, thanks to the influence of his two patrons, Sieyes was named chaplain to Madame Sophie, the king's aunt. This dignity was not destined to last: Madame Sophie died the following year, and Sieyes's position died with her. But this blow to his career was compensated for when de Lubersac was named bishop of Chartres in that same year of 1780 and named Sieyes his vicar general. Sieyes became a significant figure in the government of the diocese, handling much business for his bishop. In 1783 he became a canon of the cathedral chapter and in 1788 the chapter's chancellor. Beginning in 1786, he served as delegate of the diocese of Chartres at the Sovereign Chamber of the Clergy in Paris, and in 1788 he was named a representative of the clergy at the Provincial Assembly of the Orléanais. Although his advancement was never quite rapid enough to satisfy him, Sieyes in fact made a good career in the church and eventually secured a comfortable income.

In spite of these successes, Sieyes harbored resentments. After all, it had been only the lack of alternatives that persuaded him to enter a career in the church, an institution for whose mission he had no sympathy. He seems to have shared the antipathy to religion that was so common among the philosophes. Thus he could write, in a note probably penned during his seminary years, that "religion . . . was the first enemy of man." As a consequence of religious sentiments, Sieyes maintained, "the perfectibility of man is arrested, his efforts diverted; rather than increasing his knowledge and his pleasures on earth, these are transported and led astray in the heavens."[13] In his biographical notice of 1794, Sieyes's recollections of his entry into

13. Bredin, *Sieyès,* pp. 53–54, quoting AN, 284 AP 2.

the church inspired a passionate outcry. The young Sieyes, the notice says,

> could not help groaning about his youth so cruelly sacrificed, about so many tyrannical bonds that would strangle his sad future. . . . And how can we fail to pity that multitude of tender children . . . ! No sooner have these innocent creatures begun to count among the beings capable of cultivation than barbarous but widely applauded cares, aided by paternal prejudices, tear them pitilessly out of their natural courses, elevating them it is said: but in fact sacrificing them, without regard for wisdom, to an inhuman, sepulchral system, where the most miserable of teachers make a study of torturing them physically and morally, in order to fashion them, to tame them into the service of I know not what chimeras. [14]

According to the same biographical notice, Sieyes found religion so distasteful that he had studiously avoided undertaking religious functions during his clerical career, never having preached or taken confession. Trapped in an inhospitable profession, he made the best of it by becoming what he called an "ecclesiastic-administrator" rather than an "ecclesiastic-priest." [15]

Not only did Sieyes have to pursue a career in a church whose doctrines he found profoundly antipathetic, but he had to seek advancement within the church in the only way it was available: by attaching himself to aristocratic protectors. Juridically speaking, the clergy was a single order or estate in Old Regime France: whether born as commoners or as nobles, men were raised by their ordination as priests into the First Estate of the kingdom. In principle, their assumption of holy orders erased the merely worldly distinctions that had previously divided members of the Second and Third Estates. But in practice, noble status meant just as much within the clergy as in lay society. Advancement to high ecclesiastical office was incomparably easier for a cleric born noble than for one born common. A bright and ambitious commoner cleric like Sieyes was destined to see many mediocre sons of nobles promoted to high offices that were

14. *Notice sur la vie de Sieyes*, pp. 12–13.
15. Ibid., p. 11.

unattainable to him. Worse, because nobles occupied all the most prestigious and lucrative positions in the church, even the lesser offices available to commoners could only be reached by means of patronage. The ambitious commoner had no choice but to ingratiate himself with a nobleman, whose inevitable successes would lead to desirable benefices for his clients.

For a proud, indeed vain, man like Sieyes, this game of advancement through patronage was painful and humiliating. Some of the resentment he felt toward his patrons comes through in letters he wrote to his father in the years before obtaining his position at Chartres. In June 1773, when Césarge had failed to get him a benefice, Sieyes wrote, "My protector is consoling himself with the master stroke he has just failed to pull off. His lack of success certainly causes him less pain than it does me. If the thing had gone as he had hoped, I would have become *everything* instead of which I am *nothing*."[16] This language of "everything" and "nothing" would be echoed in the opening pages of *What Is the Third Estate?*

In April 1778, when he was still waiting for the promised benefice as canon of Tréguier and hoping for an appointment as chaplain to Madame Sophie, he wrote to his father in fury.

> My bishop has toyed with me. He is not so delicate as to render me services which he cannot turn to his own profit. His design is to make me his henchman in Tréguier. That is the only reason that could explain his blatant failure to speak for me, making me fail to get Madame Sophie and astonishing all my friends. My friends know very well that the first place vacant at Madame Sophie's was due to me. Here is the joke: in announcing that the first places to come vacant were decidedly destined for others than me, he told a story about how he had pleaded in my favor before the Princess, who seemed solicitous of me. I pretended to be duped, but the devil will not be fooled. . . . If my plan were not to assure myself at all events of the canonate at Tréguier I would have told him what I thought. Patience. I have often had someone go back on their word or promise, without astonishing me, but this time I was surprised. I thought I saw my interest

16. Octave Teissier, *Documents inédits: La Jeunesse de l'abbé Sieyès* (Marseille, 1879), p. 8.

united with his in a position that would call me to Versailles. But he has changed. . . . He has told the abbé de Césarge to relate to me a hundred things about this subject that would turn the head of a newcomer. I no more believe in those people's promises than in the predictions of the almanac. But I have the appearance of believing, because I can do no better.[17]

In a letter of the following month he added: "I depend on events and can do nothing by myself. It is my bishop's job to place me and he has nothing to offer."[18]

Such complaints were commonplace enough in the privileged society of prerevolutionary France.[19] Virtually all the major institutions of the Old Regime—the church, the army, the courts, the royal administration—were dominated by nobles, whose patronage was the key to success for impecunious provincials like Sieyes. Powerless to advance on the basis of his own merits, Sieyes had no choice but to hold down his anger and pretend to believe his patrons even when they trifled with his career. To progress from a "nothing" to an "everything" required that he remain the loyal and grateful client, subordinating his will to the whims of an aristocratic patron, who alone had the power to get him a satisfying and financially rewarding position. But his enforced passivity—"I depend on events and can do nothing by myself"—merely compounded his rage and sense of humiliation. His violent hatred of the aristocracy undoubtedly grew out of his early experiences in the French church.

If Sieyes's rise to a secure and responsible position in the church was slow, embittering, and tortuous, his political rise was meteoric. Roused by the vigorous debates of 1788, he began writing his first pamphlet, entitled *Views on the Means of Execution Which the Representatives of France Will Be Able to Use in 1789*, in the summer of that year.[20] By the time it was completed his views had already been radicalized, and he began forthwith his second pamphlet, *An Essay on*

17. Ibid., pp. 14–15.
18. Ibid., p. 16.
19. As Keith M. Baker remarks in his article "Sieyès" in François Furet and Mona Ozouf, eds., *A Critical Dictionary of the French Revolution*, trans. Arthur Goldhammer (Cambridge: Harvard University Press, 1989), p. 313.
20. *Vues sur les moyens d'exécution dont les représentans de la France pourront disposer en 1789* (n.p., 1788). This is reprinted in Dorigny, *Oeuvres de Sieyès*.

Privileges, followed, in November and December, by *What Is the Third Estate?*[21] *An Essay on Privileges* and *Views on the Means* were published at the end of 1788 and *What Is the Third Estate?* at the very beginning of 1789. By the end of the winter of 1789, Sieyes was a celebrity. He was welcomed into the salons of the capital, helped guide the electoral campaign of patriots as a member of the shadowy Committee of Thirty, and was chosen as a deputy of the Third Estate from Paris. Because the Parisian elections to the Estates-General took place later than elections elsewhere, Sieyes arrived in Versailles near the end of May, when the Third Estate was already at loggerheads with the king and the nobility.

The ordinance calling the Estates-General had granted the widespread claim for a doubling of the Third, but it remained silent on the crucial question of whether votes would be taken by order or by head. When the king opened the Estates on 5 May, he made no mention of voting methods but asked each order to proceed separately to a verification of its delegates' credentials. The Third refused, fearing that to do so would provide a precedent for voting by order. Rather than organizing itself as a separate house, it insisted that verification take place in a common session of all three orders. The nobility, which staunchly opposed voting by head, quickly declared itself organized as a separate house. But the delegation of the clergy, which contained many parish priests who sympathized with the position of the Third Estate, also put off action. Negotiations with the king, the clergy, and the nobility proved fruitless, and the situation had reached an impasse by early June, when Sieyes joined the deliberations of the Third Estate.

It was Sieyes who suggested the way out. On 10 June he proposed that the delegates of the Third take the initiative and "summon" the other orders to join them; should the others refuse, a roll call of all deputies irrespective of orders would be held, and those absent would be considered to be in default. By this action the Third Estate would,

---

21. *Essai sur les privilèges* (n.p., 1788). This pamphlet is reprinted in Emmanuel Sieyes, *Qu'est-ce que le Tiers état? precédé de l'Essai sur les privilèges,* critical ed. Edme Champion (Paris, 1888). A new edition of the Champion volume with a preface by Jean Tulard has been published (Paris: Presses Universitaire de France, 1982). The pamphlet is also reprinted in Sieyès, *Ecrits politiques,* and in Dorigny, *Oeuvres de Sieyès.*

in effect, assume the position of the nation's representative assembly, with or without delegates of the other orders. This was not precisely the action that Sieyes had suggested at the end of *What Is the Third Estate?* but it was close. There he had maintained that because the Third Estate was in fact the entire nation its representatives could simply declare themselves the National Assembly and proceed to elaborate a constitution by themselves. Sieyes's proposal of 10 June was slightly more modest in that it foresaw at least some of the deputies of the First and Second Estates joining forces with the Third. But by "summoning" the other orders and declaring that those who did not answer the call would forfeit their positions, Sieyes's motion proposed that the Third Estate arrogate to itself the power to act as the constituent assembly of the nation.

Some of the deputies of the Third were wary of the radicalism of this proposal; after some debate, an amendment, which Sieyes accepted, changed the word "summon" to the less forceful "invite." But the amended motion was passed and the roll call began on the twelfth of June. A few parish priests joined the assembly on the thirteenth, and more trickled in on the fourteenth and fifteenth. On the fifteenth, Sieyes rose again and proposed that the assembly adopt a fitting title. He suggested the clumsy and rather timid "Assembly of the Accredited and Recognized Representatives of the French Nation." A long debate ensued. The great orator Mirabeau proposed "Representatives of the People," but this was rejected because it could be read as implying that they were representatives of only a portion of the nation (of "the people" as opposed to the nobility and the clergy); the moderate Mousnier proposed "Representatives of the Greater Part of the French Nation Acting in the Absence of the Lesser Part," which was rejected for its pusillanimity. Finally a deputy suggested simply "National Assembly"—the term Sieyes himself had used in *What Is the Third Estate?* On 17 June, Sieyes's amended motion passed, and the former representatives of the Third Estate, joined by a handful of defectors from the clergy, became the National Assembly.[22] These two motions of 10 June and 17 June began the

22. This account is based on Georges Lefebvre, *The Coming of the French Revolution*, trans. R. R. Palmer (Princeton: Princeton University Press, 1947), pp. 81–83, and Lynn Hunt, "The National Assembly," in *The French Revolution and the Creation of*

decisive transfer of sovereignty from the king to the nation. At this crucial turning point in the French Revolution, it was the abbé Sieyes who led the way.

This juridical revolution of June 1789 was the period of Sieyes's greatest ascendancy. Following the victory of 17 June, Sieyes was elected to the National Assembly's Committee on the Constitution and was charged by the committee with preparing a draft of the Declaration of the Rights of Man and Citizen.[23] Although the version eventually adopted by the Assembly in September was considerably shorter and eliminated Sieyes's didactic philosophical preface, his draft was immensely influential.[24] But Sieyes's ascendancy was not destined to last. Only an indifferent orator, Sieyes had a weak voice and seldom spoke in the Assembly's debates. He was an essentially solitary figure, much respected but not a leader in day-to-day politics. Following the night of 4 August, when the Assembly abolished all privileges in a long and feverish session, Sieyes bitterly criticized the Assembly's majority for abolishing the clerical tithe. Most of his erstwhile allies found this position inexplicable—he was, after all, the nation's most celebrated enemy of privilege. In the wake of this speech, he found himself denounced as a hypocrite who cared more about his own income and that of his fellow priests than about the regeneration of the nation.

After his speech on the tithe on 10 August 1789, Sieyes never regained his preeminence in the National Assembly. Nevertheless, he continued to serve on the Committee on the Constitution, where his influence remained substantial. He was the chief designer of the momentous administrative reorganization of France, which destroyed the old, widely varying provinces and replaced them with new, equally sized units known as departments. He also played an important role in the radical reform of the clergy and was a major participant in debates on reform of the legal system. But after

---

Modern Political Culture, vol. 1, *The Political Culture of the Old Regime*, ed. Keith Michael Baker (Oxford: Pergamon Press, 1987), pp. 410–13.

23. This draft was published as *Préliminaire de la constitution françoise: Reconnoissance et exposition raisonnée des droits de l'homme et du citoyen* (Paris, 1789).

24. The profound influence of Sieyes on the Declaration that was eventually adopted is made clear in Marcel Gauchet, "Rights of Man," in Furet and Ozouf, *Critical Dictionary*, pp. 818–28.

10 August the leadership of the Assembly passed definitively to other hands.

The National Assembly finally completed its constitution for the nation and disbanded in September 1791. Because it had decided that none of its members could stand for election to the new Legislative Assembly, Sieyes retired from active politics until September 1792, when he was elected to the National Convention, a new constitutive assembly put in place after the insurrection of 10 August had overthrown the monarchy and established a republic. Sieyes was not very active in the Convention, which quickly became involved in fierce partisan battles. Although he was closer to the moderate Girondin faction than to the radical Montagnards, he voted for the death of the king in December 1792. During the ensuing period of the Terror, Sieyes said and did little. Asked later what he had accomplished during this time, he is said to have responded "J'ai vécu"—"I lived."

Sieyes reemerged as a significant political actor during the constitutional debates that followed the execution of Robespierre in thermidor 1794. Chastened by the experience of the Terror, Sieyes, who had begun by emphasizing the supreme power of the legislature, now argued above all for the importance of limiting the power of the state and protecting individual liberty. He proposed a constitutional scheme that would divide power between four distinct bodies. There would be a Government that would carry out laws and that could propose new laws that it deemed necessary, a Tribunate that would propose laws on behalf of the people, a Legislature that would pronounce upon laws proposed by the Government or Tribunate, and a Constitutional Jury that would adjudicate any complaints that laws were contrary to the constitution.[25] But his fellow legislators voted down his project and in 1795 established a new republic generally known as the Directory. Sieyes was elected to the legislature established by the new constitution and was chosen by his fellows as one of

25. Emanuel-Joseph Sieyes, *Opinion de Sieyes, sur plusieurs articles des titres IV et V du projet de constitution, prononcé à la Convention le 9 thermidor de l'an troisième de la République* (Paris: Imprimerie nationale, 1795), and *Opinion de Sieyes sur les attributions et l'organisation du Jury Constitutionnaire proposé le 2 thermidor, prononcé à la Convention le 18 du même mois, l'an 3 de la République* (Paris: Imprimerie nationale, 1795). Both are reprinted in Dorigny, *Oeuvres de Sieyès*.

the Directors who formed the executive of the republic. But Sieyes, who regarded the new constitution as a monstrosity, declined to serve and retreated into a passive and ambiguous opposition to the regime. Following the republican coup d'état of fructidor against the newly elected monarchist legislative majority, in September 1797 Sieyes was named president of the republic's lower house, the Council of Five Hundred. This time he agreed to serve. In 1798 he was named ambassador to Prussia. In 1799 he returned to Paris and became a member of the Directory. Later that year, he helped to engineer the coup d'état that brought to power the young general Napoleon Bonaparte—who quickly gained effective control of the state and within a few years officially ended the Republic, establishing himself as emperor. Sieyes failed to retain any significant influence under Napoleon, although he was appointed to the Senate and became a count of the Empire. With the defeat of Napoleon in 1814, he was exiled to Belgium. He returned to France shortly after the Revolution of 1830 and died in Paris in 1836 at the age of 88.

An Enigmatic Personality

The man who led this remarkable life left behind a reputation for inscrutability. Little is known about his private life. He seems to have lived simply and to have shunned company. He never married, even after formally renouncing the ecclesiastical condition in 1792. In an era when scandalous journalism was rife and lecherous abbés were common, no rumors circulated about his sexual life. In this respect, at least, he was perhaps better suited to a clerical career than he recognized. His papers contain much information about his reading and his intellectual pursuits but almost nothing about his personal relations. He seldom shared his opinions with others and seems to have held most of humanity in disdain.

Even some of his closest associates regarded him as cold and vain. Talleyrand remarked that "Men are in his eyes chess-pieces to be moved. . . . They occupy his mind but say nothing to his heart." Barras, who served with Sieyes in several legislative bodies, pictured him as supremely egotistical, "closing his eyes when he spoke, the better to listen to himself and to enjoy more fully the wisdom of his eloquence, his face wrinkled like a cooked apple." His friend Benjamin Constant wrote that "his disdain for mediocrities, the sense that they were of a different nature than himself, rendered them insupportable to him." Mignet, who knew him under the Empire, noted that "his views turned naturally into dogmas. . . . one had always to accept either his thoughts or his dismissal." Madame de Staël, who admired him greatly, remarked that "the human race displeased him, and he knew not how to treat it. One would say that he wished to deal with something other than men, and that he would renounce everything, if only he could find somewhere on earth a species more to his taste." He was, moreover, inclined to paranoia, and complained bitterly—occasionally even in his public speeches—about how he was calumniated and persecuted. Commenting on these paranoic tendencies, Sainte-Beuve, who spent some time working on Sieyes's papers and who knew him in his old age, concluded that he suffered "a malady of the sort that affected Rousseau and other solitary great thinkers."[26] It is hard to imagine a man so cold, distant, and misanthropic playing so important a political role in any other era; surely only the French revolutionaries' passion for reasoned abstraction gave Sieyes his continuing influence in public life.

Sieyes's extreme privacy and inscrutability make him a poor candidate for traditional biography. In fact, none of his biographers has managed to bring him to life as a person; they trace his political career and his thought but cannot penetrate his emotional life.[27] His reclusive habits and the virtual absence of personal correspondence in his papers render him a permanent enigma. Happily, this book is not a biographical study but a study of a political text. In interpreting *What Is the Third Estate?* and some of Sieyes's other writings, I shall sometimes refer to their author's biography. But the point of such excursions into biography will be to elucidate the texts or the contexts in which they were written; the person of the abbé will be as remote at the end of my tale as at the beginning.

---

26. All of these quotations are culled from Bredin, *Sieyès,* pp. 14–15.

27. For example, Albéric Neton, *Sieyès, d'après des documents inédits* (Paris: Perrin, 1901); J. H. Clapham, *The Abbé Sieyès: An Essay in the Politics of the French Revolution* (London: P. S. King and Son, 1912); Bastid, *Sieyès et sa pensée*; and Bredin, *Sieyès*.

Sieyes and the Historiography of the French Revolution

This book appears in the midst of a kind of renaissance of Sieyes studies that has been stimulated by recent developments in French revolutionary historiography. The predominantly social interpretation of the Revolution that held sway from the 1930s through the 1960s has been replaced over the past decade and a half by a new, predominantly political and intellectual interpretation. As a consequence, the abbé Sieyes and his political doctrines have come to seem increasingly crucial to the revolutionary phenomenon.

The social interpretation of the French Revolution was given its "classical" formulation by Georges Lefebvre in the late 1930s and was sustained into the 1970s by a younger generation of historians, headed by Albert Soboul.[28] These historians, most of them socialist or communist in politics, were profoundly influenced by Marxian categories. They saw the French Revolution as a bourgeois revolution that destroyed the remnants of feudalism and cleared the way for full-scale capitalist development. Thus Soboul began his great thesis on the *sans-culottes:* "The French Revolution constitutes, together with the English revolutions of the seventeenth century, the culmination of a long economic and social evolution that made the bourgeoisie masters of the world."[29] This perspective led them to see the Revolution as driven by class struggles that arose from the economic and social conditions of the time. Their sympathies were above all with the poorest classes—Lefebvre wrote mainly about the peasants and

28. Georges Lefebvre, *Quatre-vingt neuf* (Paris, 1939); see also *Les paysans du Nord pendant la Révolution française* (Lille, 1924; repr. Bari: Laterza, 1959); *Questions agraire au temps de la Terreur* (Strasbourg, 1932); *La grande peur de 1789* (Paris, 1932); and *La Révolution française* (Paris: Presses Universitaires de France, 1951). The English translation of *Quatre-vingt neuf* is Lefebvre, *Coming of the French Revolution.* Other translations are *The Great Fear,* trans. Joan White, introd. George Rudé (New York: Vintage Books, 1973), and *The French Revolution,* trans. John Hall Stewart and James Friguglietti, 2 vols. (London: Routledge and Kegan Paul, 1962–64). See also Albert Soboul, *Précis d'histoire de la Révolution française* (Paris: Editions Sociales, 1970), and Soboul, *Les Sans-culottes parisiens en l'an II: Mouvement populaire et gouvernement révolutionnaire, 2 juin 1793–9 thermidor an II* (Paris: Librairie Clavreuil, 1962). Translations are *The French Revolution 1787–1799: From the Storming of the Bastille to Napoleon,* trans. Alan Forrest and Colin Jones (London: NLB, 1974), and *The Parisian Sans-Culottes and the French Revolution, 1793–1794,* trans. Gwynne Lewis (Oxford: Oxford University Press, 1964).
29. Soboul, *The Parisian Sans-Culottes,* p. 1.

Soboul about the urban *menu peuple* (little people)—but they also shared Marx's grudging admiration for the bourgeoisie and implacable hatred for aristocrats. They had relatively little interest in the juridical and political ideas of the revolutionary leaders, which they regarded as ideological justifications for bourgeois class rule.

The abbé Sieyes actually figured prominently in some of these accounts, especially in Lefebvre's *Coming of the French Revolution,* which places him beside Mirabeau and Lafayette as a great leader of the early Revolution.[30] This is perhaps not surprising: by stirring up hostility against the nobles and by leading the deputies of the Third Estate to their seizure of power, Sieyes played a particularly crucial role in what Lefebvre regarded as the preeminently bourgeois phase of the bourgeois revolution, as distinct from the aristocratic phase that initially weakened the absolutist state in 1787 and 1788, and the revolts of the peasants and the urban poor that broke the resistance of the king and aristocracy in July and August 1789.

In a revealing article written in 1939 in response to Paul Bastid's monumental intellectual biography of Sieyes,[31] Lefebvre discussed the abbé at some length. He disagreed sharply with Bastid's claim that Sieyes's ideas were intellectually consistent. Lefebvre asserted that they were in fact utterly inconsistent, that over the course of the revolution he had moved from advocating unlimited popular sovereignty located in a unified legislature to supporting a minutely subdivided government with a strong executive and a legislative authority scattered among several distinct bodies. Whatever unity his thought possessed "was not internal: it came to him from outside, from the preoccupation of assuring the domination of the bourgeoisie."[32] He elaborated:

Sieyes is the man of that bourgeoisie which, in 1789, overturned the aristocracy to replace it purely and simply with its own political and social authority: liberal in 1789; supporting democracy in the year II only impatiently and momentarily

30. Lefebvre, *Coming of the French Revolution,* pp. 69–70.

31. Bastid, *Sieyès et sa pensée.*

32. Georges Lefebvre, "Sieyès," in *Etudes sur la révolution française,* 2d ed., introd. Albert Soboul (Paris: Presses Universitaires de France, 1963). The article was originally published in *Annales historiques de la Révolution française,* 1939, pp. 357–66.

until it was crushed by counterrevolution; liberal again in 1796; accepting military dictatorship in the year VIII when it realized that the struggle against aristocracy was not complete and that it had no other recourse, since it rejected a new dictatorship based on the popular masses.[33]

Sieyes was, in other words, the theorist of the interests of the bourgeoisie, and because the class's interests changed over the course of the Revolution, so did the theories. It is, Lefebvre remarks, "impossible to comprehend the actions of Sieyes unless one views him from a social perspective. He was the incarnation of the bourgeoisie and it is in this that his historical greatness resides."[34]

This recourse to an essentially mystical notion of Sieyes as somehow incarnating the bourgeoisie is emblematic of the fundamental flaw in Lefebvre's overall interpretation. His argument that the French Revolution was a bourgeois revolution was ultimately tautological. As in the passage quoted above, the interest or the will of the bourgeoisie is not identified separately from what the Revolution accomplished. We are told that the bourgeoisie was liberal in 1789, cautiously supported democracy in 1793, was liberal again in 1796, and supported military dictatorship in 1799. But we are offered no evidence that these were the desires of the bourgeoisie, other than that these political tendencies in fact won out. The unstated assumption is that because these tendencies won out, they must have been supported by the bourgeoisie—because, after all, the Revolution was a bourgeois revolution. The argument about Sieyes contains a similar sleight of hand. Although they have no surface unity, his thoughts and actions are unified from a "social perspective" because they are those of the bourgeoisie as a whole. But we are told nothing of how or why, by what social process or intermediaries, Sieyes became the bourgeoisie incarnate. We know that he incarnated the bourgeoisie only because his own intellectual and political twists and turns so neatly matched those of the Revolution as a whole. Once again, the bourgeoisie turns out to be identical, in Lefebvre's account, with the Revolution it is assumed to have made.

It was precisely this tautological, a priori character of Lefebvre's

33. Lefebvre, "Sieyès," p. 156.
34. Ibid., p. 153.

and Soboul's arguments that proved most vulnerable to attack. Much of the initial assault was undertaken by English-speaking historians. Alfred Cobban, in his corrosive *Social Interpretation of the French Revolution,* argued persuasively, often using the very research findings of Lefebvre and his disciples, that the representatives of the Third Estate who carried out the "bourgeois revolution" were above all lawyers and minor government officials, not capitalists; that it was the peasants who overthrew the remnants of feudalism, while the bourgeois, who had often managed to purchase or lease seigneurial rights, resisted their suppression as long as possible; that the ruling class that emerged from the Revolution was a class of wealthy landowners, not industrial capitalists; and that the revolution had the net effect of retarding, rather than speeding up, French industrialization.[35] Shortly afterwards, George V. Taylor argued that the French bourgeoisie of 1789 in fact had economic interests indistinguishable from those of the nobility, and Elizabeth Eisenstein's close reading of Lefebvre's *Coming of the French Revolution* demonstrated that the supposed "revolutionary bourgeoisie" who intervened in 1789 to launch the Revolution was actually composed of a mixed group of bourgeois, nobles, and clerics who were united by political ideals, not class interests.[36] By the early 1970s, scholars the French would call "Anglo-Saxon empiricists" had thoroughly dismantled the once unified revolutionary bourgeoisie and its formerly distinct aristocratic opponents into a congeries of overlapping fragments. This empirical scattering deprived Lefebvre's history of its central protagonists; by the mid-1970s the classical social interpretation had effectively collapsed.

The victory of the anglophone empiricist social historians was thorough. But it was not lasting, largely because they proved better at demolition than at reconstruction. The spoils of the historiographical battle were seized, instead, by historians advocating a new intellectual and political interpretation of the French Revolution,

35. Alfred Cobban, *The Social Interpretation of the French Revolution* (Cambridge: Cambridge University Press, 1964).
36. George V. Taylor, "Noncapitalist Wealth and the French Revolution," *American Historical Review* 71 (1967): 469–96; and Elizabeth Eisenstein, "Who Intervened in 1788? A Commentary on *The Coming of the French Revolution,*" *American Historical Review* 70 (1965): 77–103.

and above all by the French scholar François Furet. Furet had coauthored (with Denis Richet) a non-Marxist general history of the Revolution, published in 1965–66. In 1970, responding to an attack on this work by Claude Mazauric, Furet published a long, blistering, and highly effective polemic against the classical interpretation, at that time still dominant in France. He claimed that in the hands of Soboul and Mazauric the history of the Revolution had degenerated into a "revolutionary catechism" that sacrificed the search for historical truth to a vigilant defense of orthodoxy. Although Furet's critique included plenty of empirical detail, his approach was always more philosophical than that of his English and American allies and more attuned to the problem of reconceptualizing the Revolution as a whole.

Furet's decisive intervention was *Penser la Révolution française,* published in 1978.[37] Here Furet developed a highly original political-cultural interpretation that has established the dominant framework for revolutionary studies ever since. Furet argued that the most important questions about the Revolution had to do not with struggles between social classes but with the sudden irruption of a novel democratic political ideology that claimed to break totally with all historical precedent. The emergence of democratic politics was both the prime epochal significance of the French Revolution and the explanation of the Revolution's peculiar dynamics. Furet argued that from the opening of the Estates-General in 1789 to thermidor in 1794, social dynamics—"the conflict of interests for power"—were completely displaced by politico-cultural dynamics—"a competition of discourses for the appropriation of legitimacy."[38] The Revolution "ushered in a world where mental representations of power governed all actions, and where a network of signs completely dominated political life."[39] According to Furet, at the center of this network of signs was the abstract notion of a pure people's will, paired inevitably with a conviction that the expression of this will was constantly frustrated by an "aristocratic plot." It was the dynamic combination

37. Paris: Gallimard, 1978. An English translation is François Furet, *Interpreting the French Revolution,* trans. Elborg Forster (Cambridge: Cambridge University Press, 1981).
38. Furet, *Interpreting the French Revolution,* p. 49.
39. Ibid., p. 48.

of illusory efforts to enunciate the people's will and escalating denunciations of the aristocratic plot that drove the Revolution steadily to the left, Furet argued—not struggles between bourgeois and nobles or pressure from the Parisian *sans-culottes.*

The panache and originality of Furet's argument, together with his powerful institutional position in the Ecole des Hautes Etudes en Sciences Sociales—the most prestigious center of historical studies in France—set revolutionary historiography on a new path.[40] By the early 1980s, the principal questions were no longer social, since Furet had expelled social causality from the core events of the Revolution, but concerned political ideology. What were the guiding beliefs of the revolutionaries? How did the notion of a total break with the past get invented? Who elaborated the central conceptual schemas of the Revolution, and why were their ideas taken up so enthusiastically? What were the phases of ideological development in the Revolution? How did the ideas relate to questions of practical politics? How have the crucial conceptual and political innovations of the Revolution affected subsequent French history? In the wake of *Penser la Révolution française,* the Revolution's extraordinary ferment of political ideas, which had been largely ignored by both the classical and the empiricist social interpretations, suddenly moved to center stage. The result has been a major outpouring of works on the cultural or intellectual history of French revolutionary politics.[41] At their best—for example, in Keith Baker's *Inventing the French Revolution* or Lynn Hunt's *Politics, Culture, and Class in the French Revolution*—these works restore a vivid sense of the profound cultural and intellectual transformations that the Revolution entailed.[42] But

40. On Furet's career and influence, see Steven L. Kaplan, *Adieu 89* (Paris: Fayard, 1993), esp. pp. 673–706.

41. An exhaustive bibliography of such works cannot be given here. Two collective projects probably best exemplify the range of writing in the genre: Furet and Ozouf's *Critical Dictionary,* and a collection of articles based on a series of conferences held in the years leading up to the Revolution's bicentennial. These articles are published in three volumes under the collective title *The French Revolution and the Creation of Modern Political Culture,* vol. 1, *The Political Culture of the Old Regime,* ed. Keith Michael Baker (Oxford: Pergamon Press, 1987); vol. 2, *Political Culture of the French Revolution,* ed. Colin Lucas (Oxford: Pergamon Press, 1988); and vol. 3, *The Transformation of Political Culture, 1789–1848,* ed. François Furet and Mona Ozouf (Oxford: Pergamon Press, 1989).

42. Keith Michael Baker, *Inventing the French Revolution: Essays on French Political*

some of the work in this genre comes perilously close to traditional intellectual history, focusing on accurate reconstruction of ideas for their own sake rather than on using political texts to interrogate the revolutionary experience as a whole.

In this atmosphere the abbé Sieyes and his ideas took on a new historical importance. Now that he was no longer cast as a mere spokesman for bourgeois interests, his political thought became worthy of study in its own right; indeed, in the new interpretive climate it could be seen as a key to the Revolution's central dynamic. Because Sieyes was perhaps the most resolutely philosophical of the major political actors in the French Revolution, and because his ideas incontestably had a major influence on the Revolution's course, his career and writings have become the subject of a minor industry. The years since 1985 have seen two new editions of his collected political writings; a new edition of *What Is the Third Estate?*; Bredin's full-scale biography; Murray Forsythe's comprehensive study of his political thought; a French doctoral thesis on his ideas about political representation; and a mounting number of scholarly articles and book chapters.[43] Most of these works treat Sieyes primarily as a political

Culture in the Eighteenth Century (Cambridge: Cambridge University Press, 1990); and Lynn Hunt, *Politics, Culture, and Class in the French Revolution* (Berkeley and Los Angeles: University of California Press, 1984).

43. Sieyès, *Ecrits politiques,* and Dorigny, *Oeuvres de Sieyès*; Emmanuel-Joseph Sieyès, *Qu'est-ce que le Tiers état,* ed. Jean-Denis Bredin (Paris: Flamarion, 1988); Bredin, *Sieyès*; Forsythe, *Reason and Revolution*; Colette Clavreul, "L'Influence de la théorie d'Emmanuel Sieyès sur les origines de la représentation en droit public," thèse de doctorat d'Etat, Université de Paris, 1986. Recent articles include Baker, "Sieyès," in Furet and Ozouf, *Critical Dictionary*; Colette Clavreul, "Sieyès, Emmanuel Joseph, 1748–1836, 'Qu'est-ce que le Tiers Etat,'" in *Dictionnaire des oeuvres politiques,* ed. François Châtelet, Olivier Duhamel, and Evelyne Piser (Paris: Presses Universitaires de France, 1986), pp. 747–57; Clavreul, "Sieyès et la genèse de la représéntation moderne," *Droits: Revue française de théorie juridique* 6 (1986): 45–56; Pasquale Pasquino, "Emmanuel Sieyès, Benjamin Constant et le 'Gouvernement des Modernes': contribution à l'histoire du concept de représentation politique," *Revue française de Science politique* 37 (1987): 214–29; Pasquino, "Citoyenneté, égalité et liberté chez J.-J. Rousseau et E. Sieyès," *Cahiers Bernard Lazare* 121–22 (1988–89): 150–61; Pasquino, "Le Concept de nation et les fondements du droit public de la Révolution: Sieyès," in François Furet, *L'Héritage de la Révolution française* (Paris: Hachette, 1989), pp. 309–33; Marcel Dorigny, "La Formation de la pensée économique de Sieyès d'après ses manuscrits (1770–1789)," *Annales historiques de la Révolution française* 6 (1988): 17–34; Georges Benrekassa, "Crise de l'ancien régime, crise des idéologies: Une année dans la vie de Sieyès," *Annales: Economies, Sociétés,*

theorist, discussing his ideas about representation, national sovereignty, citizenship, or liberty. Here as elsewhere in the current wave of revolutionary historiography, the history of the Revolution risks becoming a chapter in the history of political philosophy. Forsythe, who states that his chief interest is in reconstructing Sieyes's "system of ideas," has pursued this goal most methodically, but he is not alone in this tendency.[44]

It should be clear from the very subject of this book that I too have been influenced by the turn from social to intellectual interpretations of the French Revolution. I fully accept the critique of Lefebvre and Soboul and am convinced that the Revolution cannot be understood apart from the language and conceptual vocabulary of the revolutionaries. This book is resolutely textual in method and focus; in many respects it is yet another example of the French Revolution as intellectual history. Indeed, many of the arguments developed in the book were first worked out for a series of lectures that I gave in Furet's seminar in Paris. But at the same time, I am attempting to mount a modest challenge to what I regard as a mistaken tendency in the current historiographical school to eliminate social considerations from revolutionary history and from the study of revolutionary texts.

This tendency is present in even the most impressive works in the new genre. François Furet's *Penser la Révolution française* is a par-

Civilisations 44 (1989): 25–46; Ramon Maiz, "Nation and Representation: E. J. Sieyes and the Theory of the State of the French Revolution," working paper no. 18, Institut de Ciències Politiques i Socials, Barcelona; and Jacques Guilhaumou, "Sieyes, lecteur critique de l'article 'Evidence' de l'Encyclopédie (1773)," *Recherches sur Diderot et sur l'*Encyclopédie 14 (1993): 125–144. The first two volumes of *The French Revolution and the Creation of Modern Political Culture* contain several articles that treat Sieyes extensively: see Lynn Hunt, "The 'National Assembly,' " pp. 403–15; Keith Michael Baker, "Representation," pp. 469–92; Bronislaw Baczko, "Le Contract social des français: Sieyès et Rousseau," pp. 493–514; and Lucien Jaume, "Citoyenneté et souveraineté: le poids de l'absolutisme," pp. 515–34, in vol. 1, Baker, ed., *Political Culture of the Old Regime*; and see Ran Halévi, "La révolution constituante: les ambiguités politiques," pp. 69–85; William H. Sewell, Jr., "Le Citoyen/la citoyenne: Activity, Passivity and the Revolutionary Concept of Citizenship," pp. 105–124; and Patrice Gueniffey, "Les Assemblées et la représentation," pp. 233–58, in vol. 2, Lucas, ed., *Political Culture of the French Revolution.* Antoine de Baecque's *Le Corps de l'histoire: Métaphores et politique (1770–1800)* (Paris: Calmann-Lévy, 1993) contains a brilliant chapter entitled "Sieyès docteur du corps politique: la métaphore du grand corps des citoyens," pp. 99–162.
44. Forsythe, *Reason and Revolution,* p. 2.

ticularly clear case. In this book, Furet was locked in mortal combat against the classical social interpretation. One of his major efforts was to establish that social determinations of the sort that preoccupied Lefebvre, Soboul, and Mazauric—that is, class interests derived from relations to the mode of production—were essentially irrelevant to the major issues of revolutionary history. As we have seen, he argued that the semiotic dynamic of revolutionary political rhetoric completely displaced such social determinations during the crucial period from 1789 to 1794. But as often happens in polemic, Furet in effect accepted his enemies' definition of the terrain: he implicitly defined the social in the same narrow and reductionist way as it was understood by his Marxist opponents. Because social determinants as posited by a reductionist form of Marxism proved irrelevant to revolutionary history, Furet made the unwarranted inference that the explanations lay solely in politics and ideas, to the exclusion of social considerations.

It may well be that class interests in an orthodox Marxist sense were only tangential to the political struggles of the French Revolution, although the massive peasant uprisings of the summer of 1789 stand as a continuing challenge to this claim. But orthodox Marxism has no monopoly on conceptualizing the social. The human sciences, including their Marxian variants, have developed many ways of thinking about humans as social beings: not only Marx's concepts of class and mode of production but also Weber's status hierarchies and forms of rationality, Malinowski's social structures, Gramsci's hegemony, Goffman's interaction rituals, Thompson's experience and agency, Foucault's power/knowledge and disciplinary regimes, Durkheim's social integration and collective representations, Braudel's structures, conjunctures, and events, Giddens's duality of structure, Geertz's cultural systems, and Bourdieu's habitus and symbolic capital, to name only a few. If we adopt a broader definition of the social, then the French Revolution fairly bristles with social determinations and social consequences that in the work of Furet and his school are either ignored or reduced to political ideology.

Keith Baker, in his pathbreaking *Inventing the French Revolution*, is more aware than Furet of alternative concepts of the social. But he too, in the end, reduces the social to the intellectual. Baker, however, has the merit of performing this reduction by explicit argument rather than simply by fiat. He posits what he calls "political culture" as the object of his investigation and offers a "linguistic" definition of the term. His definition

> sees politics as about making claims; as the activity through which individuals and groups in any society articulate, negotiate, implement, and enforce the competing claims they make upon one another and upon the whole. Political culture is, in this sense, the set of discourses or symbolic practices by which these claims are made. . . . It constitutes the meanings of the terms in which these claims are framed, the nature of the contexts to which they pertain, and the authority of the principles according to which they are made binding. It shapes the constitutions and powers of the agencies and procedures by which contestations are resolved, competing claims authoritatively adjudicated, and binding decisions enforced. Thus political authority is, in this view, essentially a matter of linguistic authority: first in the sense that political functions are defined and allocated within the framework of a given political discourse; and second, in the sense that their exercise takes the form of upholding authoritative definitions of the terms within that discourse.[45]

Baker's definition of political culture develops a powerful argument for the fundamental significance of political language. But one might question whether the incontestable fact that political claims are elaborated in language necessarily implies that political authority is "*essentially* a matter of linguistic authority." This definition, in short, contains a hint of linguistic reductionism.

The hint is expanded to a matter of principle in the following paragraph, where Baker explicitly considers the anticipated objection that such a definition "denies the relevance of social interests to political practice, seeking instead to privilege a symbolic realm over the realities of social life." He answers this objection by denying

> that there are social realities independent of symbolic meanings: All social activity has a symbolic dimension that gives it meaning, just as all symbolic activity has a social dimension that

45. Baker, *Inventing the French Revolution,* pp. 4–5.

gives it point. This is to argue that claims to delimit the field of discourse in relation to nondiscursive social realities that lie beyond it invariably point to a domain of action that is itself discursively constituted. They distinguish, in effect, between different discursive practices—different language games—rather than between discursive and nondiscursive phenomena.[46]

Here Baker begins with a point I fully endorse: that there are no social realities independent of symbolic meanings. But from this premise, he derives the reductive conclusion that social realities can adequately be characterized as "discursive practices" or "language games." This, it seems to me, does not follow. The fact that all human activities are structured by and bring into play linguistic or paralinguistic meanings does not imply that those activities are *nothing but* the production of meaning, or that a linguistic conceptual vocabulary can describe them adequately. Indeed, Baker's own language of social and symbolic "dimensions" of activities seems to imply that there is more to the human world than making meaning: "All social activity has a symbolic dimension that gives it meaning, just as all symbolic activity has a social dimension that gives it point." I take the second clause of this sentence as meaning that symbolic activity typically both shapes and is shaped by phenomena not reducible to symbolic meanings—for example, interpersonal communication networks, direct coercion, competition for scarce resources, or patterns of spatial contiguity and dispersion. To me, Baker's language of dimensions implies that all domains of action are constituted simultaneously and indissolubly by both "social" and "symbolic" considerations—that the shaping of the social by the symbolic and the symbolic by the social is fully mutual and reciprocal.

The problem is that Baker follows up only one side of this reciprocal relationship. In the sentence quoted above, the social and the symbolic are contrasted as two distinct but interdependent dimensions of action. But in the two sentences that follow, Baker transmogrifies the social into the symbolic. He asserts that what are usually thought of as "social realities" are themselves "discursively constituted," but he does not add that what are usually thought of

46. Ibid., p. 5.

as discursive realities are themselves socially constituted. By this means, he effectively reduces the social to the discursive and turns the claim that all symbolic activity has a social dimension into a tautology: that all symbolic activity has a symbolic dimension. In this way, Baker erases the social dimension of human action that he initially introduced into his account, freeing himself to conceptualize the French Revolution as fully constituted by an evolving counterpoint of linguistic claims.

Textuality and the Social, or the Social in the Text

This evacuation of the social from the Revolution is combined, in both Furet and Baker, with a particular strategy of textual analysis. If they reduce the complexities of social life to language, they tend to reduce the political texts they study to their logic. At a time when literary critics and a vocal minority of intellectual historians are calling for deconstructive readings of texts, readings that try to undermine or disperse what have been taken to be the texts' clear, normative, and intended meanings, the Furet school remains true to an older style of textual analysis.[47] At their best, these analyses are extremely powerful; they bring into sharp focus the texts' major contributions to the ongoing political debate and illuminate their authors' fundamental philosophical assumptions. But rather than bringing to the surface the partially suppressed multiplicity of voices that always coexist in a text, they try to discern each text's central tendency, its essential intellectual argument. Even in Baker's *Inventing the French Revolution,* which takes great pains to recapture the multiplicity of prerevolutionary political debate, the complexity of the whole is achieved by reanimating a clamoring diversity of individually coherent political voices.

My strategy in this book will be different, although I will begin with a style of argument much like that of Baker or Furet. Chapter 2 is a detailed analysis of the central political argument of *What Is the*

47. The most vocal of this minority of intellectual historians has been Dominick LaCapra. See his *Rethinking Intellectual History: Texts, Contexts, Language* (Ithaca: Cornell University Press, 1983); *History and Criticism* (Ithaca: Cornell University Press, 1985); *History, Politics, and the Novel* (Ithaca: Cornell University Press, 1987); and *Soundings in Critical Theory* (Ithaca: Cornell University Press, 1987).

Third Estate? that entails a close reading of the pamphlet's political rhetoric. This is followed in chapter 3 by an attempt to uncover the fundamental intellectual assumptions of Sieyes's pamphlet and to reconstruct from fragmentary sources the central thrust of his political philosophy. But in the second half of the book I will move from reconstructing to deconstructing the coherence of *What Is the Third Estate?* by dwelling on the multivocality that surfaces in even this remarkably well made text. In chapters 4 and 5 I probe incoherences, many of them on the text's margins, trying to show how discordant notes sounded in brief passages or expelled from the body of the work to its footnotes undermine its central arguments and render the author's intentions and the texts' meanings ambiguous and murky.

Rather than composing a single unified narrative, I trace out five successive overlapping narratives with five quite different heroes. I begin with a triumphalist plot in chapter 2, in which Sieyes successfully harnesses the French Revolution to his own intentions by writing a perfectly conceived political pamphlet. Chapter 3 begins with the plot continuing in this vein, but ends with a tragic twist. There I show how Sieyes's long meditations on political economy provided the intellectual foundations both for his great pamphlet and for a brilliant, original, and comprehensive political vision elaborated in subsequent speeches and writings—but a vision that Sieyes was never able to state in systematic form and that his fellow revolutionaries refused to take seriously. In chapters 4 and 5, I take a deconstructionist turn and trace out two successive tragic, or perhaps tragicomic, plots, in which Sieyes's genius cannot save him from the flaws inherent in his own intellectual and emotional makeup and/or from the necessarily unstable relationship between language and the world. Chapter 4 argues that Sieyes's own hatred of the aristocracy blinded him and his readers to the real consequences of an attack on privilege, making it possible for them to destroy a social order from which they had derived substantial benefits. Chapter 5 shows how Sieyes's meditations on political economy, which provided the basic foundations of his argument in his pamphlet, also led him to misrecognize the nature of productive relations in eighteenth-century France and to fear the democracy that *What Is the Third Estate?* had done so much to install. Finally, in the epilogue, I sketch an ironic plot, in which Sieyes's own rhetorical inventions escape his control to animate a succession of democratic movements utterly at odds with his own political intentions.

But if my approach to texts is influenced by techniques and perspectives of deconstructionist literary criticism, it also departs significantly from normal deconstructionist practice. The fundamental difference is that I insist on the importance of social determinants or influences in texts.[48] The central enterprise of deconstruction has been to reveal the instability of all linguistic meaning. It has located this instability in the signifying mechanisms of language itself, claiming notably that because the meaning of a linguistic sign always depends on a contrast with what the sign is opposed to or different from, language is haunted by traces of the very terms it excludes. Consequently, the meaning of a text can never be fixed; attempts to secure meaning can only defer, never definitively exclude, a plethora of alternative and opposing readings. Deconstruction is the practice of exhuming and displaying a disorderly multitude of meanings hidden beneath the tidy surface of a text.

Because every text can be shown to contain (or fail to contain) constantly proliferating meanings, deconstruction extends and blurs the boundaries of texts. Indeed, in its most expansive form deconstruction makes all the world a text, arguing that language cannot refer to anything external to itself but only to an endless chain of ever shifting linguistic meanings. To search for extratextual influences on texts is illusory, since that which is claimed to be outside textuality is itself known through and constituted by its linguistic representations. Derrida's aphorism in *Grammatology* pushes this position to its logical extreme: *"Il n'y a pas de hors-texte"*—freely trans-

48. For a more fully elaborated argument parallel to the one set forth here, see the ovulary article by Gabrielle M. Spiegel, "History, Historicism, and the Social Logic of the Text in the Middle Ages," *Speculum* 65 (1990): 59–86. Various literary critics, most of them working in an explicitly Marxist tradition, have also attempted to bridge the gap between deconstruction and the social. See, e.g., Fredric Jameson, *The Political Unconscious: Narrative as a Socially Symbolic Act* (Ithaca: Cornell University Press, 1981); Michael Ryan, *Marxism and Deconstruction: A Critical Articulation* (Baltimore: Johns Hopkins University Press, 1982); Gayatri Chakravorty Spivak, *In Other Worlds: Essays in Cultural Politics* (New York: Routledge, 1988).

lated, "nothing is extratextual."[49] This radical epistemological claim has important practical consequences for textual analysis. Some of the key questions that historians and literary scholars have traditionally brought to texts—for example, about the intentions of their authors or about their social referents or social impact—are rendered nonsensical by radical deconstruction. Within its epistemology, the intentions of a text's author or the social referent and impact of the text must be understood as mere illusions produced by the endless play of signification.

Yet it seems possible to welcome the deconstructionist insight that textual meaning is multiply unstable without accepting the disappearance of either author, referent, or extratextual world. Although I am convinced that any claimed access to the world is inevitably mediated by linguistic or paralinguistic codes, I cannot see why it should be less philosophically acceptable to posit than to deny extratextual realities. To deny them is to make an ontological claim no more capable of proof than the claim that extratextual realities exist. Since either claim can only be a working supposition about the world, not a statement of fact, the relevant question is what such claims make thinkable and unthinkable. The deconstructionist position, by freeing interpreters from their former obsessions about authorial intention and social referent, has had the salutary effect of encouraging a deeper inquiry into the mechanics of meaning production in texts and text analogs. But I believe that it also discourages the investigation of other, no less important issues.

I think we need to complement deconstructionist insights by conceptualizing text production as action in a social world—as undertaken by socially situated authors, with the intention of influencing the thoughts and behavior of other persons.[50] Texts should be

49. Jacques Derrida, *Of Grammatology* (Baltimore: Johns Hopkins University Press, 1974), p. 158.
50. My approach has certain affinities with that of Quentin Skinner, e.g., in "Meaning and Understanding in the History of Ideas," *History and Theory* 7 (1969): 3–53, and "Some Problems in the Analysis of Political Thought and Action," *Political Theory* 2 (1974): 277–303. However, I disagree with his extreme rationalism, which rules out of court any consideration of the emotional content and context of texts. I would like to thank Michael P. Moody, a student in Carlos Forment's undergraduate seminar at Princeton University, for pointing this out to me in his excellent paper on my manuscript.

seen as social products that have social consequences. They are linked to extratextual realities both through their authors, who creatively use existing linguistic conventions to carry out their socially formed intentions, and by readers, who are influenced by texts but who also interpret them—again, creatively—in terms of their own socially specific identities and interests. The meanings of texts, and therefore their social effects, are never securely and unambiguously inscribed in their language but depend on the ambiguous motives and contradictory social locations of both authors and readers. An approach that sees texts as media of social action can both profit from deconstructive strategies in analyzing the multiple social meanings of texts and show how the social situations in which texts are produced and interpreted lead to the multiplication of linguistic meaning. Indeed, I believe that the impossibility of fixing meaning arises as much from the contested character of the social actions in which language inevitably is employed as from any internal mechanics. The instability of language seems to me inseparable from the inherent contradictions of motivated social action.

Historians commonly pursue the social dimension of texts by investigating the social and institutional circumstances out of which ideas or texts arise: the social recruitment of authors, the history of knowledge-producing institutions, the sociology and economics of the media in which ideas circulate, or the systems of patronage that afford access to publics. Work of this sort, often dubbed "social history of ideas," typically spends more time studying the social structures and processes that produce texts than analyzing the texts themselves. Such studies have made important contributions to intellectual history in general and to eighteenth-century French intellectual history in particular.[51] But while my sense of the social context in which Sieyes lived, read, and wrote is much influenced by work in this genre, my approach is more definitively textual. The object of my study is *What Is the Third Estate?*, not the social history of French revolutionary political discourse. I do not systematically

---

51. See, e.g., Robert Darnton, *The Business of Enlightenment: A Publishing History of the Encyclopédie* (Cambridge: Harvard University Press, 1979); Darnton, *Literary Underground*; Daniel Roche, *Le Siècle des lumières en province: Académies et académiciens provinciaux* (Paris and The Hague: Mouton, 1978); and Rogier Chartier, *The Cultural Origins of the French Revolution* (Durham, N.C.: Duke University Press, 1991).

investigate the various social and institutional practices that made *What Is the Third Estate?* possible and shaped its content and style. The bulk of my book is devoted to a close reading of Sieyes's texts that is generally focused more on political than on social contexts. I turn to possible social influences only as they are suggested by my textual analyses, and my references to social influences or mediations are usually brief and allusive. My strategy is to show that even a study focused resolutely—indeed, almost obsessively—on puzzles of textual interpretation cannot avoid, or can only avoid with peril, articulations between texts and the social world. By pushing textual readings to their limits, I wish to demonstrate the unavoidable presence of the social in the text, shaping its metaphors, influencing its rhetorical strategies, and guaranteeing—or undermining—the stability of its categories.

I attempt to portray *What Is the Third Estate?* as a complex and unstable product of diverse and overlapping social, intellectual, linguistic, and political processes. I see the pamphlet as arising out of both the socially formed intentions of its author and the conflicting politico-linguistic conventions of late-eighteenth-century France. I probe instabilities of textual meaning and attempt to trace them to multivocalities and silences built into the pamphlet's language, to ambiguities in authorial intention, and to conundrums of reference to the world. I examine the relationship between author and readers, showing how Sieyes built on his own experience to create a rhetoric that captured the passions and frustrations of his intended readers, but also how he failed to persuade them of his most cherished philosophical ideas. In my epilogue, I sketch out how his revolutionary rhetoric was eventually appropriated by quite differently located readers, who used it to undermine the political positions Sieyes had meant to advance and to attack the social groups he had meant to empower. I attempt to cast *What Is the Third Estate?* as a powerful and unpredictable social act, a complex but fateful intervention in the French Revolution. I aspire both to illuminate the stakes and dynamics of that crucial episode and to investigate, in the context of the Revolution, broader questions about the powers and limitations of political language.

I attempt to place *What Is the Third Estate?* in the context of a particular social location and a particular sociopolitical project. The term "bourgeois revolution" is currently in utter disrepute; to use it in my title is something of a provocation. I use it, however, in a different sense than did Lefebvre and Soboul. I do not see the French Revolution as having been achieved by or as having brought to power a bourgeoisie in the Marxian sense. Capitalism was only in its childhood in France in 1789, and the capitalist class was small, not conscious of itself as a socioeconomic group, and not particularly active in the Revolution. I use the term bourgeois in a different, more diffuse, and more eighteenth-century sense as signifying a class of urban, non-noble, educated, well-to-do property-owners. This, I submit, is how Sieyes himself employed the term in the quotation I use as this book's epigraph. Sieyes was born into the lower regions of this social category, experienced many of its frustrations, and, as I try to show in chapter 2, addressed *What Is the Third Estate?* quite precisely to its members.

In invoking "a rhetoric of bourgeois revolution" in my title, I do not mean to claim that the French Revolution was a bourgeois revolution in the sense that it constituted a triumph of this or any other bourgeoisie. I mean to make the much narrower claim that the particular political rhetoric developed by the abbé Sieyes was written from the perspective of and meant to appeal to this Old Regime category of wealthy non-nobles. I will try to demonstrate that both the coherence and the incoherence of Sieyes's rhetoric make more sense if we see his writing as motivated by (among other things) an attempt to gain predominant political power for this diffuse social grouping and to give it a unity in politics that it lacked in ordinary life. Sieyes's powerfully anti-aristocratic political rhetoric, his use of political economy as a basis for the Third Estate's claim to power, his profound ambivalence about privileges held by non-nobles, and his hopelessly contradictory views about citizenship—all of these features of his rhetoric testify to his ultimately unsuccessful attempt to invent a politics in which wealthy non-nobles would be the natural governing class of a unified nation.

The model of society that Sieyes held out to this diffuse eighteenth-century bourgeoisie was also "bourgeois" in a more anachronistic nineteenth-century sense: it assumed that production, exchange, and consumption were the fundamental bases of the social and political order. Sieyes's political vision, more than that of any other actor or theorist in the French Revolution, was based on the emerging discourse of political economy. The bourgeois, for Sieyes, is above all the producer, who, in the words of my epigraph, employs "his entire intelligence and all his strength for our present service" and who uses "the resources of his industry" to sustain our current and future enjoyment, rather than basing his life on memories of past grandeur. If wealthy non-nobles were the natural governing class of the nation, it was, according to Sieyes, because they occupied the key positions in the nation's productive apparatus.

But the "revolutionary bourgeoisie" to whom Sieyes directed these arguments never fully embraced this portrait of themselves and of their title to political leadership, and after 1792 they more commonly cast themselves as ancient Romans and Greeks, resting their claims on virtue rather than on productivity. If Sieyes managed to rouse wealthy non-nobles with *What Is the Third Estate?* he was unable, in the end, to convince them that they were a bourgeoisie in the sense that their nineteenth-century successors or twentieth-century historians would have recognized. That the eighteenth-century bourgeoisie failed to recognize itself in Sieyes's political-economic mirror reveals the depth of the gulf—economic, social, cultural, and political—separating it from the bourgeoisie of the nineteenth century. As I have argued elsewhere, it was largely the social, political, and intellectual transformations launched by the French Revolution, but not completed until the 1830s and 1840s, that made a model of society based on economic classes plausible.[52] The abbé Sieyes invented a rhetoric of bourgeois revolution that was brilliant and original, perhaps even prophetic. But it was not until long after the Revolution that a rhetoric based on political economy attained anything like hegemony in French political discourse.

52. Sewell, *Work and Revolution.*

2

WHAT IS THE THIRD ESTATE?

RHETORIC IS CONVENTIONALLY DEFINED AS THE ART OF persuasion. *What Is the Third Estate?* was one of the most persuasive texts ever written. The task of this chapter is to analyze the rhetoric of *What Is the Third Estate?* in some detail. I shall examine the sequence of Sieyes's argumentation, his strategy for changing the terms of contemporary debate, his distinctive figurative language, and his appeals to the emotions of his readers. By doing so I hope to show how the pamphlet helped to motivate both a political and a social revolution in the summer of 1789.

Sieyes neatly sets forth the framework of his pamphlet in his brief prologue. My account of his argument will be easier to follow if this framework is kept in mind.

> The plan of this book is fairly simple. We must ask ourselves three questions.
> (1) What is the Third Estate? *Everything.*
> (2) What has it been until now in the political order? *Nothing.*
> (3) What does it want to be? *Something.*
> We are going to see whether the answers are correct. . . . We shall next examine the measures that have been tried and those that must still be taken for the Third Estate really to become something. Thus, we shall state:
> (4) What the Ministers have attempted and what the privileged orders themselves propose to do for it.
> (5) What ought to have been done.

> (6) Finally, what remains to be done in order that the Third
> Estate can take its rightful place.[1]

The six headings specified in the prologue correspond to the six
chapters of the pamphlet. The reader is apprised at the outset of the
pamphlet's structure.

The introduction's briskness and clarity set the tone for the entire
pamphlet. But in spite of Sieyes's direct and epigrammatic style, his
exposition is complex and multileveled. I believe that the key to the
success of the pamphlet was Sieyes's ability to weave together several
quite distinct levels of argument into a coherent whole, all within a
simple, comprehensive framework. *What Is the Third Estate?* was
simultaneously a seemingly conventional contribution to an ongoing
debate, a treatise on abstract political philosophy, an identification
and denunciation of a class enemy, and a statement of social metaphysics, all harnessed to a timely and specific program for revolutionary action. Moreover, while its immediate purpose was to motivate
citizens to support a specific political strategy, it also implicitly
carried a far more radical message: that to achieve political liberty,
the entire social order would have to be transformed. In this sense,
What Is the Third Estate? was an argument for a social as well as a
political revolution.

The structure of Sieyes's argument will be easier to grasp if we
begin with his rhetoric of political revolution, which leads to the
major practical goal of the pamphlet: a seizure of power by the
deputies of the Third Estate. Sieyes's rhetoric of political revolution
begins in earnest in the third of his six chapters and constitutes the
bulk of the pamphlet as a whole—109 of the 127 pages in the first
edition. Understanding the development of this political argumentation will make clearer the purposes of his rhetoric of social revolution, which he launches at the very beginning of the pamphlet.

---

1. Sieyes, *Qu'est ce que le Tiers état?* pp. 119–20. For an English edition see Sieyès,
What Is the Third Estate?, trans. M. Blondel. My translations of quotations generally follow Blondel, but I have not hesitated to make changes where I felt they were
necessary. Henceforth, references to *Qu'est-ce qu le Tiers état?* will be given in
parentheses following quotations in the text. All such references are to the Zapperi
edition.

A Contribution to Ongoing Debate

One of Sieyes's crucial strategies was to take up the political issues of the day and twist them in a far more revolutionary direction. He began with the contemporary debate and the political institutions it assumed, but he ended by subverting and surpassing both conventional political discourse and conventional institutional practice. *What Is the Third Estate?* was a contribution to the debate that was raging in 1788 and 1789 about what form the newly convoked Estates-General should take. It was, in the first instance, an argument on behalf of the widely voiced, quite conventional demand for a doubling of the Third—that is, giving the Third Estate twice as many representatives as either of the others—and for taking votes by head rather than by order.

These demands are the subject of the pamphlet's third chapter, entitled "What Does the Third Estate Want to Be? *Something.*" But Sieyes's advocacy of these demands was far from conventional. Interspersed in his energetic arguments for these demands are continuing criticisms of their timidness and insufficiency. He claims that "the Third Estate is still very backward in this matter, by comparison not only with the enlightenment of those who have studied the social order, but even with that mass of common ideas that form public opinion" (134). He remarks that while the Third "wishes to become *something,*" it is asking to become "the least thing possible" (134). He complains that the Third Estate has been "raised in a superstitious or obligatory respect for the nobility" (135); "The more one considers this subject, the more one sees the insufficiency of the three demands of the Third" (137); "I cannot refrain from repeating once more that the timid inadequacy of this claim is an after-effect of times gone by" (144). In fact, by the time the reader has finished the chapter, Sieyes has undermined the position for which he ostensibly has been arguing almost as effectively as he has refuted the arguments of the Parlement and the privileged orders. At the end of chapter 3, he is explicit: "It is impossible to accept the claim of the Third Estate *or* to defend the privileged classes without turning some indisputable ideas upside-down" (151–52). Instead of concluding the chapter with a vindication of the standard demands of the Third Estate, he announces that the time has come to leave timidity behind and "to proclaim what is true and just in its full strength" (152). In other words, Sieyes *begins* by making common cause with his readers—by arguing for the Third Estate's already familiar demands. But his real purpose is to move his readers beyond these demands to a far more radical position.

A Refutation of Proposed Remedies

Chapter 4 of the pamphlet is devoted to ridiculing "What the Government Has Attempted, and What the Privileged Propose in Favor of the Third Estate." Its purpose is to demonstrate the utter inadequacy of all the proposals offered since the beginning of the current political crisis. Sieyes begins with proposals made by the government. The first, made by the prime minister, Calonne, in 1787, called for the convocation of new Provincial Assemblies which were to apportion a new land tax, and which were to be chosen by all property holders independently of the Estate to which they belonged. This proposal wins a limited assent from Sieyes, who claims that it could have established "a genuine national representation" (153). But the promising initiative was botched by Calonne's successor, Loménie de Brienne, who spoiled it by reintroducing separate chambers for the three orders. Moreover, the two "Assemblies of Notables," which were summoned to act on the ministers' reform proposals, "produced nothing of value for the Third" (156). These assemblies, called by Calonne in 1787 and by Necker (who succeeded Brienne) in 1788, were composed almost exclusively of great nobles and clergymen and rejected all of the prime ministers' reform proposals. Two years of efforts by the government, hence, came to naught.

Unable to get reforms through the Assemblies of Notables, the government finally agreed to call a meeting of the Estates-General. The nobility initially welcomed this decision, but once the furor about the "doubling of the Third" arose, nobles began to have second thoughts. Now that they doubted their ability to control the Estates-General, nobles began to offer a renunciation of their tax privileges, which would solve the financial crisis and obviate the need for an Estates-General altogether. Sieyes is scathing about these proposals.

He insinuates that in "offering a voluntary surrender" the nobles "hoped to avoid the necessity of making it a legal act of justice." They hoped to distract the Third Estate from "the necessity of being *something* in the Estates General, . . . to buy, at the cost of a forced renunciation, the continuation of all remaining abuses and the hope of increasing them still further" (159). The last-minute renunciation was unacceptable; after all, tax advantages were but one of the manifold privileges enjoyed by the nobles. Such privileges as the nobles' exclusive right to bear arms, unequal penalties in criminal courts, and exclusive access to lucrative public offices would remain intact unless the Estates-General managed to expunge them from the French constitution.

But there remained a final danger. If the nobles could no longer halt the Estates-General, they could attempt to persuade France to accept a constitution modeled upon England's, in which the nobility would have one chamber to itself and could also hope to obtain a dominant position in the second chamber. Sieyes ridicules this proposal. Not only did French social institutions differ sharply from English ones, but the English constitution was deeply flawed in its own right. The House of Lords "can hardly be regarded as anything but a monument to Gothic superstition," and the House of Commons is "imperfect in all its elements, as the English themselves admit" (172). In forming their constitution, the French should imitate "the model of the good and the beautiful" rather than imitating an imperfect English copy of that model. The true model "is not less well known today than it was to the English in 1688. . . . Must the products of the political art at the end of the eighteenth century be no better than those of the seventeenth? The English proved equal to the enlightenment of their time, let us not prove unequal to the enlightenment of ours" (175).

A Statement of Abstract Political Theory

Having dismissed what the government, the privileged orders, and the Anglophiles have proposed, Sieyes asks what ought in fact to have been done. To answer this, Sieyes says, "we must go back to basic principles, always more powerful than all the achievements of genius" (178). He therefore launches into a brief but remarkably cogent

statement of abstract political philosophy. This philosophical statement begins with an implicit borrowing from Jean-Jacques Rousseau, but it also introduces a crucial modification of Rousseau's
theories. In chapter 5 Sieyes constructs a novel philosophical position, one that not only is coherent in itself but also lends itself to a
practicable strategy for political revolution.

The crucial question before the nation in the disputes of 1788 and
1789 was who had the authority to determine its constitution.
According to Sieyes, the claim that fundamental constitutional questions could be determined by an Assembly of Notables, or by the
king, or even by an Estates-General, is absurd. Only the nation itself
can decide on its constitution. To arrive at this conclusion, Sieyes
employs a radical conception of the nation and its sovereignty similar
to Rousseau's in *The Social Contract*.[2] Sieyes, however, mentions no
political philosopher by name; he argues for his proposals as sheer
self-evident truths, not as the conclusions of some authoritative
thinker. The nation, according to Sieyes (and Rousseau) is not to be
understood as being defined by the laws, procedures, and customs
sanctioned by its history. The nation has its origin in a social contract
that transforms an aggregate of isolated individuals into a unified
social body with a single general will. The nation formed by the
social contract is composed of the entire body of citizens, and its will
is sovereign. "The nation," as Sieyes puts it, "is prior to all, it is the
source of everything. Its will is always legal; it is the law itself"
(180). In other words, the nation remains prior to any constitution
and its government serves only at the pleasure of the national will.
"In whatever fashion [a nation] wills, it is sufficient that its will
appear for all positive law to dissolve before it as before the source and
supreme master of all positive law" (183).

This conception of the nation as perpetually empowered to exercise
its sovereign will over the constitution had definite implications for
the debate at hand in France. In particular, it implied that when a
nation was to decide constitutional questions, it could not be bound
by any preexisting constitutional provisions.

2. Jean-Jacques Rousseau, *The Social Contract*, trans. Maurice Cranston (Harmondsworth, England: Penguin Books, 1968).

Can it be said that a nation, by an initial act of its will which is entirely independent of any procedural limitations, can bind itself thereafter to expressing its will only in certain determined ways? . . . A nation can neither alienate nor forbid to itself the right to will; and whatever its decisions may be, it cannot lose the right to change them as soon as its interest so requires. . . . Even if it could, a nation *must* not subject itself to the shackles of a definite procedure. That would put it in danger of losing its liberty forever, for tyranny, under the pretext of giving the people a constitution, would only need a momentary success to bind it so closely by procedural rules that it would lose the ability to express its own will. (182–83)

The implication of this argument was clear: the Estates-General, limited as it was by the division of the nation and its representatives into three orders and by the archaic procedural rules accumulated over the centuries, was hardly competent to determine the nation's constitution. The nation must decide constitutional questions by the pure exercise of its sovereign will, unconstrained by any preexisting constitutional forms. "Whose task is it to decide? The nation's, independent as it necessarily is of any positive forms. Even if the nation had an Estates-General that met regularly, this constituted body would not be competent to judge in a dispute concerning its own constitution" (184).

Sieyes's adoption of a basically Rousseauean conception of the nation, hence, gave him a powerful philosophical argument against the political competence of the Estates-General. No representative body based on the division of the French people into three separate and hierarchically arranged orders could legitimately express the national will. But when it came to the question of how the nation's will was to make itself known, Sieyes found Rousseau's ideas considerably less helpful.[3] This was because Rousseau was profoundly suspicious of representative government. He insisted that "sovereignty cannot be represented, for the same reason that it cannot be

3. For the relationship between Rousseau's and Sieyes's views on representation, see "Representation Redefined," chap. 10 in Baker, *Inventing the French Revolution,* esp. pp. 235–51.

alienated; its essence is the general will, and will cannot be represented." Thus he claimed that the English, who believed that their representative form of government assured their freedom, were actually free only during the brief moment of parliamentary elections.[4] "The moment a people gives itself representatives it is no longer free, it no longer exists."[5] On this matter Sieyes departed radically from Rousseau. He argued that a constitution must be elaborated by a body of representatives. And he based this argument on an implicit claim that representation, far from an alienation of sovereignty, was the essential form that sovereignty took in the large and advanced countries that made up contemporary Europe.

Sieyes's views on representation, and his implicit differences with Rousseau, are made clear in his own version of the story of the emergence of political society from the state of nature. Sieyes distinguishes three epochs in the formation of political society.

In the first epoch, we assume a greater or lesser number of isolated individuals who wish to unite. By this fact alone they already form a nation: they have all the rights of a nation and it only remains for them to exercise them. This first period is characterized by the play of *individual* wills. The association is the work of these wills; they are the origin of all power.

The second epoch is characterized by the action of the common will. The associates want to give consistency to their union; they want to fulfill its aim. They therefore discuss and agree among themselves on public needs and on means of satisfying them. We see that here power belongs to the community. Individual wills are still its origin and still form its essential elements; but considered separately, they would be powerless. Power resides only in the aggregate. The community must have a common will; without *unity* of will it would never become a willing and acting body. (178)

Up to this point, Sieyes's story is more or less a synopsis of Rousseau's social contract. Previously isolated individuals form a

4. Rousseau, *The Social Contract,* p. 141.
5. Ibid., p. 143.

nation by a conscious act of association—a social contract. The social pact launches a second epoch of human history, in which the nation becomes an aggregate body with a single general will. The entire nation, the community as a whole, now exercises a plenitude of power over public affairs. But Sieyes's story of the third epoch is distinctly un-Rousseauean.

> Let us step forward in time. The associates are too numerous and occupy too large an area to exercise their common will easily by themselves. What do they do? They separate out whatever is necessary to attend to and satisfy public requirements; and they confer the exercise of that portion of the national will, and consequently of the national power, on a few of their number. Here we arrive at the third epoch, that is to say, the epoch of *government exercised by agents* [*par procuration*]. . . . I distinguish the third epoch from the second because it is no longer the *real* common will that acts, but a *representative* common will. (178–79)

The third epoch is necessitated by the nation's growth in population and area, which eventually makes action by the whole community impossible. In this third epoch, long since reached by the major countries of Europe, the real common will is replaced by the representative common will and exercised by bodies of delegates. Rousseau, of course, agreed that it was impossible to assemble the sovereign community in one place in the large nations that characterized Europe in his day. But he regarded these nations' practice of representation as evidence that they were no longer capable of liberty. Sieyes's view was quite different. For him the "representative will" that characterized modern societies was no less legitimate than the "real will" of the simpler, archaic societies they replaced. It was the form that the national will was bound to take in the large, wealthy, and complex societies of modern Europe.

But in the matter of determining the nation's constitution, a particular sort of representative body was required.

> The *ordinary* representatives of a people are charged, within existing constitutional forms, with exercising that portion of

the common will that is necessary for the maintenance of a good administration of society. Their power is limited to the affairs of government.

Extraordinary representatives will have whatever new power it may please the nation to give them. Because a great nation cannot assemble itself physically whenever extraordinary circumstances make this necessary, it must confer upon extraordinary representatives the powers required on such occasions. . . .

A body of extraordinary representatives takes the place of an assembly of the nation. Of course it need not be charged with the *plenitude* of the national will; it requires only special powers, and only in rare cases. . . . [The extraordinary representatives] are put in the place of the nation itself in order to determine the constitution. They are as independent of constitutional forms as the nation would be. It suffices for them to will as individuals would will in the state of nature; whatever the manner in which they were appointed as deputies; whatever their means of assembling and deliberating . . . ; their common will is as valid as that of the nation itself. (184–85)

Faced with a constitutional crisis, what should a nation do? It should choose an extraordinary representative body that stands in place of the nation itself. These deputies of the people should then deliberate and decide; just as individuals in the state of nature unite their wills to form a social pact, so the deputies unite theirs to make a constitution for the nation. "Their common will," Sieyes insists, "is as valid as that of the nation itself" (185). Thus Sieyes uses a Rousseauean definition of the nation and sovereignty to demonstrate that the current political impasse is so deep a constitutional crisis as to be irresolvable by any of the remedies yet suggested by the government. But Sieyes supplements Rousseau with a theory of legitimate representation, showing how a properly constituted representative body, one that refused to observe the distinction between the three orders, could validly express the people's will and provide the nation with a binding and legitimate constitution.

What, then, ought to have been done to resolve the constitutional crisis of the French monarchy? Not the convocation of an Estates-General. The Estates-General would be incompetent to act even if the Third were doubled and votes taken by head; as a representative body observing the distinction between orders and convoked under the forms of the old constitution, it could not represent the nation in formulating a new constitution. Rather, the monarch ought to have asked the nation to choose and to send to the capital an extraordinary assembly of deputies charged specifically with determining the constitution. But the Estates-General had, in fact, been convoked. Representatives of all three Estates were already being chosen, and in a few months they would begin to meet in Versailles. Is it not, Sieyes asks, too late to worry about "what ought to have been done?" "To this," he answers, "I reply . . . that the knowledge of what ought to have been done may help us to know what must be done" (191) in the current circumstance. The discussion of abstract political philosophy, in other words, prepares the reader for the revolutionary strategy outlined in the final chapter, entitled "What Remains to Be Done?"

A Revolutionary Program

In the sixth and final chapter of *What Is the Third Estate?* Sieyes develops an intensely practical and specific revolutionary strategy for the representatives of the Third Estate. In fact, he lays out two alternative strategies, both consistent with his statement of abstract political philosophy.

The goal, of course, was to assemble a body that represented the nation without regard to preexisting constitutional forms and divisions. In chapter 5, Sieyes had declared that the nation must be found "there where it exists, in the forty thousand parishes that embrace all the territory, all the inhabitants, and all those who pay taxes to support the common good" (187). The Estates-General could not claim to represent the nation so defined because half the delegates represented not the territory and people that constituted the nation but a tiny minority of privileged nobles and clerics. But this defect was not true of the body constituted by the representatives of the Third Estate. They could speak for the immense majority of the French people—some twenty-five million, as against the mere two hundred thousand represented by the deputies of the First and Second Estates. From this it follows that the delegates of the Third

Estate are actually "the authentic trustees of the national will" (201). If they were to meet alone, quite apart from the deputies of the other two Estates, they would be able "to speak without error in the name of the entire nation" (201). The representatives of the Third Estate would be entirely within their rights to declare themselves the National Assembly and to proceed without further ado to prepare a constitution for the nation. Such is Sieyes's first strategy: "The Third should assemble separately; it will not cooperate with the nobility and the clergy, nor will it vote with them, either by *order* or by *head*. . . . It is alleged that the Third Estate cannot form the *Estates-General* by itself. So much the better! It will form a *National Assembly*" (197).

This first revolutionary strategy brilliantly utilizes the philosophical arguments that Sieyes develops in chapter 5. The deputies of the Third Estate were, of course, chosen under a procedure that recognized only their ability to place before the king the wishes of the lowliest estate of the realm. But in *What Is the Third Estate?* Sieyes invites the deputies to imagine themselves as something much grander; he uses the elixir of political philosophy to transform the delegates of an inferior order in a hierarchical state into the sole and rightful bearers of the nation's sovereign will.

Nevertheless, Sieyes admits that this strategy, while philosophically justified, might be impolitic in practice—it might seem, as he puts it, "a little too abrupt" (202). "Our intention, in demonstrating to the Third the full extent of its resources, or rather of its rights, is not to convince it to employ them in all their rigor" (202). Thus, Sieyes proposes a second strategy. The Third Estate can simply use the meeting in Versailles to explain to the people of France the urgent necessity of convoking not an Estates-General but a body of extraordinary representatives specifically charged by the nation with fixing its constitution. Until such an extraordinary assembly is convoked, the Third Estate must refuse to constitute itself as a separate order of the Estates-General. Sieyes writes, "It will take no definitive decisions; it will wait for the nation to judge the great contention that divides the three orders. Such a course is, I admit, the most straightforward, the most magnanimous, and consequently the best suited to the dignity of the Third Estate" (203).

Hence, even though the government did not respond to the

constitutional crisis by doing what should have been done, the representatives of the Third Estate possess the means necessary to rectify the situation and provide France with a constitution. By preference, they should act magnanimously, refusing to act as an inferior order in an assembly of three estates and instead addressing to the public their plea for a proper extraordinary representation. But should this fail, they possess the rightful authority to declare themselves what they actually are: freely chosen representatives of the vast majority of the nation and thus capable of forming a National Assembly by themselves and giving a valid constitution to France.

A Script for the Revolution

Sieyes deploys his political arguments brilliantly over the course of the final four chapters of *What Is the Third Estate?* In chapter three he draws his readers in by supporting the conventional demands of the Third Estate, then proceeds to criticize the inadequacy of these demands. In chapter four he goes on to demonstrate that neither the government nor the nobility can be trusted to come up with a solution favorable to the Third Estate. This prepares the reader for a philosophical exposition of the true nature of the nation, its representation, and its constitution in chapter five, where he develops a political philosophy that points toward a solution to the constitutional crisis. Finally, in chapter 6 he shows how even the improperly constituted Estates-General can be utilized by the Third Estate to revolutionize the constitution and abolish the privileged status of the clergy and the nobility.

The cogency and effectiveness of Sieyes's argumentation can hardly be doubted. After all, a modified version of his strategy was eventually adopted by the representatives of the Third Estate. In the beginning they refused to constitute themselves as a separate order and used their sessions to appeal to public opinion. Finally, they took the second, more "abrupt" course and declared themselves the National Assembly—in a motion authored by Sieyes himself. *What Is the Third Estate?* provided a surprisingly accurate political script for the Revolution.[6]

6. I borrow this term from Keith Michael Baker, "A Script for a French Revolution:

A Rhetoric of Social Revolution

The French Revolution was not merely a political revolution, and *What Is the Third Estate?* was not merely a political document. Sieyes's deft political argumentation was certainly a crucial element in the success of his pamphlet. But I believe that the originality and power of *What Is the Third Estate?* arose equally from what might be called its rhetoric of social revolution. By the term "rhetoric of social revolution," I mean to include a number of related things: rhetoric that challenged the superior social prestige and extrapolitical power of nobles and clerics; rhetoric that harnessed private social grievances and resentments to public political issues; and rhetoric that criticized or called into question the basic architecture of the Old Regime's social order. Most of this rhetoric of social revolution was carefully crafted by Sieyes to motivate his readers to pursue his desired political goals. In this sense, his rhetoric of social revolution was all "political" rhetoric, and it had much of the sureness of touch that characterized his rhetoric of political revolution. In *What Is the Third Estate?* Sieyes linked a very specific and practical political program to the identification and denunciation of a class enemy. One of the distinct achievements of his pamphlet, I believe, was to harness to the "patriot" program for liberal political reform the energy of bourgeois resentment against aristocrats.

But whereas Sieyes appears to have envisaged the goals of his political rhetoric with remarkable clarity, the goals of his social rhetoric seem somewhat cloudier. The social rhetoric certainly was calculated to move his readers toward his by now familiar political goal: establishment of a national assembly free of distinctions of orders and empowered to adopt a new constitution. But it also implied more far-reaching and diffuse social goals: the abolition of honorific distinctions between nobles and laymen and the establishment of equality before the law, to be sure, but also, it would seem, the abolition of all forms of legal privilege, the reform of social manners, and a shift of both social and political power from idle aristocrats to a productive bourgeoisie. The means of reaching these goals

---

The Political Consciousness of the Abbé Mably," chap. 4 in *Inventing the French Revolution,* pp. 86–106.

was never spelled out in *What Is the Third Estate?* and it was often quite unclear what the goals might mean in practice. Although the social passions stirred up by the pamphlet certainly were powerful and politically effective, they were also volatile and unpredictable. In this respect, *What Is the Third Estate?* partook of and contributed to the gathering storm of social discontent that propelled the French Revolution into the uncharted waters of an anti-aristocratic social revolution.

An Identification of the Enemy

To see how Sieyes's pamphlet channeled the French Revolution toward an assault on the aristocracy, we must remember that attacks on the privileges of the nobility were only one of a swarm of themes in the political discourse of the pre-Revolution. However, *What Is the Third Estate?* focuses insistently on this single issue. Thus, in chapter two, Sieyes absolved the monarch of any blame for the sad condition of France. Indeed, he claimed that "it is a great mistake to believe that France is a monarchy. With the exception of a few years under Louis XI and under Richelieu and a few moments under Louis XIV when it was plain despotism," the history of France is actually the history of the court. "And what is the court but the head of this vast aristocracy which overruns every part of France . . . ?" The people, Sieyes remarks in chapter 2, "has always considered the King as so certainly misled and so defenseless in the midst of the active and all-powerful court, that it has never thought of blaming him for all the wrongs done in his name" (132–33). Thus absolved, the king is discreetly shuffled off the stage, not to be called on again until chapter 5, when Sieyes affirms that the king, although not competent to decide what France's constitution should be, undoubtedly has the right, as "first citizen," to convoke an extraordinary constituent assembly of the nation's representatives (190).

It was, of course, hardly original to absolve the very popular Louis XVI from wrongdoing. But blaming the *court* for whatever wrongs were committed in the King's name was a specific political choice. It was more common in the immediate prerevolutionary period to blame not the court but the king's *ministers*. Indeed, in his first pamphlet, written only a few months earlier, Sieyes himself had railed against ministers at some length.[7] But *What Is the Third Estate?* is virtually silent about so-called "ministerial despotism," one of the great political catchphrases of the day. This was for good reason. To blame "ministerial despotism" would have been to make common cause with the aristocracy—as represented, for example, in the Parlements and the Provincial Estates—against the power of the crown and the royal bureaucracy. About this Sieyes was explicit: he began his last chapter with the declaration that "the time is past when the three orders, thinking only of defending themselves against ministerial despotism, were ready to unite against the common enemy" (192). By attacking the court, Sieyes was rejecting such an alliance and laying all blame for political oppression and malfeasance at the door of the aristocracy.

A Statement of Social Metaphysics

The importance of the social theme in *What Is the Third Estate?* is indicated by the order in which Sieyes's arguments are presented. His strictly political argument does not begin in earnest until chapter 3. Chapters 1 and 2 are used to establish what Sieyes sees as a prior point, on which the weight of the political argumentation depends: that the Third Estate, in fact, constitutes a complete nation, while the nobility has a totally parasitical relationship to society.

The pamphlet begins rather oddly for a political tract. Rather than invoking the current crisis, chapter 1 launches into a classification of the nation's population into abstract socioeconomic categories. The first words of chapter 1 are, "What does a nation require to survive and prosper? It needs *private* activities and *public* services." The private activities, Sieyes continues, are carried out by four classes of citizens.

> (1) Since land and water provide the basic materials for human needs, the first class, in logical order, includes all the families connected with work on the land. (2) Between the initial sale of goods and the moment when they reach the consumer or user,

---

7. Emmanuel Joseph Sieyes, *Vues sur les moyens dont les représentants de la France pourront disposer en 1789* (n.p., 1789), e.g., pp. 4–6, 10, 62. This pamphlet is reprinted in Dorigny, *Oeuvres de Sieyès.*

goods acquire an increased value . . . through the incorporation of varying amounts of labor. In this way, human industry manages to improve the gifts of nature. . . . Such are the activities of the second class of persons. (3) Between production and consumption, as also between the various stages of production, a variety of intermediary agents intervene, to help producers as well as consumers; these are the shopkeepers and merchants. . . . Such is the function of the third class of persons. (4) Besides these three classes of useful and industrious citizens who deal with *things* fit to be consumed or used, society also requires a vast number of special activities and of services *directly* useful or pleasant to the *person.* This fourth class embraces all sorts of occupations, from the most distinguished liberal and scientific professions to the lowest of menial tasks. Such are the labors which support society. But who performs them? The Third Estate. (121–22)

These seemingly innocuous opening paragraphs are, in fact, the foundation of Sieyes's argument. They are placed at the outset of the pamphlet because they provide, in concrete exemplary form, the metaphysical underpinnings of his contention that the Third Estate is "everything." By dividing the population into *four* categories, Sieyes was implicitly overthrowing the traditional division of the population into *three* hierarchically ordered Estates. The three Estates were ranked according to their proximity to spirit, which, in the traditional scheme of things, was thought of as the source of order in the world. The clergy, who cared for spiritual matters, were the highest order; nobles, who magnanimously defended the realm and gave counsel to the prince, were the Second Estate; and commoners, who worked with their hands for material gain, were the Third. Sieyes's classification proposes a different ultimate source of order— nature—and ranks the four classes according to their proximity to it: from agriculture (direct cultivation of products of nature), to industry (transformation of natural products by labor), to commerce (exchange of these manufactured goods), to services (which entail no physical products at all). But Sieyes's classes are strictly nonhierarchical; otherwise, how could the fourth class, the one most remote from nature, contain both the most distinguished liberal professions and the lowest of menial tasks? In his classification of the population, Sieyes shifts the definition of society from a spiritually based hierarchy to a collection of producers united by their common work on nature. Within this obliquely announced social metaphysics, there was literally no place for the nobility.

Of course, the nobility could always object that its service to society was in its traditional sphere of public affairs, not in Sieyes's private activities. So immediately after setting out his fourfold classification, Sieyes attacked this argument head-on. Nineteen-twentieths of public services are, in fact, also performed by the Third Estate. In fact, "only the well-paid and honorific posts are performed by the privileged order" (122). And this, rather than a magnanimous service to the public, is actually a "social crime" (122). Because aristocrats have a monopoly on such posts, their work is badly done: "Are we unaware that any work from which free competition is excluded will be performed less well and more expensively? . . . Without [the nobility] the higher posts would be infinitely better filled. . . . If the privileged have succeeded in usurping all well-paid and honorific posts, this is both a hateful iniquity towards the generality of citizens and an act of treason to the commonwealth" (122–23). In this passage, Sieyes refutes the nobility's last claim to usefulness.

The conclusion, then, is that the nobility is *nothing:* "It is not part of our society at all; it may be a burden for the nation, but it cannot be part of it" (124). The Third Estate, by contrast, is *everything.*

> Who then is bold enough to maintain that the Third Estate does not contain within itself everything necessary to constitute a complete nation? It is like a strong and robust man with one arm still in chains. If the privileged order were removed, the nation would not be something less but something more. What then is the Third Estate? Everything, but an "Everything" that is fettered and oppressed. What would it be without the privileged order? It would be a free and flourishing everything. Nothing can function without the Third Estate; everything would work infinitely better without the others. (124)

The point of the first chapter of *What Is the Third Estate?* is to establish the social nullity of the aristocracy. Given Sieyes's implicit metaphysical definition of society as a collection of producers united by common work on nature, the nobility has no real existence. As Sieyes puts it in a footnote, "Whatever the society, there exist only private and public professions. Nothing else exists except nonsensicalities, dangerous fancies or pernicious institutions" (124). The nobility, therefore, can only be thought of as something foreign to society. It is, Sieyes asserts, "foreign to the nation because of its *idleness*" (125). Worse than foreign, it is, in fact, an enemy. Its pretensions constitute "a social crime, a veritable act of war" (122), "an act of treason to the commonwealth" (123); the privileged are "no less enemies of the common order than are the English of the French in times of war" (140). This same essential point is made over and over by Sieyes's metaphorical representations of the nobility: as "Barbary pirates" preying on legitimate commerce (140), as a "horrible disease eating the living flesh of an unfortunate man" (211), and as "vegetable parasites which can only live on the sap of the plants that they impoverish and blight" (125). And Sieyes twice performs the wishful thought experiment of removing the aristocracy from the nation, once in the first chapter and once in the last: "If the privileged order were removed, the nation would not be something less but something more" (124); and later, "How fortunate it would be for the nation if so desirable a secession could be perpetuated! How easy it would be to do without the privileged!" (194)

At the very beginning, then, Sieyes establishes the fundamental point of his pamphlet upon which all his later political arguments are built. Given Sieyes's metaphysical assumptions, the nobility is a social nullity; its domination of state and society is therefore a crime and an act of war. Foreign, parasitical, cancerous, it must be obliterated for the nation to be healthy and free. If the reader accepts Sieyes's denunciation of the nobility as an enemy of the nation, his political conclusions are almost impossible to resist. The Third Estate must constitute the political as well as the social nation, and the representatives of the Third Estate are the sole legitimate representatives of the national will. Thus, the first two chapters of *What Is the Third Estate?* provided a social motivation for the political arguments of the remaining chapters. At the same time, Sieyes provided the revolution with a specific program of social revolution—abolition of the privileges of the nobility.

An Appeal to Class Resentment

I stated earlier that the specific contribution of *What Is the Third Estate?* to the French Revolution was to harness the energy of bourgeois class resentment against aristocrats to the patriots' program for liberal political reform.[8] I think I have by now established that it was calculated to intensify resentment against the aristocracy. But was this resentment specifically *bourgeois?* Explicitly, of course, the aristocracy is always portrayed as the enemy of the entire Third Estate, which was the whole nation. But in practice, Sieyes makes no appeals to lower levels of the Third Estate; for example, he never mentions the very real grievances of peasants or of artisans. He does, however, make a very specific appeal to the wealthy and educated non-nobles of the cities, whom we can speak of, in an eighteenth-century sense, as "the bourgeoisie."

Perhaps the clearest case is in chapter 3, where he refutes the argument that "the Third Estate does not contain enough intelligent or courageous members competent to represent it" and therefore "has no option but to call on the greater enlightenment of the aristocracy": "So ridiculous a statement deserves no answer. Look at the *available* classes in the Third Estate; and like everyone else I call "available" those classes where a sort of affluence enables men to receive a liberal education, to train their minds to take an interest in public affairs. Such classes have no interest other than that of the rest of the People. Judge whether they do not contain enough citizens who are educated, honest, and worthy in all respects to represent the nation properly" (143–44). Here Sieyes clearly is attempting to win the assent not of the entire Third Estate but only of those who can imagine themselves as fit to represent the nation. Their pride is further indulged by the implication that they are animated entirely by public-spiritedness: they "have no interest other than that of the rest of the People." The bourgeoisie is here presented as the natural representative of the nation as a whole.

8. In speaking of "class resentment" here and elsewhere, I use the term class in a purely colloquial sense. I do not mean to imply that either the bourgeoisie or the nobility was a class in the Marxian sense of the term—that is, a group standing in a particular and antagonistic relation to the means of production. Class resentment here means simply a resentment against a category of persons who are perceived as claiming to be superior to one's own category.

But far more pervasive than this positive appeal to the *amour propre* of the bourgeoisie are Sieyes's negative appeals to bourgeois resentment against the overbearing pride of aristocrats. Over and over again, Sieyes remarks how the Third Estate, in spite of its utility, its competence, and its enlightenment, is constantly subjected to humiliation by aristocrats: "The Third Estate must submit to every form of contempt, insult, and humiliation. To avoid being completely crushed, what must the unlucky non-privileged person do? He has to attach himself by all kinds of contemptible actions to some magnate; he prostitutes his principles and human dignity for the possibility of claiming, in his need, the protection of a *somebody*" (129). The language of pride and humiliation is ubiquitous. Insult, base, prostitute, servitude, humiliate, vile, fear, degrade, shame, opprobrium, coward, villein, bondage, despise, flattery, mock, brazen, pride, contempt, honor, infamy: such words burst from Sieyes's pen on page after page, from one end of the pamphlet to the other. Throughout the development of the argument, the bourgeois reader, who is assumed to be male, is reminded over and over that his pride has been wounded by those who hold him in contempt, that the necessity of passively accepting the dictates of aristocrats endangers his manly honor. By the end of the pamphlet, not only has he been convinced that the principle of aristocracy vitiates the state and society and that the Third Estate possesses the means to reconstruct France on a sound basis; he has also been goaded into fury at the aristocrats' insufferable pride.

It is interesting to note that Sieyes successively increased the number of passages that included language of pride and humility or expressions of fury at the aristocrats' arrogance in the second and third editions of *What Is the Third Estate?*, which were published in the spring of 1789.[9] He seems to have been responding to the success of his rhetoric of social resentment by pouring it on thicker than ever. In any case, the tone of his pamphlet became increasingly ferocious. This may be seen at the very end of the pamphlet. His first two editions ended combatively enough, with a metaphor comparing aristocrats to a life-draining disease:

9. Additions of this sort may be found on pp. 125, 126–27, 128, 129, 131, 133, 140, 160, 162, 165, 194–95, and 196. Zapperi notes all changes introduced into the text in its various editions.

> Do not ask what is the appropriate place for a privileged class in
> the social order. It is like deciding on the appropriate place in
> the body of a sick man for a malignant humor that torments
> him and drains his strength. It must be *neutralized*. The health
> and the order of the organs must be restored, so as to prevent the
> formation of noxious combinations that vitiate the essential
> principles of life itself. (218)

But in the third edition, Sieyes adds to this a stinging taunt calculated to prod his bourgeois reader into rage.

> But the word has gone round: you are not yet fit enough to be
> healthy! And to this aphorism of aristocratic wisdom, you give
> credence, like a pack of orientals consoling themselves with
> fatalism. Sick as you are then, so remain! (218)

The Pamphlet's Rhetorical Structure

How, then, can we characterize the overall rhetorical structure of
What Is the Third Estate? The pamphlet is divided into two sections.
The first, which comprises the first two chapters, is devoted to
establishing the social nullity of the aristocracy. It is the primary
locus of what I have called Sieyes's rhetoric of social revolution. The
second, much longer, section, which comprises chapters 3 through
6, is the principal locus of his rhetoric of political revolution. Its goal
is to move the reader from support for the conventional demands of
the Third Estate to support for revolutionary action by the Third
Estate's delegates to the Estates-General.

The chief role of Sieyes's rhetoric of social revolution is to motivate
his political conclusions. By identifying the aristocracy as the essential cause of France's political woes, and by demonstrating that the
aristocracy is a social nullity, absolutely without metaphysical standing, Sieyes prepares his readers to accept his radical political conclusion that the Third Estate can rightfully arrogate to itself sovereign
power to determine the nation's constitution. In this sense, the social
argumentation is a means to a political end. But this means-ends
relationship can also be read the other way around. Once the representatives of the Third Estate have made themselves the National
Assembly, what ought their program to be? Sieyes does not raise the

point, since the goal of the pamphlet is to make possible a seizure of power by the representatives of the Third Estate. Yet an implicit program is set forth in Sieyes's first two chapters. The National Assembly must abolish privilege so as to recognize and to constitute the nation legally as what it truly, metaphysically, is: a community of citizen-producers united by their work on nature. In other words, while Sieyes's social argumentation is a means to a political end, his political arguments, once they succeed, in turn become the means to an implied social end. The ultimate but unvoiced goal of *What Is the Third Estate?* is a fundamental transformation of the social order. Finally, from the beginning to the end of the pamphlet, Sieyes stokes up social passions capable of driving forward both his avowed political and his unavowed social revolutions by drawing out the resentment and piquing the wounded pride of the bourgeoisie. In this sense, Sieyes was what Marxist historians of the Revolution have always thought him to be: a prophet of a bourgeois social revolution.

A Revolutionary Bourgeoisie?

But what sort of "bourgeoisie" was Sieyes appealing to? After all, it is by now generally accepted that the members of the upper Third Estate who led the French Revolution were by no means an industrial and commercial bourgeoisie frustrated by the fetters imposed on them by feudal property relations. Most historical research of the past three decades has argued that the supposed "revolutionary bourgeoisie" had a culture and a mode of life that distinguished it little from the nobility. Many of the most prominent bourgeois even had the same relation to the means of production as nobles in that their revenues, like those of the nobility, were derived above all from what George Taylor calls "proprietary wealth." The "revolutionary bourgeoisie," like the nobility, was largely a rentier class.[10] Historians have also established that the prerevolutionary nobility was by no means a closed caste; upward mobility from the upper reaches of the Third Estate to the nobility remained substantial right to the end of the Old Regime.[11] Nor were nobles and wealthy commoners divided

10. Taylor, "Noncapitalist Wealth."
11. David D. Bien, "Manufacturing Nobles: The Chancelleries in France to 1789," *Journal of Modern History* 61 (1989): 445–86.

by impenetrable social barriers; they participated in the same salons, Masonic lodges, and provincial academies. [12]

If all this was true, why should wealthy commoners have been moved by the burning resentment expressed in the pages of *What Is the Third Estate?* What were Sieyes and his readers angry about? The mystery does not seem difficult to penetrate. Revisionist historiography has tended to assume that if the bourgeoisie and the aristocracy were not distinct classes in a Marxist sense and if wealthy commoners could still rise into the nobility, then there was no reason for relations between the nobility and the bourgeoisie to be fraught with conflict. The French Revolution, therefore, could only be a political, not a social, revolution. I think this line of argument is based on a false premise. While it certainly is true that Old Regime society was much more fluid than the classical Marxist historians of the Revolution claimed, it remained profoundly hierarchical. Where elaborate hierarchy was combined with fluid social relations, social status was never secure. Even those bourgeois who had wealth, education, and good social positions had to be constantly vigilant to preserve their honor against threats from above and below. Social intercourse, consequently, was bathed in a continual cascade of disdain. Each group was subjected to multiple, if often petty, humiliations from above and returned the favor to those immediately below. In Old Regime society, disdain—and its inevitable complement, resentment—were produced abundantly by the ordinary experiences of bourgeois life. [13] And although these resentments were by no means generated solely by slights at the hands of nobles, the nobility and its privileges remained the pinnacle and the paradigm of hierarchy. The genius of Sieyes was to tap into this diffuse and omnipresent social resentment, to direct it unambiguously against the privileges of the nobility, and to harness this resentment against the nobility to a specific political program. By doing so, Sieyes helped induce prosperous bourgeois who were deeply integrated into Old Regime social

12. Daniel Roche, *Le Siècle des lumières en province: Académies et académiciens provinciaux, 1680–1789,* 2 vols. (Paris: Mouton, 1978).
13. One historian who has made much of this kind of resentment as a source of radical politics among old regime journalists and men of letters is Robert Darnton. See his *Literary Underground,* esp. chap. 1, "The High Enlightenment and the Low-Life of Literature," pp. 1–40.

hierarchies to embrace a revolution that would destroy the social world as they had known it.

The brilliance of Sieyes's combined rhetoric of political and social revolution may be judged by its extraordinary efficacy. *What Is the Third Estate?* crystallized the resentments of the politically active elite of the Third Estate and charted the political course of the Revolution through the crucial summer of 1789. Moreover, it presaged and prepared the climactic night of 4 August, when the National Assembly abolished the privileges of the aristocracy and the clergy, destroyed the vestiges of feudalism, and established equality of citizens before the law. The night of 4 August was the logical culmination of Sieyes's revolutionary script.

3

POLITICAL ECONOMY, SOCIAL CONTRACT, AND

REPRESENTATION: THE FOUNDATIONS OF

SIEYES'S POLITICAL THOUGHT

HAT IS THE THIRD ESTATE? WAS A RHETORICAL tour de force. Like most truly persuasive texts, however, its power was not based solely on rhetorical cunning, but on conceptual innovations as well. Two of the most crucial arguments of the pamphlet—Sieyes's exclusion of nobles from the nation on the grounds that they did not work and his grafting of representation onto a Rousseauean theory of popular sovereignty—had precisely this quality of conceptual novelty. In *What Is the Third Estate?* Sieyes proved himself to be a political philosopher of some originality as well as a master rhetorician. Like most of the major pamphleteers and orators of the French Revolution, Sieyes was familiar with Greek and Roman history and with the works of Rousseau, Montesquieu, Locke, Grotius, and other political theorists. Where he differed from most of his peers was in his intimate knowledge of the emerging discourse of political economy. This difference was the foundation of his originality: the arguments Sieyes used to exclude nobles from the nation and those he employed to combine national sovereignty with representation were drawn directly from political economy.

Although other pamphleteers borrowed ideas from political economy, such ideas were rarely central to their arguments. Sieyes was not, for example, the first to claim that the Third Estate did all of the nation's useful work, nor the only one to conclude that the Third therefore constituted the true nation. Such assertions, which certainly rested implicitly on political-economic ideas, were actually fairly common in the countless pamphlets written in the months before the opening of the Estates-General. But in other pamphlets, occasional and ill-developed economic notions were used as flourishes in a political argument. For Sieyes, by contrast, the idea that the Third Estate was the nation because it did all the nation's work was a logical conclusion explicitly derived from principles of political economy. Sieyes began *What Is the Third Estate?* with cogent economic arguments and used these as the logical foundation on which to erect his subsequent political reasoning.

This prominent use of political economy in *What Is the Third Estate?* was not a matter of mere opportunistic borrowing. Sieyes had read and studied the major texts of political economy long before the Revolution. Economic ideas figured centrally in nearly all of his published writings and speeches, from the prerevolutionary *Essay on Privilege* and *What Is the Third Estate?* through his speeches and writings during the Constituent Assembly on the rights of man, the tithe, the royal veto, the reorganization of national territory, and the reform of the clergy, down to the constitutional proposals he put forward after thermidor. Virtually all of Sieyes's political thought had an important economic dimension. As we shall see, Sieyes rejected not only Rousseau's ideas about representation but the entire classical model of Greek and Roman political virtue on which it was based; he argued that material well-being, not political virtue, was the proper goal of a modern European state. Sieyes embraced the modern commercial societies of his own day and used the language of political economy to elaborate a constitutional program he deemed appropriate to a commercial age. Not only did he address *What Is the Third Estate?* to a bourgeois audience, but he also attempted to fashion a state that would be governed by enlightened bourgeois officials and guided by what the nineteenth century would have called a bourgeois ethos.

Nowhere was the importance of political economy clearer than in his ideas about representation, which recent scholars have quite properly identified as his most original contribution to the political theory of the revolutionary era.[1] On this issue, Sieyes differed sharply

1. See especially Baker, "Sieyès"; Baker, "Representation"; Baczko, "Le contract social"; Clavreul, "Influence de la théorie de Sieyès"; Clavreul, "Sieyès et la représen-

from virtually all of his contemporaries. Even after the National Assembly had seized power in June 1789, most political thinkers remained trapped in a Rousseauean distrust of representation. Although members of the National Assembly had gained power as elected representatives, they continued to worry about how and whether their legislative enactments could be regarded as genuine expressions of the nation's will. Their continuing malaise about the legitimacy of representation made legislators susceptible to claims— by fellow legislators, journalists, or popular orators—that they had betrayed or ignored the will of the people.

François Furet has argued that this fundamental mistrust of the principle of representation made possible a continuing escalation of claims to enunciate the national will. He identifies this escalation as the chief mechanism of radicalization in the Revolution. The dominant mistrust of representation was, by this reckoning, a major source of the Terror. One reason that students of revolutionary political theory have been so fascinated by Sieyes is that he was the only major French thinker of the period who entirely escaped the Rousseauean trap and argued clearly and consistently for the legitimacy of binding action by representatives. Keith Baker, in the final paragraph of *Inventing the French Revolution,* intimates that had Sieyes's concept of representation been accepted by other political actors, the history of the Revolution might have been very different and far less bloody. According to Baker, the National Assembly's "repudiation of Sieyes's arguments for a theory of representation" meant that "in the long run, it was opting for the Terror."[2]

Sieyes's espousal of government by representatives was based on his musings about political economy, and especially on his thoughts about the division of labor. Sieyes did not explicitly set forth this political-economic foundation when he argued for the legitimacy of representation in *What Is the Third Estate?* But its presence as an assumption is evident from his prerevolutionary notes and his later speeches and writings. Several recent studies of Sieyes's political ideas have made it clear that political economy provided him with the

---

tation moderne"; Gueniffey, "Les Assemblées et la représentation"; Pasquino, "Sieyès, Constant et le 'Gouvernement' "; Pasquino, "Concept de nation"; and Maiz, "Nation and Representation."

2. Baker, *Inventing the French Revolution,* p. 305.

means of escaping the Rousseauean trap; his theory of representation was based on the concept of the division of labor.[3] I will try to demonstrate in this chapter that Sieyes's reliance on political economy went very deep, perhaps deeper than most of his recent interpreters have guessed.

In this chapter I will argue that political-economic principles served as the indispensable foundation of two crucial arguments of *What Is the Third Estate?*: that nobles were not part of the nation and that representatives of the people were fully, indeed uniquely, competent to express its will. But I will also try to show that Sieyes had a surprisingly coherent and original underlying vision of political economy, one that differed markedly from those of both the French Physiocrats and the Scottish political economists. At the core of this vision was a particular theory of the social contract. Although Sieyes never developed his economic ideas systematically, I will argue that he managed to combine social contract theory with political economy to forge a unique perspective on the constitutional issues that faced the French during the Revolution.

A Long Apprenticeship

Sieyes's engagement with political economy was deep and sustained.[4] As early as 1774, when he was still a student in the seminary of Saint Sulpice in Paris, he actually prepared for publication what was intended as the first installment of a tract on political economy. The tract as a whole was entitled "Letters to the Economists on Their Political and Moral System," and the completed portion was the "First Letter: On Riches." Its publication was to be undertaken by supporters of the reformist minister Turgot, but the minister's fall from office disrupted their plans, and the tract languished unpublished in Sieyes's papers.[5] Sieyes never again attempted to publish a

3. See n. 1.
4. An excellent introduction to the economic thought of Sieyes is Dorigny, "Formation de la pensée économique de Sieyès."
5. "Lettres aux économistes sur leur système de politique et de morale," AN, 284 AP 2, dossier 10. The term "économistes" referred at the time specifically to the school of writers now usually called the Physiocrats. The "Lettres" has recently been published in Sieyès, *Ecrits politiques*, pp. 25–44. Zapperi points out that before the publication plans collapsed, Sieyes had obtained permission from the royal censor to publish this work (p. 19).

work on political economy, but over the entire period from 1770 to the eve of the Revolution he continued to read widely in the economists' works. He took many notes and jotted down reflections on a wide variety of political-economic issues. These notes are available in Sieyes's papers in the Archives Nationales in Paris, and a number of the most important have been published recently in a collection of Sieyes's writings edited by Roberto Zapperi.[6]

Except in his "Letters to the Economists," Sieyes's economic ideas are scattered and are presented in only fragmentary form. His published pamphlets and speeches from the revolutionary period contain a number of observations about political economy, but because these works were all directed to specific political ends, his economic ideas are stated only in brief. His notes from the prerevolutionary period are far more elaborate and abundant, but they present very difficult problems of interpretation, not the least of which is Sieyes's difficult hand. The most interesting of these notes are very brief, usually just a paragraph or two, and are penned on small sheets of unbound paper. The individual notes, which are virtually never dated, are grouped together in folders in the archives. Some of these folders have been given brief titles and dates by Sieyes—for example, "Political contours written in 1774 and 1776,"[7] or "Political Economy 1772"[8]—but others are simply labeled "Varia,"[9] or "Scattered, diverse, and incomplete notes on subjects of political economy,"[10] with no indication of dates. Moreover, the small, undated sheets of paper could easily have found their way from one folder to another during the long years since they were initially written by Sieyes; for this reason, most of the notes cannot be dated firmly. It is therefore virtually impossible to assess how Sieyes's thinking about political economy may have changed over time.

6. The story of Sieyes's papers is sketched in Marquant, *Les Archives Sieyès*. Most of the papers now in the Archives Nationales had disappeared from view after being consigned to Sieyes's nineteenth-century biographer Hippolyte Fortoul and were only discovered again among the papers willed to the Archives Nationales in 1959 and 1964 by Fortoul's descendants. The notes on political economy are in Sieyes, *Ecrits politiques*, pp. 45–90.
7. AN, 284 AP 2, dossier 15.1
8. AN, 284 AP 2, dossier 6.
9. AN, 284 AP 3, dossier 1.2.
10. AN, 284 AP 2, dossier 13.

But the difficulties do not end with the uncertainty about dates. The notes are generally very brief and often cryptic. They are genuine notes, addressed by the author to himself and not to the public. They served to sketch out ideas, to aid his memory, to fix fugitive thoughts. Some are as much works of fantasy as of science or philosophy. Because Sieyes did not intend these notes for public consumption, he made no effort to impose coherence on them; what is said in one note, or indeed in one paragraph, is sometimes taken back in the next. The notes, in short, are filled with fascinating, astute, and occasionally puzzling observations. Carefully interpreted, they significantly enrich our understanding of Sieyes's thought. But what is missing from the notes as well as from Sieyes's published political writings is any systematic development of his ideas. Even his "Letters to the economists," which comes closest of any of his writings to a treatise on political economy, is mainly a critique of the Physiocrats rather than a systematic exposition of his own concepts. It should not be surprising that in this scattered mass of documentation there are plenty of contradictions. Some of these contradictions arose from the changing contexts in which Sieyes recorded his reflections about economic life; others, no doubt, resulted from alterations in his views over time. But I also think that his economic thought is permanently marked by certain fundamental ambivalences. The goal of this chapter is to sketch out the fundamental premises of Sieyes's ideas about political economy, to search for unifying themes more than contradictions and ambivalences. But contradictions will certainly be apparent in the text of this chapter, and some of them will be pursued more tenaciously in chapter five.

The Marks of Modernity

Sieyes's thinking about political economy was based on an explicit acceptance of modernity, which he understood as the predominance of economic motives and interests over all others—moral, religious, military, or political. But this fundamental acceptance was not without certain afterthoughts, as can be seen from a passage in his speech on the question of the proposed royal veto, delivered in the National Assembly in September 1789.

Modern European peoples bear little resemblance to the an-
cients. Among us it is always a question of commerce, agriculture, manufactures, etc. The desire for riches seems to have
made the great states of Europe into nothing but vast work-
shops where people think more about consumption and production than about happiness. Hence political systems, today, are
founded exclusively on labor: the productive faculties of man are
all; we hardly know how to profit from moral faculties, which
could, nevertheless, be the most fertile source of real happiness.
We are therefore forced to see, in the largest number of men,
nothing but laboring machines [*machines de travail*].[11]

Sieyes clearly marks his distance from Rousseau and from all other
philosophers and politicians who looked for inspiration to the ancient
republics of Greece and Rome. Because modern Europeans care only
about production and consumption, the political systems of ancient
peoples, which had entirely different goals, could no longer serve as
useful models. But even while accepting the necessity of political
systems appropriate for the European societies of his era, he also
registered doubts about the real worth of modern preferences. Far
from speaking, as did Adam Smith, for example, of the growth of
consumption as the source of happiness, Sieyes implicitly opposes it
to happiness: modern Europeans "think more about consumption
and production than about happiness." Similarly, he contrasts the
productive faculties to the moral faculties, remarking that the latter
"could, nevertheless, be the most fertile source of real happiness." All
of this implies that the interest in production and consumption that
dominates modern European peoples gives rise only to inferior forms
of happiness, that "real happiness" is more moral than economic.
This implication is vividly fortified in the final sentence, which
seems to say that moderns no longer see humans as moral beings but
merely as "laboring machines."

Such doubts are unusual in Sieyes's writings. They do not occur
elsewhere in his major political pamphlets or speeches and are rare in
his notes, most of which accept a society based on economic motiva-

11. *Dire de l'Abbé Sieyes sur la question du veto Royal*, pp. 13–14; published in Sieyes,
Ecrits politiques, p. 236.

tions as their point of departure. But there is one note with a completely different spirit. Sieyes entitled it "Greece, Citizen, Man."

Happy Greece! All my observations irritate me, I return to you, I find again in the pictures you offer me the true image of man in the state of society. Alas, how we have degenerated! What depravity among my fellow men!

I think no one will disagree if I say that citizens no longer exist because there is no longer a society governing itself in all the purity of original liberty; but if I moan that I no longer see *men*, there will be complaints. We pay little attention to the fact that there are only a small number, very small, of free and thinking heads who still perpetuate the reduced dignity of the human species. Leave a few European capitals and search everywhere. See if in the well-to-do classes there is a single individual who is not the slave of some great one, the enemy of his fellows, a despicable animal, even though trained in a few copied social antics [*singeries sociales*] lacking in sense or sensibility. Among the unfortunates devoted to painful labor, producers of others' pleasures who receive barely enough to sustain their suffering and needy bodies, in that immense crowd of biped instruments, without liberty, without morality, without intellectuality, possessing only hands that gain little and a soul absorbed, serving them only in suffering . . . are these what you call men? Is there one among them who would be capable of entering into society? . . . I return to my imagination, to my democratic colonies, I contemplate the imposing and well-organized mass. . . .

The qualities that make a man are to be *sociable* and not servile; to be capable of becoming an integral part of society, or a citizen; to conserve in his soul the sentiment of equality; not to have lost the spring of his soul and his mind; to be enraged against the insolent, against the tyrant and against the coward; to be above superstitions of all kinds, but especially above this vile nobility and the masters of nations.[12]

This note is highly exceptional in the works of Sieyes, in style as well as in content. It begins with emotional exclamations in the

12. Sieyes, *Ecrits politiques*, p. 81, and AN, 284 AP 5, dossier 4.

manner of Rousseau ("Happy Greece! . . . Alas, how we have degenerated! What depravity among my fellow men!")—a rhetorical device uncommon in Sieyes's works, which normally deal in irony spiced with occasional indignation rather than effusions of sentiment. The content is no less Rousseauean: the degeneration of men from their pristine condition; the wealthy as slaves of the powerful, full of "copied social antics lacking in sense or sensibility"; the poor reduced to "biped instruments, without liberty, without morality, without intellectuality." Sieyes's nostalgia for the simpler, more virtuous society of Greece, which contradicts his normal matter-of-fact acceptance of "modern" nations bent on production and consumption, is palpable in this note.

One might hypothesize that this was an effusion of the young Sieyes, whereas the mature man had come to accept modern society on its own terms. But the note is not definitively datable, and there are reasons to think it may have been written relatively late. Jotted down on a single unbound sheet, it is contained in a carton of Sieyes's papers dating from 1792 through the beginning of the Empire, but in an undated dossier entitled simply "Scattered and incomplete notes." It seems probable, but far from certain, that the notes gathered there date from the same period as the political papers contained in the other dossiers in the carton, but none of the notes in the dossier are dated, nor can any of them be dated unambiguously by their subject matter or references to events. All are of the same type found in Sieyes's prerevolutionary papers. There is, moreover, little in the language of this note that might help us to date it. However, the final line, denouncing the nobility, seems rather out of place at any time after 1789, when the term "nobility" was largely replaced by "aristocracy," especially in unfavorable usages. In the end, it is impossible to hazard more than a plausible guess about the date of composition of this note. But whenever it was written, its existence, together with his remarks in the speech on the royal veto in September 1789, indicates that there was a bit of Rousseau under the skin of this apparently committed modernist—that he, like so many of his fellow revolutionaries, had experienced regret about the fact that economic motives had come to predominate over motives of political and moral virtue in the societies of his epoch.

But Sieyes, whether from a real sympathy for the goals of contemporary societies or from a resigned realism, embraced the world the political economists had revealed in their works. Sieyes strove to construct a state and a constitution appropriate for a society devoted to production and consumption. This set him off sharply from most other revolutionary political leaders, whose conscious political model was the patriotism of classical Greece and Rome.

The Labors that Support Society

Sieyes based his version of political economy on a fundamental principle: "It is labor that forms wealth."[13] This is the thesis he maintains against the Physiocrats in his "Letters to the Economists" of 1774. The doctrine of the Physiocrats was quite different: that the fecundity of the earth is the true source of wealth, whereas industrial or commercial labor is sterile. Sieyes insisted that labor was as necessary to agricultural as to industrial production. Agricultural products, which the Physiocrats called "simple productions," were not simple at all. "The earth only yields them to our solicitations, to our labors, to our investments."[14] In industry, as in agriculture, wealth is always the product of natural forces managed and applied by human labor: "Is it not nature that reddens and softens the iron that the blacksmith exposes to the action of fire? Can we, without recurring to the power of nature, decompose what it has composed, unite what it has separated? Does not a large part of our food consist of mixtures that nature has yielded to us separately? In the art of production as in all others, man seizes one part of the forces of nature, with which he subdues another part."[15] Or as he puts it in one of his notes, "The difference between the product of currently cultivated land and that of a still wild country whose productions are so little appropriate to the needs and the tastes of man should be considered as the progress of labor. Everything comes from industry; nature is only the instrument of art, and it is the same in manufactures."[16] Industry, which Sieyes intends in its eighteenth-century meaning of steady

13. Sieyes, "Lettres," in *Ecrits politiques*, p. 32, and AN, 284 AP 2, dossier 10.
14. Sieyes, "Lettres," in *Ecrits politiques*, p. 40.
15. Ibid.
16. Sieyes, "Extension de l'industrie rurale," in *Ecrits politiques*, p. 74, and AN, 284 AP 3, dossier 1.2.

and assiduous work, is what creates wealth. Nature, including land, is only made productive by the application of art, that is, human ingenuity applied to the world.

Sieyes sees labor at the very origin of human society. In his "Letters to the Economists," Sieyes performs an original twist on social contract theory by characterizing society as an association of laborers formed for the effective production of wealth.

> Every man wishes to be happy, that is, to enjoy himself as he pleases. Enjoyment consumes goods; an ever-acting force that produces new ones is therefore needed. . . . We must employ all our efforts to assure and increase the reproduction of goods that require the aid of our labor. This particular goal becomes that of all society; could it have any other end than that of its members? An association is only a more perfect means to obtain with greater profusion and more certainty what each desires, wealth. Therefore society, independently of the power of nature which produces goods, must have a *living force* coproductive of wealth, and it is necessary that the elements of that force, united by society, produce more than they would if they remained isolated. The sum of the labors of all citizens forms the living force. If there is a citizen who refuses his portion of activity he renounces his rights; no man may enjoy the labor of others without exchange. General labor is therefore the foundation of society, and the social order is nothing but the best possible order of labor.[17]

Here Sieyes presents a highly original supplement to the theory of the social contract, one that has resemblances to both Locke's and Rousseau's but is distinct from either. Locke, of course, sees society as arising out of labor. Placed in the state of nature, men (I use the masculine advisedly) labor to satisfy their wants. Their labor on nature creates property in things. "The acorns he picked up under an oak, or the apples he gathered from the trees in the wood" became the property of the man whose labor was expended in gathering them, as did "as much land as a man tills, plants, improves, cultivates, and

17. Sieyes, "Lettres," in *Ecrits politiques,* p. 32.

can use the product of."[18] For Locke, the motivation for the social contract is the protection of property. Government arises when individuals in the state of nature band together, deciding that they need a neutral and impartial magistrate to secure their liberty to use their property as they see fit.

Sieyes, like Locke, begins with the individual and his wants. Because enjoyment consumes goods, humans must labor "to assure and increase the reproduction of goods." But the society created by these laboring individuals is significantly different from Locke's. Locke sees the social contract as creating a minimal state, whose goal is to guarantee men's natural rights of liberty and property. In Locke's social contract, labor stands at the origin of society, but once government has been formed, questions of production and consumption cease to be of concern to the state; they are consigned entirely to the private sphere. Sieyes, as can be seen in several of his writings, agrees that society has been formed for the protection of the liberty and property of the individual.[19] But in addition, he attributes to the association born of the social contract a more positive function. "An association," he asserts, "is only a more perfect means to obtain with greater profusion and more certainty what each desires, wealth." Just as individuals in the state of nature procure enjoyment by their labor, so a principal goal of the society they create is the more effective production of wealth. The act of association that removes people from the state of nature creates not only a government to protect property and adjudicate conflicts but also "a living force coproductive of wealth," which is composed of "the sum of the labors of all the citizens." This sum of labors forms a "general labor" that assures that the associates will "produce more than they would if they remained isolated." Here the obvious parallel is not with Locke but with the "general will" of Rousseau. Just as the general will is more than the sum of the individual wills of the associates, so Sieyes's "general labor" performed in society accomplishes far more than the sum of what the individual laborers could do if they worked alone.[20] Not

18. John Locke, *Two Treatises of Government,* 2d ed., ed. Peter Laslett (Cambridge: Cambridge University Press, 1967), pp. 329–30, 332.
19. See especially Sieyes, *Préliminaire de la constitution françoise.*
20. Rousseau, *The Social Contract.*

only, as in Locke, does individual labor on nature stand at the origin of society, but the general labor created by the act of association remains "the foundation of society" long after the social contract has been enacted. Indeed, Sieyes describes the "social order" that results from the contract as "nothing but the best possible order of labor."

The "living force" of "general labor" produces more wealth by two means: by the division of labor in civil society and by the action of the government. Having established that "the social order is only the best possible order of labor," Sieyes continues:

> Here is the progress of this order. First, each man acquires alone nearly all his goods. Their number increases with the means, and as these become more complicated, divisions of labor form; the common advantage requires this, because laborers are less distracted by cares of the same nature than they would be by occupations of different kinds; they therefore tend to produce greater effects with fewer means. The divisions are multiplied continually by virtue of this law of all work: improve the effect and diminish the expense.[21]

The existence of society makes possible the division of labor, which increases the production of wealth, and increasing wealth stimulates further division of labor. The division of labor, which only becomes possible in society, is a powerful source of ever-increasing wealth.

But the formation of society also implies the formation of a government, which assures a further rise in wealth.

> I must note the great division between productive labors and coproductive labors, to prevent the confusion of certain readers about political and public labors. How do they [coproductive labors] produce wealth, one will ask? By assuring the fruit of labor, and by diminishing the need for means. They are coproductive like merchants, haulers, citizens occupied by useful sciences, educators, etc. The labors of these classes . . . have been separated from the general mass of productive labors which they encumbered and which they served much better in this state of division. The goal of all these divisions is always to

---

21. Sieyes, "Lettres," in *Ecrits politiques*, p. 33.

produce a greater sum of goods and their order follows . . . the general law: improve the effect and diminish the expense.[22]

Elsewhere Sieyes insists that public works are a major source of the wealth of a nation: "Roads, canals, ports, assuredly make a nation richer than if it were deprived of them."[23] The development of government, of administration, of public functions, is a consequence of the same principle of the division of labor that animates civil society. Public labors are a form of "coproductive labors," analogous to the work performed by merchants, haulers, educators, or scientists. Coproductive workers do not engage in direct production; rather, they organize the work of society and render it more productive. The division of public from private labors, like any other division of labor, improves the effect and diminishes the cost of the production of goods.

It was in 1776 that Adam Smith, the Scottish philosopher and political economist, published *The Wealth of Nations,* which is generally regarded as the definitive elaboration of the concept of the division of labor. Yet in 1774, two years before the publication of Smith's book and seven years before its first translation into French, Sieyes had already adopted two of Smith's most important principles: that labor was the source of all wealth and that the division of labor was the most fruitful source of economic progress. He had, moreover, integrated these political-economic notions into the dominant form of discourse in contemporary political theory: social contract theory. This combination of social contract and political economy served as a foundation of his argument in *What Is the Third Estate?* If societies are formed to assure and increase the production of wealth, it is evident that those who refuse to cooperate in this endeavor place themselves outside the social contract. Once again, the parallel with the contractual theories of Locke or Rousseau is very close, but once again, something new has been added. In Locke and Rousseau, those who refuse to obey laws place themselves outside of society and renounce their rights: they become enemies who are subject to laws of war. In his "Letters to the Economists," Sieyes had already stated the parallel

22. Ibid.
23. Ibid., p. 32.

economic principle explicitly: "If there is a citizen who refuses his portion of activity he renounces his rights; no man may enjoy the labor of others without exchange."[24] The premise from which Sieyes concluded that the Third Estate was *everything* and the nobility *nothing* was already in place in 1774: in a society where labor is everything, the idler is a criminal and an enemy. We cannot know whether Sieyes was already thinking of nobles as early as 1774. But it is clear that he had already developed the principles of political economy that would exclude idlers from society.

The Division of Labor

Clearly, the principle that all wealth is created by labor serves as a major basis for the crucial conclusion of *What Is the Third Estate?*: that the Third Estate was everything and the nobility nothing. But this conclusion was also based on two other principles of political economy: the division of labor and free competition.

Sieyes, as we have seen in chapter 2, begins *What Is the Third Estate?* with a discussion of the different types of labor necessary for a nation "to subsist and prosper." He distinguishes four categories of "private labors" and a fifth category of "public functions" (121). The four classes of private labors are ranked according to their proximity to nature. Agriculture is the first class because it consists in cultivating the productions of nature itself. The second class is industry, which transforms the products of nature into useful goods. The third class is commerce, which exchanges goods, and the fourth is services, which neither makes nor distributes physical products but performs other activities useful to persons. For Sieyes, the private labor necessary to a nation, all of which is performed exclusively by the Third Estate, is a divided labor, performed by distinct categories of persons. It is by the cooperation of the four classes that the wealth of society is produced. But although the labor is divided, all classes of workers are equally necessary and equally useful. Sieyes makes it clear that he sees no distinctions of superiority or inferiority among these four classes by noting that the fourth class, which is farthest from nature, includes an array of labor that ranges "from the *most distin-*

24. Ibid.

guished scientific and liberal professions to the *least esteemed* domestic services" (121). Hence, the division of labor is not a question of dividing supposedly vile from supposedly distinguished functions, as was the case in the division between the three estates of the realm. All private labors were productive, useful, and honorable.

These questions of the nature and division of the classes that cooperated in national labor occupied much of Sieyes's attention in the years prior to the revolution, particularly between 1774 and 1776.[25] The principal question in many of his notes was precisely whether certain classes of labor were or were not superior to others. Above all, he attempted to refute the physiocratic idea that the land was the only source of wealth, with the corollary that proprietors of the land constituted a superior class in the nation. This is the subject, for example, of a note entitled "Legislative power badly distributed in England," written between 1774 and 1776.

The opposing complaints that the different classes make every day in England make me think that the English constitution has made a big mistake in its distribution of legislative power. One should begin by dividing the nation into as many great classes as there are distinct interests: 1. the landowners and all their tenants, 2. all those who appropriate raw materials for our uses, and those who are employed with the circulation of wealth, 3. moral culture, etc. These three classes joined to executive power should govern the legislation in any well ordered state. It is therefore necessary that each of them have the right to elect its representatives, and if such were the order of things I am persuaded that we would no longer see this continual war between the manufacturers and merchants on the one side and the landowners on the other. From this point of view the economists are dangerous. How can landowners alone be regarded as true citizens and the rest as wage-earners [*gagistes*] who should contribute neither to the costs nor to the cares of administration? This would sacrifice twelve million men to two million tyrants at most. Even in our ideas, we have not shaken

25. A number of notes devoted to this subject are included in a notebook entitled by Sieyes "Délinéamens politiques écrits en 1774 et 1776" [Political delineations written in 1774 and 1776] AN, 284 AP 2, dossier 15.

off the barbarism of our worthy ancestors the *Welches*, the *Cauques*. We will remain *Welches* until we abandon our absurd opinions *about the nobility*, about the House of Lords, etc., until we have the good sense to understand in the organization of a society only the nerves, the muscles, etc. that actually make it up and not the bizarre fashions that only shield its surface from the eyes of the base and servile. Classes must be divided according to the different interests.[26]

There are two point to remark in this note. First, Sieyes distinguishes three "distinct interests" in society: an agrarian class, an industrial and commercial class, and a third class that is engaged in moral culture. These classes, he proposes, should have an equality of influence in legislation. But we also see a major reason for his hostility toward the Physiocrats and their doctrine that only the land produces wealth: favoring landed proprietors would mean favoring the nobility. This note suggests that when Sieyes defends labor as the true source of wealth, he is motivated in part by his hostility to nobles.

Sieyes went so far as to imply, on occasion, that agriculture was perhaps less productive than industry. This is the import of a note entitled "The product of the arts is more abundant and renders greater profits," also written between 1774 and 1776. By "arts," Sieyes means the mechanical arts, or manufacture.

---

26. Sieyes, *Ecrits politiques*, p. 59, and AN, 284 AP 2, dossier 15. Emphasis in original. *Welche*, sometimes spelled *velche*, is a term derived from the German *welsche*, an adjective which means Latin, Romance, French, Italian, or, by extension, foreigner. According to *Le Robert: Dictionnaire de la langue française* (Paris, 1985), it was used in the eighteenth century to mean "an ignorant Frenchman, full of prejudices. By extension: A man who is ignorant, credulous, and without taste." Voltaire made frequent use of the term in precisely this sense. For example, in a letter of 1764, he declared that the French nation "emerged from barbarism" only because of the efforts of a few authors of genius—Corneille, Racine, Boileau, Pascal, and Bossuet—who "changed the *Welches* into Frenchmen" (*Voltaire's Correspondence*, ed. Theodore Besterman [Geneva: Institut et Musée Voltaire, 1960], 54:200). In another letter of the same year he wrote, "I tremble for the *Encyclopédie*, rest assured that it will be stopped no sooner than it is printed. Belles-lettres are in the tomb, the French will no longer be more than *velches*, they will have Duchap, the Opéra Comique, and the decrees of the Parlement" (ibid., p. 251). I have been unable to determine the meaning of Sieyes's term *Cauques*, although the context implies that its meaning must be analogous.

The most civilized and opulent nations are far superior in their progress in the arts and very little in what they can do in agriculture. Rural labor is neither divisible, nor perfectible as are manipulations in arts. If a rich nation places more of its investments and knowledge there [in agriculture], the surplus scarcely pays for the expenses and high prices. Soon there is nothing more to conquer in this endeavor. One must turn toward the arts, perfecting them. You will obtain preference in the general markets and you will render the nations your tributaries. Thus the net product of the arts is unlimited, individual consumption is greater, and the arts furnish three quarters.[27]

There is, thus, an occasional urban and anti-agricultural penchant in Sieyes's political economy.

In spite of this, he sometimes designated agriculturists as the first class of society. This is the case in an undatable note called "Industrious classes."

There should be a word to characterize the general goal of this superfluity of men who present all kinds of products in order to gain their part in reproduction.

I would call it the secondary class, because its labors only come second to nutrition, because they are supported by reproduction, and above all because this class has for its general goal to *second* all of society, because it only works to embellish and augment the sum of pleasures.

All classes, moreover, are coproductive, they all tend directly or indirectly to give birth to greater reproduction. If there were a term to express all these ideas, to wit: that which aids reproduction and serves consumption, which seasons the enjoyment of nutrition and furnishes all other physical enjoyments (as for enjoyment of means, that comes from instruction, from enlightenment), one would have to use it by preference. Not having one, we must attach a clear idea to some known word which could take the place of the one we wish for. We say daily: tax *industry*, the *industrial* class, in opposition to taxing real estate, the proprietors of land. This word industry is of all

27. Sieyes, *Ecrits politiques,* p. 60, and AN, 284 AP 2, dossier 15.

words in usage the one containing the largest part of the ideas which we need to fix. It is not exact in that industry can signify also the other labors of society, since the nourishers and the politicians also make use of their industry, but nothing prevents us from understanding by this word the ideas expressed above.

I would therefore say the secondary or industrious class.[28]

As is so often the case in Sieyes's notes, the text is occasionally obscure. Here Sieyes speaks of three classes: first a class of nourishers (that is, agriculture, which nourishes everyone); the secondary or industrious class (that is, that which "seasons the enjoyment of nutrition and furnishes all other physical enjoyments"); and a third class of "politicians" (who, he says, also make use of their industry). He also implies the existence of a fourth class, once again the intellectuals, those who furnish "the enjoyment of means." This time commerce (a fifth class?) is not mentioned, although perhaps it is to be included under the term industry. In any case, even though he designates the industrious class as secondary and the nourishers as primary, he insists that "all classes, moreover, are coproductive, they all tend directly or indirectly to give birth to greater reproduction"—that is, to greater wealth and population. The primary class, in other words, is in no way superior to the secondary class.

As his notes demonstrate, Sieyes's terminology and typology of the division of labor into large classes varied considerably. They sometimes varied even within a note, as in the case of "Productive classes . . . all those who work," another note written between 1774 and 1776.

In fact only *personal services* and *tutelary* services do not directly produce wealth, if by wealth we understand *all objects* and all salable qualities. The carter, the merchant add by their labors useful qualities; these qualities, even if only local, circumstantial, temporal, etc., are genuinely useful, the final value is established on the basis of all these considerations. . . . Thus all labor that governs any one of these elements and is able to render it useful is in truth a creator of wealth, as much as is the artisan who imposes useful qualities in the object itself. Be-

28. Sieyes, *Ecrits politiques,* p. 52.

cause, whether these qualities are internal or external to the object, the essential point is that they not be external to needs or to enjoyment. No matter how one wishes to deepen this question, one cannot avoid recognizing that personal service is as productive and even more directly so than *objective* labor; it is directly occupied with enjoyment. Even though real service is entirely a matter of wealth, these two services are equally salable, but the *real* is felt indirectly through its product, and the *personal* is appreciated directly by the very person who consumes it. Is not the goal of wealth to afford enjoyment? Well then, personal service affords it either by itself (industrious classes) without assistance, or with the assistance of objects (auxiliary classes) . . . , by preparing the subject, by giving him useful qualities, since by their means the wealth consumed produces in a prepared subject far more precious enjoyments. This service is to persons what plowing is to the land.

All classes are relatively coproductive, and directly productive, because they give some of the elementary values that compose salable value.[29]

In this note Sieyes uses shifting vocabularies and makes shifting distinctions—between personal and tutelary services, between personal and objective or real work, between industrious classes and auxiliary classes. His observations do not add up to a unified typology. But he does successfully establish a significant point: that personal services are just as productive of wealth as labor that "imposes useful qualities in the object itself."

It is clear, then, that Sieyes had pondered questions of the division of labor in some depth long before the publication of *What Is the Third Estate?* The pamphlet resounds with echoes from his notes. The number and denomination of the classes who did society's useful labor was extremely various in his notes; it is not clear when he arrived at the four classes of private labors that he distinguished in *What Is the Third Estate?* But one idea never varied: in all his notes, as in the pamphlet, Sieyes insisted that whatever kind of work they performed, all who worked were to be regarded equally as productive citizens.

29. Ibid., p. 55, and AN, 284 AP 2, dossier 15.

Free Competition

The notes we have examined thus far do not take up the question of whether the nobility did useful work. After all, even the most traditionalist of the nobles would have agreed that commoners performed the lion's share of the productive work of society. But they regarded the commoners' work, the production of material satisfactions, as vile, whereas their own contributions to the nation, in the military, the judiciary, and the administration, were elevated—in a word, noble. The unpublished writings analyzed thus far certainly imply that Sieyes did not accept the nobility's claim to perform more elevated services. As early as 1774 in his "Letters to the Economists," he spoke of the work of government as a form of "coproductive labor" parallel to that of "merchants, haulers, citizens occupied by useful sciences, educators, etc."[30] The work of administration, defense, and government, Sieyes implies, is useful in much the same way as other sorts of work. The development of public functions arose, like other distinct labors, from the general progress of the division of labor. Their goal was to assure production of "a greater sum of goods"; their development follows "the general law: improve the effect and diminish the expense."[31]

But Sieyes's claim in *What Is the Third Estate?* was far more radical. He denied not only that the nobles' contributions to society were superior to those of the various classes of the Third Estate but that they made any valid contribution whatsoever. Although some nobles incontestably performed functions that were useful in themselves, all nobles were to be regarded as idlers who were harmful to the nation. To make this argument, Sieyes called upon a third basic principle of political economy, the principle of free competition. Unlike the principles of the division of labor and of labor as the source of all value, Sieyes had relatively little to say about free competition in his notes. This was not, in my opinion, because he regarded it as less important, but because he regarded it as unproblematic. He developed his views about labor as the source of value and about the equal utility of different kinds of labor as a continuing struggle against the dominant views of the French Physiocrats. But the Physiocrats espoused free

30. Sieyes, "Lettres," in *Ecrits politiques*, p. 33.
31. Ibid.

competition as a foundation of their system, as did Adam Smith and the other Scottish political economists. Sieyes agreed with his major political-economic interlocutors about the value of free competition. Consequently, Sieyes simply assumes the principle of free competition rather than arguing for it, both in his notes and in his published works.

At the beginning of *What Is the Third Estate?* Sieyes included "public functions" together with "private labors" as what a nation requires "to subsist and prosper" (121). He admitted that nobles were employed in public functions, although he insisted that nineteen-twentieths of public functions were performed by the Third Estate, "but with the difference that it is loaded down with all the really difficult work, with all the tasks that the privileged order refuses to perform. Only the lucrative and honorific posts are occupied by members of the privileged order" (122).

Although the nobles perform functions that are useful in themselves, they do so in a way that contravenes the principle of free competition. By reserving to themselves the best posts in public service and excluding the Third Estate, they have created a monopoly.

> Do we not know the effects of monopoly? If it discourages those it excludes, does it not also destroy the skills of those it favors? Are we unaware that any work from which free competition is excluded will be performed less well and more expensively? . . . The supposed utility of a privileged order for public service is but a chimera; . . . without it, the superior posts would be infinitely better filled; . . . they should be the natural lot and recompense of talent and of service rendered; . . . if the privileged have succeeded in usurping all the lucrative and honorific posts, this is at once an odious iniquity for the generality of citizens and a treason to the commonwealth. (122–23)

The supposed utility of the nobility to the state is therefore in fact "a social crime against the Third Estate, a veritable act of war" (122). The absence of free competition, in short, transforms apparently useful work into a crime against the nation, obliterating the monopolists' claim to be part of society at all.

Here *What Is the Third Estate?* draws a conclusion that remains implicit in Sieyes's notes on political economy: that the principle of the division of labor is necessarily linked to free competition. It is only when professions are open to all that the various tasks of society will be filled by the most capable. If society is an association for the perfection and extension of the production of wealth, this goal can only be realized by a division of labor based upon freedom of competition within all occupations. The crucial assertion of *What Is the Third Estate?*—the claim that the Third Estate is everything and the nobility nothing—therefore depends on a model of society incorporating all three of the fundamental assumptions of Sieyes's political economy: the productivity of all labor, the division of labor, and free competition. These principles constitute the economic foundation of Sieyes's radically antinoble argumentation.

Division of Labor and Representation

Political economy also served as the foundation of Sieyes's unique theory of representation. This is not obvious from the text of *What Is the Third Estate?* but it is clear when the pamphlet is put in the context of his earlier and later writings. It will be remembered that in *What Is the Third Estate?* Sieyes developed a theory of the social contract that posited three epochs in the history of a nation. The first epoch, comparable to Rousseau's state of nature, "is characterized by the play of individual wills" (178). The second epoch, which results from the association of individual wills in a social contract, "is characterized by the action of the common will" (178). But Sieyes differs from Rousseau by positing a third epoch, which is characterized by "a *representative* common will" (179). Here is how Sieyes describes the emergence of the third epoch.

> Let us step forward in time. The associates are too numerous and occupy too large an area to exercise their common will easily by themselves. What do they do? They separate out whatever is necessary for attending to and satisfying public requirements; and they convey the exercise of that portion of the national will, and consequently of the national power, to a few of their number. Here we arrive at the third epoch, that is to say, the epoch of *government by agents* [*par procuration*]. (178–79)

This explication of the "third epoch" has definite affinities with Sieyes's account of the emergence of the division of labor in his "Letters to the Economists" of 1774, where the development of government is treated as but one example of a general specialization of functions in society. In the passage from *What Is the Third Estate?* Sieyes argues that once a nation has become too large in population and extent to assemble in one place, it separates out the functions of government and conveys them to a small number of people who specialize in attending to public requirements. As in the "Letters to the Economists," the functions of government become the distinct occupation of a portion of the population as the nation progresses. The only thing lacking in *What Is the Third Estate?* is a statement that the development of government and public administration results from the same principle of division of labor that characterizes the progress of civil society. But Sieyes's discussion of the emergence of representative government in *What Is the Third Estate?* certainly appears to be in harmony with political-economic principles he had already worked out fifteen years earlier.

The connection between division of labor and representation also appears in a prerevolutionary note written sometime in the 1780s. The note is a discussion of the work of Adam Smith.

What seems to be most applauded in France, in the work of Smith, is his first chapter on the *division of labor.* However, there is nothing in his ideas that had not become commonplace among those of our countrymen who occupy themselves with economic matters. It seems that the work appeared in England in 1776; it was announced in the *Journal des savants* of February 1777, p. 81; the first [French] translation from Yverdon is from 1781.

For myself, I had gone farther than Smith by 1770. Not only did I regard the *division* of labor *in the same trade,* that is to say, under the same superior direction, as the most certain means of *reducing costs and augmenting products;* I had also considered the distribution of the great professions or trades as the true principle of the progress of society. All of this is only a portion of my *representative order* in private relations. To have oneself/let oneself be represented is the only source of civil prosperity. . . .

> Multiply the means/powers to satisfy our needs; enjoy more,
> work less, this is the natural increase of liberty in society. But
> this progress of liberty follows naturally from the establishment
> of *representative labor.*[32]

Here Sieyes boasts not only of discovering the principle of the
division of labor before having read Smith, but of having surpassed
him already by 1770. In the note, Sieyes seems to use the term
representation as a kind of synonym for division of labor. Allowing
oneself to be "represented" in private relations, rather than doing
everything for oneself, is presented as "the source of civil prosperity."
"Representative labor" multiplies the means of satisfying our needs.
In this note, Sieyes seems to be using representation as a general
concept that covers division of labor in civil society, not only as a
principle that applies to government.

The meaning of the term "representation" in this prerevolutionary
note is somewhat obscure, but a look at some of Sieyes's speeches and
writings from the revolutionary period make his sense much clearer.
We might begin with a passage from his pamphlet *On the New
Organization of France.*

> For those who consult reason rather than books it is evident that
> among men there can only be one legitimate government. It can
> manifest itself in *two* different forms.
>
> The members of a political association wish either to govern
> themselves, or to choose some of their number to be occupied
> with the care and attention that public needs require.
>
> In the first case, it is pure, I would almost say raw democracy,
> by analogy with the raw materials and the crude foodstuffs that
> nature everywhere offers to man, but which man has everywhere
> used his industry to modify, to prepare, in order to render them
> suitable for his needs and enjoyments.
>
> Men do not unite in society to spend their idle lives in
> agreeable pastimes; they have other things to do than organiz-
> ing games and parties. Nature has submitted us to the law of
> labor. She has made the first advances to us, and then said: Do
> you wish enjoyments? Labor. It is for a more certain, more

32. Sieyes, *Ecrits politiques*, p. 62. Emphasis in original.

abundant, and more differentiated consumption, and consequently to impart greater energy to production and to guarantee and perfect his labor ever more, that man decided to unite with his fellows. Reason, or at least experience, still says to man: you will succeed more in your labors the more you learn to limit them. By concentrating all the faculties of your mind on only a portion of the totality of useful work, you will obtain a greater production with less effort and less expense. Hence arises the division of labor, the effect and the cause of the growth of wealth and the improvement of human industry. This matter is thoroughly developed in the work of Dr. Smith. This division is to the common advantage of all members of society. It applies as much to political labors as to all other types of productive labor. The common interest, the amelioration of the social state itself, cries for us to make of government a distinct profession. . . .

Hence, a purely democratic constitution not only becomes impossible in a large society, but even in the smallest state it is far less appropriate to the needs of society, far less conducive to the objects of political union, than the *representative* constitution. Such is the second legitimate form of government.[33]

Here Sieyes treats political representation as a natural extension or complement of the division of labor in civil society. Pure, or raw, democracy corresponds to a civil society in which labor is little divided. In a more advanced society, each individual specializes in a single type of labor, with the consequence that wealth greatly increases. In such a society, political labors become a specialty like any other. No longer carried out by all the citizens as in pure democracy, political labors are carried out by specialists who represent the citizens. One could say, by analogy, that in civil society, all work not done by every individual but by specialists of some kind would be "representative" labors.

In his speech on the Constitution of the Year III, Sieyes's analogy is more explicit. There he criticized the projected constitution for not having accepted sufficiently the principle of political representation.

33. *Observations sur le rapport du comité de Constitution concernant la nouvelle organisation de la France* (Versailles: Baudoin, 1789), pp. 33–35. Reprinted in Dorigny, *Oeuvres de Sieyès.*

He reproached the Convention and the "friends of the people" for believing "the representative system incompatible with democracy, as if an edifice were incompatible with its natural foundation; or as if they wished to cling to the foundation, imagining no doubt that society should condemn men to spend their entire lives camping out."[34] It is a great error, according to Sieyes, to believe "that the people should only delegate those powers that they cannot exercise themselves. . . . It is as if one wished to prove to citizens who need to write, for example, to Bordeaux, that they would retain their entire liberty much better if they reserved to themselves the right to carry their own letters."[35] Sieyes insists, to the contrary, that "it is certain that to have oneself represented in the most things possible increases one's liberty, just as accumulating diverse representations in the same persons diminishes it. Search in the private order, to see if that man is not most free who has most work done for him; just as everyone agrees that a man is more dependent on others when he accumulates more representations in the same person, to the point that he achieves almost an alienation of himself if he concentrates all powers in the same person."[36]

In this passage, Sieyes is arguing against placing too much power in a single legislative body—in part, no doubt, because he believed that the concentration of all power in the Convention from 1792 to 1794 was responsible for the development of the Terror. Instead, he urged the careful division and apportionment of governmental powers among different representative bodies: "Be careful not to attach all of your rights to the capacity of a single representative; carefully distinguish the different representative procurations you make, and be sure that the constitution does not permit any single category of your representatives to go beyond the limits of its special procuration."[37]

What is of particular interest in the context of this chapter is that he argues for his constitutional ideas by analogizing political representation to "representations" in "the private order." In a society

---

34. *Opinion de Sieyes, sur plusieurs articles des titres IV et V du projet de constitution, prononcée à la Convention le 2 thermidor de l'an troisième de la République* (Paris, year III), p. 5. Reprinted in Dorigny, *Oeuvres de Sieyès*.
35. Ibid., pp. 5–6.
36. Ibid., p. 6.
37. Ibid.

characterized by the division of labor, people do not do for themselves all that is necessary for their prosperity; rather, they have as much work as possible done for them by others, whom Sieyes characterizes as their representatives. By implication, he conceptualizes the division of labor as a system of mutual representation, with each person represented by (and therefore also a representative of) an ever greater range of people as the division of labor becomes more elaborated. Moreover, the growth of the division of labor results in an increase in individual liberty, because a person whose well-being depends on a great diversity of others is never vulnerable to the tyrannical whims of any single individual.

In an unpublished paper entitled "Bases of the social order," written a few months before his speech on the Constitution of the Year III, Sieyes argues explicitly that the division of labor and representation are one and the same: "The division of labor, of professions, etc. is simply the representative system establishing itself spontaneously; it goes hand in hand with the progress of the society it animates; it is most favorable to the production of wealth, the convenience of exchange, and the general movement of business. It has seized hold of virtually all human activities."[38] This is also the assumption that underlies one of Sieyes's declarations in his speech on the Constitution of the Year III: "All is representation in the social state. It is found everywhere in the private order as in the public order; it is the mother of productive and commercial industry, as of liberal and political progress. I would even say that representation is confounded with the very essence of social life."[39]

These writings make it evident, in short, that Sieyes based his ideas about political representation on reflections about political economy. He sees political representation as an integral part of an ever increasing division of labor. In political life as in civil society, the progress of liberty and prosperity consists in doing only what one does best and having the rest done for one by representatives to whom

38. "Bases de l'ordre social ou série raisonnée de quelques idées fondamentales de l'état social et politique: an III" [Bases of the social order or reasoned series of some fundamental ideas about the social and political state: Year III], AN, 284 AP 5.1. On the argument of the "Bases," see Forsythe's discussion in *Reason and Revolution,* pp. 142–46.

39. *Opinion de Sieyes, sur plusieurs articles . . . du projet de constitution,* p. 5.

one has delegated the tasks and the powers necessary to carry them out. In both spheres, representation should be everywhere. The good political constitution, hence, is a logical extension of the proper organization of the private economy. Although Sieyes developed his notion of the connection between political representation and the division of labor most fully in speeches and writings after the publication of *What Is the Third Estate?* what he says in these later works is entirely consistent both with his discussion of representation in the great pamphlet and his brief jottings in his unpublished note on Adam Smith and the division of labor. Just as his later, more fully developed theory of representation clearly depends on his conception of the division of labor, so his easy and emphatic acceptance of representation in *What Is the Third Estate?* as the natural means of expressing the sovereign will of the French people was a product of his earlier ruminations about political economy. Sieyes's ability to move beyond Rousseau's hostility to representation arose from his long and varied meditations, in the 1770s and 1780s, on the problem of the division of labor. Once again, Sieyes's political thought was founded on a vision of the human condition that derived from political economy.

Sieyes and Adam Smith

But to say that Sieyes's vision derived from political economy is not very precise. In the late eighteenth century, the discourse of political economy was various and highly contested. Sieyes was not a devotee of any particular camp but worked hard to develop his own distinct positions. As we have seen, he began his reflections on political economy with a close reading of the Physiocrats, but soon became critical enough of their doctrines to attempt a public refutation in his "Letters to the Economists." His ideas were much closer to those of Adam Smith. Smith's political economy, like that of Sieyes, revolved around three principles: the productivity of labor, free competition, and the division of labor. This resemblance is hardly accidental: it is clear that Sieyes read Smith carefully and appreciatively. But it is also clear that Sieyes had arrived at his basic ideas by 1774, when he completed his "Letters to the Economists"—two years before Smith's *Wealth of Nations* was published. It is of course possible that Sieyes

picked up some ideas from Smith's Scottish colleague Adam Ferguson, whose *Essay on the History of Civil Society* had discussed the
division of labor in 1767.[40] But we should probably credit Sieyes
with some degree of independent discovery; after all, he claimed in
one of his notes that he had "already gone farther than Smith by
1770."[41]

Sieyes's statement that he had "gone farther" than Smith also
signals that he saw important differences between their ideas. His
note on Smith continues with the claim that

> Not only did I regard the *division* of labor *in the same trade,* that is
> to say, under the same superior direction, as the most certain
> means of *reducing costs and augmenting products;* I had also consid-
> ered the distribution of the great professions or trades as the true
> principle of the progress of society. All of this is only a portion
> of my *representative order* in private relations. To have oneself/let
> oneself be represented is the only source of civil prosperity. . . .
>
> Multiply the means/powers to satisfy our needs; enjoy more,
> work less, this is the natural increase of liberty in society. But
> this progress of liberty follows naturally from the establishment
> of *representative labor.*[42]

Here Sieyes implies that he discovered an important principle—the
distribution of the great professions or trades—that had escaped
Smith. I believe that tracing out this difference between Sieyes and
Smith can help to define the specificity of Sieyes's views about
political economy.

Sieyes claims to have surpassed Smith because the latter's discussion of the division of labor was focused above all on division of tasks
within a single trade or manufacture. Thus Smith gives as his
principal example the manufacture of pins, in which "one man draws
out the wire, another straights it, a third cuts it, a fourth points it, a
fifth grinds it at the top for receiving the head; to make the head
requires three distinct operations; to put it on is a peculiar business,
to whiten the pins is another; it is even a trade by itself to put them

40. Adam Ferguson, *An Essay on the History of Civil Society, 1767,* ed. Duncan Forbes
(Edinburgh: University of Edinburgh Press, 1966).
41. Sieyes, *Ecrits politiques,* p. 62.
42. Ibid.

into the paper."[43] This minute division of tasks greatly increases the number of pins a given group of workers can produce in a day. If workers "had all wrought separately and independently," they could not have made more than twenty pins a day; but in a manufactory based on a minute division of labor, ten workers could make "upwards of forty-eight thousand" every day.[44] The division of labor within a manufacture could produce such seemingly miraculous increases in productivity for three reasons: "the increase in dexterity in every particular workman; . . . the saving of time which is commonly lost in passing from one species of work to another; and . . . the invention of a great number of machines which facilitate and abridge labor."[45] Sieyes, by contrast, was interested above all in what he called "the distribution of the great professions or trades," which he claimed was "the true principle of the progress of society."

On the face of it, Sieyes's claim to have found the true principle of social progress seems to betray an incomprehension of one of Smith's most important discoveries. Smith claimed to have uncovered the real mechanism of the increase in productivity of human labor precisely by viewing the process of production from close up, by carefully demonstrating in detail how the division of labor perfected products and shortened the time required to produce them. Most important of all, Smith saw the principle of division of labor within the trade as being linked to an entire system of economic laws. Thus, the division of labor, and hence the productivity of labor, is determined, according to Smith, by the extent of the market. The greater the extent of the market, the more advanced the division of labor. And it is the action of this same market that regulates the level of prices and the quantity of demand and supply for various goods. For Smith, the principle of the division of labor was an integral part of a systematic theory of the economy as a natural phenomenon governed by scientific laws. Sieyes does not seem to have recognized the power of Smith's systematic economic theory. From the point of view of Smith, Sieyes seems to have it backwards: rather than seeing the division of labor as only a means to the end of increasing wealth, he

43. Adam Smith, *The Wealth of Nations,* introd. Andrew Skinner (Harmondsworth: Penguin Books, 1982), p. 110.
44. Ibid.
45. Ibid., p. 112.

sees division of labor as the desirable end that is produced by rising wealth.

This difference can be seen even in the note that brings Sieyes closest to Smith's theories. The note is entitled "Perfection of labor, by the division of labor." I suspect that the note was inspired by a reading of Smith, since it follows his arguments very closely, but unfortunately it is undatable.

> Divide or distinguish the different operations that combine to form a product of any kind, and attribute them to different agents. . . . The hands acquire more facility, more dexterity; by habituation, one learns, (1) not to spend one's time and force in useless movements, (2) to train them in useful movements, (3) to *do better* what one does. The object is better disposed to its *goal,* better disposed to the utility of those who use it. . . . *intelligence, attention, manual dexterity.* Attention directed to a smaller space observes better, grasps relations, which leads to invention of means, of machines, and the choice of circumstances that abridge effort. . . . a saving of time lost in starting up, in coming and going, in taking up and quitting different operations. . . .[46]

Up to this point we have precisely Adam Smith's observations about the advantages of the division of labor. But the consequences that Sieyes draws from this analysis of division of labor are not Smith's. Rather than speaking of the abundance of goods, their low price, and the resultant increase of human happiness, he speaks of "the formation of different classes of persons, for they only begin to be distinguished by their employment at different tasks; the perfection of the human species, because if each individual occupied himself with all the objects of his consumption, all individuals would resemble one another, and society would not leave behind its infancy."[47] Sieyes jumps directly from the technical advantages of the division of labor to social and moral consequences—classes of persons, perfection of the human species—rather than to economic ones. Moreover, perfection of the species is implicitly (and tautologi-

46. Sieyes, *Ecrits politiques,* p. 63. Emphasis and ellipses in original.
47. Ibid.

cally) defined as heterogeneity in human personality; a society is recognized as still being in its infancy by the fact that its individuals are all alike.

Thereafter the note goes on to rejoin Adam Smith's argument, now speaking of the advantages of commerce and the consequences of commerce for the division of labor.

> The difference of natural aptitudes and circumstances of labor occasions different products; good sense leads to exchange; the possibility of exchange leads to a particular occupation; from this arises division of labor. The product is proportional to demand, and as a consequence the division of labor is soon stopped where the demand is not sufficient to employ all the time of an individual. By contrast, it goes forward and the perfection of society with it, in the most populated places, in the places where communications are open, easy, etc.; hence society must have been perfected more rapidly in Egypt, China, Bengal, etc.
>
> If by *commerce* we mean the *possibility of exchange,* it is right to attribute to it all possible advantages.
>
> By division of labor, we mean first of all that of the arts, the trades, the professions; next, that of the diverse operations that make up the same trade.[48]

Once again the sequence is the same: we begin with the advantages of commerce and with the principle that the division of labor is limited by the extent of the market. But once again we move on to the global perfection of society, presumably still defined as increasing social diversity, rather than to specifically economic consequences. And the final sentence of the note indicates that even when he had just jotted down the major points of Smith's economic argument, Sieyes persisted in his privileging of division of labor between trades over division of labor within manufactures. Sieyes remains more fascinated by the division of populations into different occupational groups than by the productivity gains and economic growth that result from an ever finer division of tasks in the workplace.

The reason for this fascination can be ferreted out, I believe, by

48. Ibid.

returning to the final sentences of the note in which Sieyes claimed to have "gone beyond" Adam Smith. "Multiply the means/powers to satisfy our needs; enjoy more, work less, this is the natural increase of liberty in society. But this progress of liberty follows naturally from the establishment of *representative labor*."[49] Here Sieyes celebrates the advantages of commerce and division of labor, which, as Adam Smith would agree, multiply the means to satisfy our needs, enabling us to consume more while working less. In Sieyes's view, however, the increase in wealth is not an end in itself, but a means to something more important: a progress of *liberty*, which he claims follows naturally from the establishment of "representative labor." When Sieyes claimed to have surpassed Smith by discovering that the "distribution of the great professions or trades" was "the true principle of the progress of society," he seems to have had a different criterion of progress than Smith's. Smith had only recognized that "division of labor within the same trade" was "the most certain means of reducing costs and augmenting products," while Sieyes had seen that the multiplication of distinct professions or trades—which he called "representative labor"—resulted in a progress of liberty.

Sieyes never elaborated in print precisely how the division of labor between professions led to a progress in liberty, but it is possible to piece together his thinking by looking at various fragmentary statements. We might begin with his speech on the Constitution of the Year III. There, it will be remembered, he argued that in both the private and public spheres, liberty is maximized by developing a complex network of representations. He denounced as "greatly prejudicial" the reigning error

> that the people should only delegate those powers that they cannot exercise themselves. . . . It is as if one wished to prove to citizens who need to write, for example, to Bordeaux, that they would retain their entire liberty much better if they reserved to themselves the right to carry their own letters. . . . Can one derive true principles from such an incorrect calculus?
>
> It is certain that to have oneself represented in the most things possible increases one's liberty, just as accumulating diverse representations in the same persons diminishes it. Search

49. Ibid.

in the private order, to see if that man is not most free who has most work done for him; just as everyone agrees that a man is more dependent on others when he accumulates more representations in the same person, to the point that he achieves almost an alienation of himself if he concentrates all his powers in the same individual.[50]

In Sieyes's view, people are most free when they depend upon many other persons for their well-being and least free when they depend upon few. A person suspended in a diverse web of interdependencies will have many refuges and resources against anyone who attempts domination, but a person who is dependent on only a few will be far more vulnerable. The more advanced the division of labor, the more complex and multiple the web of interdependencies. It therefore follows that an increased division of labor between trades, which makes it possible for persons to rely on many others to satisfy their diverse needs, will enhance liberty and decrease the possibilities for private or public tyranny.

This web of interdependencies arises freely from peaceful conventions between rational humans. Our needs incline us to engage in mutually useful exchange, and it is therefore natural for us to form free contracts, which are the basis of the division of labor. In 1793, in an article entitled "On the Interests of Liberty in the Social State and in the Representative System," Sieyes wrote:

> The common interest is to consider and treat one another reciprocally as means, and not as obstacles, to our happiness, for if the will of another, by an indelible decree of nature, stands among the most powerful means that she offers us to arrive at our ends, the same voice teaches us that it is to the will of the other that our will should be addressed, not to his weakness. . . . In a word, as a consequence of force, one sees only domination, oppression, resistance, and all the evils that oppress humanity. If, on the other hand, we approach one another under the sign of free exchange, if we unite on the basis of natural law and fidelity to our engagements, think of the order

---

50. *Opinion de Sieyes, sur plusieurs articles . . . du projet de constitution*, pp. 5–6.

of things that will result. Your mind can scarcely imagine the course of human prosperity that will open up before our view.

It is, hence, by the sole means of reciprocal and free engagements, so necessary to happiness, to the liberty of all, that men work together.[51]

The development of many distinct occupations, which arises from reciprocal and free engagements, also increases liberty by increasing our powers. In this same article, Sieyes distinguished between two aspects of liberty: "liberty of independence" and "liberty of power."[52] Liberty of independence is freedom from oppression by others; liberty of power is a person's ability to accomplish things. Both sorts of liberty were necessary for humans, but few politicians recognized the significance of the liberty of power. Without liberty of power, however, liberty of independence would be useless. How, Sieyes asks, could a man "satisfy his continually resurgent needs, how could he exercise his actions in a useful fashion, if he had no genuine power, a sort of empire over exterior objects? . . . And what would be the use of his empire over the objects he could reach, if he were surrounded only by a dearth of useful objects? . . . The great goal of liberty is the augmentation of this power. The farther it extends, the more we become free."[53] The liberty of power, this passage implies, depends on the production of objects and on the development of means for gaining them. Hence, progress of the division of labor, which is the most potent stimulus to production and commerce, has as its effect the progress of freedom. By surrounding us with useful objects and with categories of persons whose occupations can supply us with an ever widening range of goods and services, the division of labor prodigiously expands our powers and therefore increases our liberty.

The development of liberty, as Sieyes understands it, is inseparable from the development of representation as the very principle of social life. He elaborated this in a note, apparently also written around 1793: "Liberty always consists in procuring the *greatest product* with

51. Emmanuel Sieyes, "Des intérêts de la Liberté dans l'état social et dans le système représentatif," *Journal d'Instruction Sociale* 2 (8 June 1793): 46–48.
52. Ibid., p. 36.
53. Ibid., pp. 36–37.

the *least cost,* and in consequence in having something done for one when the result will be less hardship and more enjoyment. But I say having things done [*faire faire*], not letting things happen [*laissez faire*]. Ignorant servitude is letting things happen; . . . enlightened representationism is having things done. Having things done means commissioning to do, it is choosing the more expert."[54]

Although Sieyes was actually writing about political representation in this note, its language also covers liberty in private relations. For him, "enlightened representationism" is the path to liberty in state and society alike. In both spheres, liberty arises neither from doing everything oneself nor from standing by and letting others do what they please. It results not from *laissez faire* (allowing to be done), but from *faire faire* (having done or causing to be done). Liberty is a matter of commissioning experts, by means of free contractual engagements, to do for one that which the experts can do better than oneself. The society with the greatest freedom will be that in which representation, in Sieyes's sense, dominates the largest part of social life—a society in which all are experts at some specialty and enter into engagements with a multitude of others in order to have things done well and cheaply. In such a society, everyone will have increased power to satisfy wants and none will have the possibility of tyrannizing over others. It is in this sense that Sieyes asserted, in his prerevolutionary note on Adam Smith, that the division of labor "between the great professions or trades is the true principle of the progress of society," and that "the progress of liberty follows naturally from the establishment of representative labor."[55]

The Contract and the Market

As much as Sieyes appreciated Smith and borrowed from his ideas, the gap between them remained fundamental. Although the notes analyzed in the previous section make it clear that Sieyes understood the logic of Smith's arguments, they also demonstrate that he employed the arguments to entirely different ends. Sieyes's political economy, although it shared many assumptions, arguments, and

54. AN, 284 AP 5.1.
55. Sieyes, *Ecrits politiques,* p. 62.

conclusions with Smith's, was structured by a very different intellectual paradigm. The root metaphor of Sieyes's political economy is the contract; Smith's is the market.

In this respect Sieyes was far more conventional; the contract was the dominant metaphor of social and political theory in the late eighteenth century. The notion of the social contract drew in part on an analogy with the private contracts that structured economic relations. The social contract was a consciously arrived at agreement to form a political society, and such contracts were seen by contemporary theorists as the source of all legitimate government. Likewise, the practice of representation was understood on an analogy with contracts. In choosing representatives, citizens were consciously engaging agents empowered to act on their behalf, just as private persons may contractually engage agents to represent them in business dealings. Politics, according to the contract metaphor, was everywhere a matter of consciously entering into binding agreements to protect or enhance citizens' interests.

Sieyes, in fixing on representation as a metaphor for the division of labor in private affairs, might be said to have been projecting a political notion originally derived from the sphere of production and exchange back onto the economy. But while the contract metaphor was derived in part from the legal practices of private economic life, it constructs a model of the economy quite different from Adam Smith's. By characterizing the economy as a network of representation, Sieyes stressed voluntary, rational, contractual agreements arrived at by parties who know and trust each other. Rather than attempting to produce all the goods and services necessary to subsistence and to the enjoyment of life, each individual concentrated on doing one socially valuable task—say, baking bread—while making a series of exchange arrangements with others to procure other goods and services—flour from millers, education from teachers, fruits and vegetables from farmers and grocers, loans from bankers, houses from builders, justice from judges. Sieyes's metaphor of representation constructs the economy as a series of explicit or implicit rational agreements to divide up labor in a mutually beneficial way. His basic paradigm for the economy is a network of voluntary, rational, contractual relations—a network of mutual "representations."

Adam Smith's economic world is radically different. While Smith, like Sieyes, praised free contractual relations, his basic paradigm for the economy was not the contract but the purely anonymous market, where buyers and sellers do not seek to form binding relations but merely to buy cheap and sell dear. In Smith's vision of the economy, prices and allocations of goods are determined not by rational efforts to achieve mutual advantage, but by purely selfish decisions that are transmogrified into maximum common advantage by the providential laws of supply and demand. For Smith, economic processes work anonymously and behind actors' backs, against or beyond their conscious, rational motives; it is the "hidden hand" of natural law that governs.

Sieyes, by contrast, never speaks of the natural laws of the economy, and scarcely mentions the regulation of supply and demand by the anonymous mechanism of prices. Once again, there is evidence in his notes that he understood Smith's arguments on these matters. In a brief note entitled "Balance of the market acts out of view, but surely," he produced a recognizable sketch of Smith's anonymous market: "We do not understand very well a market of circumstances and combinations whose influences determine the price. But even though we cannot follow them, they continue to act, and we *experience* the results of their balances, better perhaps than if we had done so. The action of each individual contributes to the general action, which resembles none of its elements, but which . . . determines the price."[56] But if Sieyes understood the logic of Smith's arguments, he never accepted the market as the paradigm for social life. For Sieyes the paradigm is representation; prosperity is not the happy but ironic consequence of a blind and anonymous pursuit of self-interest, but the result of contractual relations consciously established between people who know each other and who decide to rely on each other for their mutual benefit. Adam Smith's political economy is based on a vision of natural economic laws that transcend the reason and intentions of its constituent actors, so that public benefit arises from selfish deeds. In Sieyes's political economy, public good arises from intentional agreements about mutual advantage; economic progress is a consequence of reason, intentionality, and mutual trust.

Sieyes, as this analysis makes clear, was perhaps a less profound

56. AN, 284 AP 2.13.

economic thinker than Smith. Although it is true that Sieyes's political ideas were deeply influenced by his study of political economy, it is equally true that his economic ideas remained in thrall to political theory. He never fully grasped the significance of Smith's discovery that the economy could be understood as a self-sufficient system, governed by laws of its own that were utterly distinct from the principles of political science. But when viewed from the standpoint of political theory, Sieyes looks far more impressive. He elaborated, in however fragmentary form, a brilliantly novel conception of social contract theory, one in which the social contract was as much an economic as a political pact. This fragmentary new economic theory of the social contract went beyond both Locke and Rousseau in important respects. In Locke's social contract, human labor on nature stands at the origin of property and hence of the social compact that is formed to protect property. But the government that arises from the social pact is a minimal government whose sole function is to protect property from domestic and foreign depredations. Sieyes, by stressing the progressive development of division of labor that the social contract sets in motion, sees government as a positive force for enhancing the production and consumption of goods, whose secure enjoyment was a major motive for establishing government in the first place. He complements Locke's obsession with liberty of independence by stressing the development of liberty of power.

Rousseau's contract theory certainly recognized the importance of liberty of power. But it erected an ideal of government that was impossible to achieve in a modern European country like eighteenth-century France. By insisting on constant, direct, unmediated citizen control over the government and denouncing representation as an alienation of the sovereign will, Rousseau's theory could only be applied to a vast, differentiated modern state in an unstable and illusory fashion: by allowing one vocal minority or another to claim to enunciate directly the people's will. By incorporating the idea of a progressive division of labor into his social contract theory, Sieyes escaped from the Rousseauean trap and embraced representation as the appropriate way for a modern country to exercise and enhance its liberty of power without crushing its liberty of independence.

Moreover, if Sieyes was a less original economic thinker than Smith, his contract paradigm for political economy actually had some advantages over Smith's paradigm of the self-regulating market, at least on the question of the legitimate role of the state in economic life. Smith, of course, regarded the hidden hand as far wiser than any legislator, and consequently argued that governments should merely maintain public order and leave the economy to its own devices. The crucial motto was *laissez faire*—"leave alone," or more literally, "allow to be done." Sieyes's position was antithetical to Smith's. As we have seen, he regarded the key principle not as *laissez faire* but as *faire faire*—"have done" or "cause to be done."[57] Rather than believing that that government is best that governs least, he supported an active state that undertook public works and did whatever was necessary to promote prosperity. Rather than seeing the economy as a sphere clearly distinct from politics, governed by inexorable natural laws and beyond the control of the state, Sieyes saw the economy and politics as entirely continuous, with both economy and politics constituted by conscious representation and subject to rational deliberation. The political economy of Sieyes, then, is "political" in a very different and much fuller sense than Adam Smith's.[58]

It may be countered that Sieyes's contractual conception of the economy was an illusion, an inappropriate model based on political analogies that missed the real dynamics of the economic system. But something similar may be said of Smith's model. If the idea of a self-regulating economic system has made possible the discovery of economic "laws" that a contract model might have obscured, it is also true that the market model has obscured the extent to which the economy is necessarily structured by public law, subject to political manipulations, and multiply ramified in public life. The ideological implications of Sieyes's illusory contract model—government regulation on behalf of the citizenry—seem to me preferable to the ideological implications of Smith's illusory market model—giving power over all significant economic decisions to private individuals motivated by the desire for profit. A contract paradigm for political

57. "Liberté," AN, 284 AP 5.1.
58. This point is elaborated in Dorigny, "Formation de la pensée économique de Sieyès," pp. 29–33.

economy, had it been widely adopted, might have spared Europe and the rest of the world a great deal of pain in the nineteenth and twentieth centuries. A writer who has witnessed the recent depredations of Reaganism and Thatcherism may be forgiven for appreciating the advantages of a contract model of the economy over the model of the self-regulating market.

Whatever the relative merits of the market and contract models, it must be admitted that Sieyes attempted a thorough and extremely original integration of the discourses of political economy and social contract theory. This was a sustained intellectual effort, one that went back at least as far as 1770 and continued at least through the middle of the 1790s. Sieyes's painstaking meditations on political economy and contract theory provided him with the conceptual foundation on which the crucial arguments of *What Is the Third Estate?* were built. In this respect, the great pamphlet constituted only one step toward the elaboration of a full theory of the representative state and an application of the theory to practical questions of constitution making. Sieyes pursued this theoretical and constitutional project to the best of his abilities over the next several years. But in spite of the tremendous success of *What Is the Third Estate?* and in spite of Sieyes's triumph on 17 June 1789, his influence had waned sharply by the fall of that year. He argued eloquently for the principle of representation in his speech on the royal veto of September 1789, his article "The Interests of Liberty in the Social State and in the Representative System" in June 1793, and his speech on the Constitution of the Year III in March 1795. But he was never able to persuade either his fellow legislators or the general public of his views.

After 1795 he virtually ceased his speaking and writing. Once Sieyes was convinced that he could not impose his opinions through legislation, he withdrew into a sullen silence punctuated only by a few brief orations on official occasions and one last constitution, written by Sieyes and imposed by the coup of 1799, but soon discarded by Napoleon Bonaparte. Unfortunately for the development of liberal political theory, the defeated Sieyes did not take advantage of his imposed leisure to write a systematic theory of political and civil representation. His most important innovation in political philosophy—his integration of social contract theory and political economy—was never consolidated in a major treatise. However brilliant and original, his ideas about contract, representation, and political economy were ignored in their time and had little effect on the subsequent history of political thought.

4

WHAT IS PRIVILEGE? A RHETORIC OF AMNESIA

THE STORY OF PUBLIC INDIFFERENCE TO SIEYES'S BRIL-
liant theory of representation signals a transition in the
argument of this book. Up to now, it has been an inquiry
into the political and rhetorical triumph of *What Is the Third Estate?*
From now on, the emphasis will shift to the pamphlet's ambiguities
and paradoxes, nowhere more perplexing than at the apparent moment of triumph, on the night of 4 August 1789, when the National
Assembly abolished all privileges and established a new regime of
equality before the law.

As I have implied in chapter 2, *What Is the Third Estate?* not only
was an important statement of the case against privilege, but was
itself a crucial ingredient in the historical process that led to the
abolition of privileges on the night of 4 August. Yet it is unclear
precisely what Sieyes meant by privilege when he denounced it. In
What Is the Third Estate? Sieyes spoke above all of the political and
pecuniary privileges of the nobility, although the privileges of the
clergy are also mentioned. But privilege in Old Regime society
reached far beyond the nobility and clergy. From the juridical point
of view, the Old Regime state was made up of a congeries of privileged bodies, estates, and orders—not only the clergy and the
nobility, but a great diversity of communities, chartered cities,
provinces, guilds, companies, academies, bodies of magistrates, and
others—all in principle created by and subject to the will of the
prince. Privilege was, hence, a constitutive principle of the social
order; the privileges of the nobility and the clergy were only the most

spectacular instances of the multitude of privileges that made up the state and society of Old Regime France.[1] When privilege was abolished on the night of 4 August, it was not only the spectacular privileges of the First and Second Estates that were annihilated, but the entire motley tissue of privileges, great and small.

Although *What Is the Third Estate?* launched the campaign against privilege that succeeded so dramatically on the night of 4 August, Sieyes's own attitude to privileges other than those of the hated nobility are not made very clear in the text of his pamphlet. When he declaimed against privileges, what precisely did he mean to condemn? Did he wish to destroy the whole fabric of privilege or simply the particular privileges of the nobility? This chapter is an attempt to answer these questions by a close analysis of Sieyes's treatment of privilege, first in *What Is the Third Estate?* and then in his other writings. Pursuing these questions will demonstrate that the exceptionally well-made text of Sieyes's great pamphlet contains deep ambiguities—ambiguities that not only reveal some of the surreptitious powers of his pamphlet but lead us to hidden mechanisms of the political and discursive process that eventuated in social revolution on the night of 4 August.

The Question of Privilege in What Is the Third Estate?

Sieyes directed his polemic in *What Is the Third Estate?* above all against the privileges of the nobility. But a pamphlet defending the rights of the Third Estate had to address the privileges of the clergy, officially ranked as the First Estate, as well as those of the nobility, or Second Estate. Sieyes spoke of the clergy fairly often in his pamphlet, but he treated it very differently than the nobility. He never attacked

1. Roland Mousnier, "Les concepts d'ordres, d'états, de fidélité et de monarchie absolue en France de la fin du XVe siècle à la fin du XVIIIe siècle," *Revue historique* 502 (April–June 1972):289–312; William H. Sewell, Jr., "Etat, Corps and Ordre: Some Notes on the Social Vocabulary of the French Old Regime," in *Sozialgeschichte Heute: Festschrift für Hans Rosenberg züm 70. Geburtstag,* ed. Hans-Ulrich Wehler (Göttingen, 1974). The best account I have seen of what privilege actually meant in practice in Old Regime society is Gail Bossenga, *The Politics of Privilege: Old Regime and Revolution in Lille* (Cambridge: Cambridge University Press, 1991). See also Bossenga, "City and State: An Urban Perspective on the Origins of the French Revolution," in Baker, *Political Culture of the Old Regime,* pp. 115–40.

the clergy's privileges as vehemently as he attacked those of nobles. For example, although he often spoke of the privileges of "the two orders," that is, treated them together, he only rarely mentioned the particular privileges of the clergy, whereas he often mentioned particular privileges of the nobility without mentioning those of the clergy. Even more significantly, in cases where the clergy and the nobility had the same or similar privileges, Sieyes often spoke only about those of the nobility. This was especially true when his attacks were at their most violent. One example is the crucial passage where he denounced the nobles as political foreigners.

> The noble order is no less foreign to us by its *civil* and *public* prerogatives.
> What is a nation? A body of associates living under a *common* law and represented by the same *legislature*.
> Is it not obvious that the noble order has civil privileges, exemptions, even rights distinct from the rights of the great body of citizens? As a consequence it escapes from the common order, the common law. Hence, its civil rights make of it a people apart in the great nation. It is truly *imperium in imperio*.
> With respect to *political* rights, it exercises them separately as well. It has its own representatives, who are charged with no mandate from the people. Its deputies sit separately, and even if they assembled in the same chamber as the deputies of ordinary citizens, they would still constitute a different and separate representation. The nobility's representation is foreign to the nation in its principle, because its mission does not come from the people, and in its object, because it consists of defending not the general interest, but private interest. (125–26)

These arguments would apply just as well to the clergy as to the nobility; they too had civil and political privileges that separated them from ordinary citizens. Yet the clergy is never mentioned. This should make it clear that, to say the least, Sieyes's treatment of the clergy and the nobility is asymmetrical.

Moreover, even where he explicitly introduces the clergy, he occasionally manages to efface them from his argument. Sometimes this is done subtly, perhaps unconsciously; at other times the importance of clerical privilege is minimized explicitly. The two fullest discussions of the clergy and their privileges appear not in the text of *What Is the Third Estate?* but in two very long footnotes. Both attempt to minimize the danger posed to the Third Estate by the clergy and its privileges.

Near the beginning of the pamphlet, at the point where he argues that "the nobility is not a part of our society at all," Sieyes explains in a footnote that this is not true of the clergy.

> I do not mention the clergy. In my ideas, it is not an order, but a profession charged with a public duty. It is precisely because the clergy is a profession that it amounts to something among us. If the clergy were only an *order,* it would have no substance. There is nothing in a political society except private and public professions. Nothing else exists except nonsensicalities or dangerous chimeras. In its case, privileges are not attached to the person but to the function, and this is quite different. If idle benefices can be found in the Church, they constitute an abuse. All clerics must be employed in public teaching or in the ceremonies of the cult. But if one cannot be accepted as a clergyman without having survived a long series of tests, this should not cause this corps to be regarded as a separate *caste.* This word can only mean a class of men who, although they lack functions and usefulness, enjoy privileges attaching to their person by the mere fact that they exist. It is truly a people apart, but a false people which, lacking organs to keep it alive, clings to a real nation like those vegetable tumors which can live only on the sap of the plants that they impoverish and blight. The Church, the law, the army and the bureaucracy are four classes of public agents necessary everywhere. Why are they accused of *aristocratism* in France? Because the caste of the nobles has usurped all the best posts, and taken them as its hereditary property. Thus it exploits them, not in the spirit of the laws of society, but to its own profit. (124–25)[2]

2. This footnote is quite literally an unstable text. The text of the footnote quoted above is from the first and second editions, but in the third edition, published sometime in the spring of 1789 (Zapperi, in Sieyes, *Qu'est-ce que le Tiers état?*, p. 92) the note was revised. The footnote to the third edition was somewhat briefer and was cleansed of some of the most apparent obscurities of the original note, but made the same basic argument. "Here I do not speak of the clergy. If you regard it as a

Here Sieyes denies that the clergy should be regarded as a privileged order. Its status as an order is a kind of optical illusion; in reality, the clergy is a perfectly legitimate profession that carries out a useful public service. Unlike the nobility, the clergy has a real social existence. But does Sieyes really mean to claim that the clergy is not a privileged order? After all, he often designates it as one of the two privileged orders elsewhere in *What Is the Third Estate?* Moreover, the note is highly equivocal. For example, Sieyes says that "*in my ideas,* it is not an order, but a profession charged with a public service." The words "in my ideas" would seem to indicate at least that his opinion on this subject may be different from that of other Frenchmen, and it could mean that he is offering a description of the clergy as it ought to be, a kind of project for reform, rather than a description of the clergy as it actually is. He then goes on to say that "if the clergy were only an *order,* it would have no substance." The words "if the clergy were only an *order*" can be read to imply that the clergy is an order and something else besides. Sieyes's language thus seems to deny that the clergy is a privileged order, but leaves open the possibility that it may be a privileged order in addition to being a useful profession.

The equivocation doesn't end there. In this footnote, Sieyes conjures up and then effaces those characteristics of the clergy that make them seem comparable to the nobility. Thus he mentions "idle benefices" (*bénéfices oiseux*), thereby tacitly admitting that not all

---

corps charged with a public duty, it belongs to society, since any public service is part of the government. When one says that the clergy is a *profession* rather than an *order,* those ecclesiastics who are still living in the eleventh century, or who affect to think so because it suits their plans, complain that they are belittled. They are wrong. It is precisely because the clergy is a profession that it amounts to something among us. If it were merely an *order,* it would have no substance. The more the political and moral sciences advance, the more convincing becomes the proposition that, whatever the society, there exist only private and public professions. When I maintain that the clergy cannot be considered an order, it is not to rank it lower than the nobility. The clergy must not be regarded as an *order* because there must be no distinction between *orders* within the nation. If however, such distinctions could be admitted, it would probably be better to grant such a privilege to men who can show proof of a sacerdotal election, rather than grant it to men whose pretensions have no other foundation than a certificate of baptism. For, after all, one can prevent an unintelligent or dishonest man from entering the church, but how can one prevent him from being born?" (124). The denunciation of the nobility as a caste of parasites who had usurped all the good posts in the public services was broken off from this note and used as an independent note appended to the next sentence (125).

clergy perform a useful public service. But he denounces them as "an abuse," which implies that idleness is a correctable perversion of the clergy's status, not a necessary and intrinsic consequence of privilege, as he claims it is among nobles. He also recognizes that the clergy has privileges. However, he claims that these privileges are "quite different" from those of the nobility, because they are "not attached to the person, but to the function." But does this justify the clergy's privileges? Sieyes does not say. Moreover, he fails to make clear in what sense the clergy's privileges are attached to the function rather than the person. Thus he says in the same footnote that a man is "admitted to the clergy" once he has passed "a long series of tests." This statement implies that the man is tested for suitability *as a person*. Quite so. And once he passes the tests, he is also admitted *as a person* to the clergy's privileges, such as exemption from the *taille* and the right to be tried by ecclesiastical rather than civil courts. As Sieyes half recognizes in this passage, members of the French clergy of the Old Regime in fact had personal privileges as clergymen quite apart from the particular clerical functions they may have performed.

Sieyes's footnote on the clergy thus turns out to be misleading, contradictory, even incoherent. But the incoherence of his discussion of the clergy in the first half of the footnote is obscured by the sharp contrast drawn between the clergy and the nobility in the second half. The equivocal privileges of the clergy virtually disappear when juxtaposed to the blatant privileges of the nobility. Real privilege, Sieyes implies, is that conferred by birth, independently of all merit. The true fault of the nobility is that it is a *caste*. Having established this assertion, Sieyes ends his awkward discussion of the clergy with a rousing denunciation of the nobility. A bogus nation of vegetable parasites, the caste of nobles has usurped all the best posts in public service as hereditary property—including those of the church. If abuses are committed by the clergy, it is subtly suggested, they are actually the fault of the nobility, which has seized the commanding heights of ecclesiastical power. Attention is shifted from the clergy to the nobility.

There is only one other place in *What Is the Third Estate?* where Sieyes speaks at length of the clergy, and that, too, is in a footnote, this time in chapter 3. Here Sieyes gives detailed calculations of the number of nobles and ecclesiastics in France in order to show that the two privileged orders constitute only a tiny minority of the population—fewer than two hundred thousand in a total population of twenty-six million. At the end of his calculations, Sieyes appends the following note.

Here I observe that if we subtract the monks and the nuns . . . from the total number of ecclesiastics, one can infer that we are left with about 70,000 men who are truly citizens, taxpayers and who have the qualifications of electors. In the nobility, if you remove women and children, who are not taxpayers or electors, there hardly remain thirty to forty thousand with the same qualifications. It follows that the clergy is, relatively to national representation, a much more sizable mass than the nobility. If I make this observation, it is precisely because it is opposed to the torrent of present prejudices. I will not bend my knee to the idol; and when the Third Estate, swept by a blind animosity, applauds a decision by which the nobility receives twice as many representatives as the clergy, I tell the Third that it consults neither reason, nor justice, nor its own interest. Will the public never be able to see otherwise than through the glass of current prejudices? What *is* the clergy? A body of agents in charge of the public services of education and worship. Change its internal administration; reform it to some extent; it still remains necessary in one form or other. This body is not an exclusive caste but is open to all citizens; this body is so constituted that it costs nothing to the state. Just calculate how much it would cost the Royal Treasury to pay only the curés, and you will be terrified at the increase of taxes that would be entailed by the squandering of Church property. Finally, the clergy cannot avoid being a *corps,* because it is part of the administrative hierarchy. The nobility, on the contrary, is an exclusive caste, separated from the Third Estate which it despises. It is not a corps of public functionaries; its privileges are attached to the person independently of any employment; nothing can justify its existence but the right of the stronger. Whereas the clergy loses privileges every day, the nobility keeps them; indeed, it increases them. Was it not in our days that the ordinance appeared requiring *proofs* for those who wished to become military officers, *proofs* not of talent or good character, but *parchment proof* of noble ancestry, thus excluding the Third from the service! It seems that the *Parlements* were originally created for the express purpose of supporting and strengthening the People against the tyranny of the barons, but the Parlements have seen fit to change their role. Very recently they have, without fanfare, made a perpetual gift to the nobility of all positions as councillors, presidents, etc. . . . Finally, which order is more to be feared by the Third Estate, the order which gets feebler day by day and of which, besides, it constitutes nineteen-twentieths, or the order which, just when it seems that the privileged classes ought to move towards the commoners, finds on the contrary means of raising itself above them? When the curés come to play the role among the clergy that is indicated by the nature of things, the Third Estate will see how much more rewarding it would have been to reduce the influence of the nobility rather than that of the clergy. (147–48)

Once again, Sieyes uses a footnote to minimize the danger of the clergy and its privileges and to draw a contrast between the clergy and the nobility. He begins by demonstrating that although it is unjust for either order to have as many representatives as the much more populous Third Estate, it is particularly unjust in the case of the nobles, because there are only half as many nobles as clerics who meet the conventional tests of citizenship—that is, who are adult male taxpayers. Moreover, the clergy, unlike the nobility, is a body of useful public functionaries, one that is supported by its own property holdings. Its existence as a distinct body is inevitable, since it is in fact an arm of the administration of the state, whereas the nobility constitutes a body only as a consequence of the privileges attached to noble birth. Unlike the nobility, the clergy is open to all citizens who have the calling and the necessary qualifications. Finally, the clergy's privileges are declining while the nobility's are increasing; the nobles have recently succeeded in monopolizing all posts as officers in the *parlements* and the military. Sieyes scolds the Third Estate for its hostility to the clergy, who should actually be regarded as potential allies against the nobility. After all, the parish clergy, who constitute ninety-five percent of all clergy, are recruited from the Third Estate, and might therefore be expected to side with the Third in the Estates-

General. Again, Sieyes does not deny that the clergy is privileged, and he explicitly brings up the possibility of reforming the clergy and changing its internal administration. But he seems to imply that the privileges of the clergy pale to almost nothing beside those of the noble caste.

This comparison between the clergy and the nobility is once again totally asymmetrical. In the first place, Sieyes actually begins this footnote by subtracting the monks and nuns from the total number of ecclesiastics, thereby eliminating at a stroke all the clergy holding "idle benefices." The remainder of his discussion therefore deals by definition with clerics who are engaged in "public services of education and worship." He treats the nobility quite differently, subtracting only women and children, but including idle adult male nobles. His claim that clerics all performed public functions while nobles did not was therefore a consequence of his initial subtractions.

More significantly, in both of these footnotes Sieyes views clerics and nobles from utterly different epistemological stances. He treats the clergy not as they were conventionally defined in Old Regime French public law—as a privileged body—but as they existed "in my ideas," in other words as the public functionaries they should become in a properly rational state. In both notes his description of the clergy is in fact a kind of thought experiment—a project for a radical reform of the clergy that purges them of the idle monastic orders, strips them of their political and pecuniary privileges, and recasts them as public servants whose functions are education and public worship. But his treatment of the nobility is quite different. Nobles are defined as a caste, a privileged body whose privileges depend upon birth. The multitude of public functions actually carried out by nobles in the army, the judiciary, and the public administration are presented not as useful services like those of the clergy but as monopolies that exclude the Third Estate from distinguished and lucrative careers.

Yet it surely was no more difficult to paint a portrait of a reformed nobility in 1788 than of a reformed clergy. If the clergy could be cast as public servants carrying out the functions of education and public worship, so the nobles could be cast either as public servants in the army, the judiciary and the state administration or as landed proprietors who oversaw the cultivation and marketing of agricultural produce. Sieyes silently refuses to carry out for the nobility the thought experiment he performs twice for the clergy. He defends the clergy by characterizing them in terms of their beneficial services but effacing their privileges; he attacks the nobility by characterizing them in terms of their privileges but effacing their beneficial services. In both of these footnotes, Sieyes does point out one genuine difference between the clergy and the nobility: that nobility is gained by birth, whereas the clergy is entered by choice and ordination. But this difference hardly explains the contrasts that Sieyes elaborates in his footnotes. Does the fact that nobles inherit their titles make their work any less useful than that of priests? Does the fact that monks choose their professions erase their idleness? Does the fact that clerics entered the church freely justify their political and pecuniary privileges? In fact, both nobility and clergy could have been described with reasonable accuracy either as privileged orders or as social categories engaged in functions useful to the nation. The sharp contrast that Sieyes draws in his footnote is a rhetorical artifice, less the result of differences between nobles and clerics than of differences between the epistemological frames he employs in the description of nobles and clerics.

Another kind of shift between the treatment accorded to the nobility and that accorded to the clergy can be found in the text of *What Is the Third Estate?* There are a few passages where faults initially attributed to the clergy are then subtly effaced from the text and attributed exclusively to the nobility. This shifting of blame takes place in the micromechanics of the text and is effected by means of specific word choices and grammatical constructions. None of these passages are of great significance in the development of Sieyes's arguments, and I suspect that the subtle effacements and reattributions were quite unconscious. I think they reveal less a conscious manipulation of linguistic detail than a subconscious or only partially conscious bias that is woven into the fabric of the text. One such passage may be found in chapter two, where Sieyes denounces the "triple aristocracy of the Church, the Sword and the Robe" that he claims has always dominated the Estates-General in the past. "Legislative power," he asserts, has been exercised entirely by "a *clerico-nobili-judicial* assembly." But to make matters worse, "all the branches of executive power have also fallen into the caste that provides the

Church, the Robe and the Sword. A sort of spirit of confraternity makes the nobles prefer each other to the rest of the nation. The usurpation is total; they truly reign (132)." Sieyes begins with the clergy and the two branches of the nobility seizing legislative power. He then adds that the executive power of the state has also fallen to the same aristocracy. But the sentence proclaiming this fact is oddly constructed: it speaks of not simply of Church, Robe and Sword, but of "the caste that provides [*qui fournit*] the Church, the Robe and the Sword." However, this "caste," which is the subject of the sentence, is not further identified. He then notes that *nobles* prefer one another to the rest of the nation. This makes it appear that the unidentified "caste" which "provides" the church, the army and the judiciary must be the nobility—which of course did provide the men who filled the leading offices in all three institutions. Finally, because of this intervening sentence, the "they" in the last sentence of this passage—those who have usurped power and in fact reign—seems to have as its referent not the clergy *and* the nobility to whom legislative and executive power fell early in the passage, but rather the nobles who prefer each other to the rest of the nation. By choice of words and the play of grammatical reference, the nobility subtly usurps the clergy's part in what had begun as a joint usurpation; the clergy's responsibility for an iniquitous act is surreptitiously effaced and attributed to the nobility.

An analogous effacement takes place at the beginning of the final chapter of *What Is the Third Estate?* There Sieyes speaks of "the pride of the first two orders," which "was irritated by the sight of the great municipalities of the realm claiming even the smallest part of the political rights that belong to the people." He goes on to remark that the "privileged" wished to use the people "as a blind instrument to extend and consecrate their aristocracy." Finally, he asks, "What will future generations say upon learning of the fury with which the second order of the State and the first order of the clergy attacked every demand of the cities?" (192). Here Sieyes passes from "the first two orders" to the "privileged"—an ambiguous term that could signify any privileged persons but that Sieyes normally uses as a synonym for the nobility—and back to the two orders. But upon his return to the two orders, Sieyes uses the peculiar expression "the second order of the State and the first order of the clergy." This expression is peculiar because Sieyes begins with "the second order of the State" rather than the first, but above all because he speaks of "the first order of the clergy" instead of "the first order of the State." This expression implies that there is more than one order of clergy, just as there is more than one order of the state. Was it simply a slip or an error on Sieyes's part? But if so, why was it not corrected in the second and third editions? The alternative hypothesis was that Sieyes wished, either consciously or unconsciously, to say that it was not all the clergy, but only the nobles among the clergy, who attacked the demands of the cities with such fury. The ambiguity of the text leaves the reader free to see the fury of the clergy as the specific product of the order of bishops, virtually all of whom were of noble extraction at the end of the Old Regime. Once again, the responsibility of the clergy for a joint deed is subtly displaced onto the nobility alone.

In short, Sieyes's pamphlet does much to minimize the danger that the clergy and its privileges posed to the Third Estate. The privileges of the clergy exist in the text, but in a spectral fashion, recognized and spoken, to be sure, when it was necessary to do so, but also erased from time to time by explicit arguments in the footnotes or by the workings of grammar and word choice in the text. And if the privileges of the clergy have only a spectral existence in the text, the other privileges of Old Regime society are entirely absent. The text of *What Is the Third Estate?* could easily lead one to conclude that Sieyes was not actually hostile to privileges in general, only to the privileges of the nobility. His objections to clerical privilege are blurred or blunted at every turn, and there is virtually no sign in the text that he was even conscious of the motley privileges of provinces, cities, guilds, academies, bodies, and communities.[3] Perhaps we are wrong to think of him as an enemy of privilege in general. Perhaps he

3. Only once does Sieyes hint that some members of the Third Estate might themselves benefit from privileges. In chap. four, he writes, "What citizens are most exposed to personal vexations at the hands of the tax collectors and the subalterns in all parts of the administration? The members of the Third; I mean of the real Third, those who enjoy no exemptions" (161). This sentence implies that, as was indeed the case, some members of the Third Estate actually benefited from the same sort of tax exemptions as the nobility. But Sieyes does not specify what sorts of privileges members of the Third Estate might hold; rather, having dropped this briefest of hints, he simply resumes his denunciations of the nobility.

really was opposed only to the hereditary privileges of the nobility—what he designated in the text by the word "caste."

Yet such a conclusion would not be easy to defend. Although Sieyes minimizes the importance of clerical privileges and sometimes even seems to excuse them, he does not attempt to justify them. His basic opposition to the political and pecuniary privileges of the clergy is not really in doubt. Moreover, his definition of the nation as "a body of associates living under a common law" implies that all privileges, not only those of the nobility, must be illegitimate. The text of *What Is the Third Estate?* is genuinely ambiguous. Precisely what Sieyes wished to oppose when he denounced privileges remains impossible to decide, at least from within this text. It therefore is imperative to look for evidence in Sieyes's other writings. The *Essay on Privileges* seems the obvious place.

The Question of Privilege in the Essay on Privileges

The *Essay on Privileges,* a pamphlet devoted entirely to the question of privilege, appeared in November 1788, just before *What Is the Third Estate?* In fact, Sieyes wrote in a note to the third edition of *What Is the Third Estate?* that his great pamphlet "may serve as a continuation of the *Essay on Privileges*" (119). We therefore would seem to have the authorization of Sieyes to look in the *Essay* for guidance as to what he means to include in the term "privilege" in *What Is the Third Estate?*

The *Essay* appears to begin as a criticism of privileges in general. At the outset, Sieyes gives a broad and admirably clear definition of privilege: "All privileges, without distinction, certainly have as their object either to give an *exception* to the law, or to give an *exclusive right* to something that is not forbidden by the law. What constitutes privilege is to be outside the common law, and one can only be outside it by one of these two means. We will examine, from this double point of view, all privileges at once."[4] For Sieyes, privilege is

---

4. Sieyes, *Qu'est-ce que le Tiers état? précedé de L'Essai sur les privilèges.* This book has been reprinted as Emmanuel Sieyes, *Qu'est-ce que le Tiers état?* ed. Jean Tulard (Paris: Presses Universitaires de France, 1982). This quotation is from pp. 1–2. All citations to the *Essai* are to the 1982 reprint of the Champion edition. Henceforth citations will be in parentheses following quotations in the text and will be designated *EP*. The *Essai* is also reprinted in Dorigny, *Oeuvres de Sieyès.*

any right or exception that places its holder outside the common law. Such a definition applies just as well to the privileges of municipalities or guilds as to the pecuniary or political privileges of the nobility, and Sieyes himself says that he intends to examine "all privileges at once."

Sieyes immediately denounces all privileges as unjust. This conclusion depends on his concept of the law, a concept typical of Enlightenment thought.

> Let us begin by asking what is the object of the law. It is undoubtedly to assure that no one will suffer an injury to their liberty or property. . . .
>
> There is a *master law* from which all others should flow: *Do no harm to others*. This is the great natural law of which the legislator gives in retail, as it were, the various applications necessary for the good order of society; this is the origin of all particular laws. Those which assure that no wrong will be done to others are good; those which serve this goal neither directly nor indirectly are necessarily bad. . . .
>
> With the help of these elementary principles, we can judge privileges. Those which have as their object to give exemptions from the law cannot be supported. Every law, we have observed, says either directly or indirectly: *Do no harm to others*. To support privileges would say to the privileged: *You are permitted to do harm to others*. . . .
>
> Similarly, we cannot give anyone an exclusive right to something that is not forbidden by the law; this would rob citizens of a portion of their liberty. Everything not forbidden by the law, we have also observed, is in the domain of civil liberty and belongs to everyone. To accord an exclusive privilege to someone over that which belongs to everyone would be to harm everyone for the benefit of someone. This would represent at once the very idea of injustice and the most absurd irrationality.
>
> All privileges are therefore, by the nature of things, unjust, odious and contradictory to the supreme purpose of all political societies. (*EP* 2–3)

All of this argumentation is presented in the first few pages of the pamphlet. The rest of the work is devoted to a more concrete criticism of privileges and their bad effects. But even though Sieyes promises that he will examine "all privileges at once," in the body of the *Essay* he writes only of the privileges of the nobility. Other privileges—those of the clergy and of other corps, communities, provinces, and municipalities—are never so much as mentioned, even though they too are either exemptions from the common law or exclusive rights to things not forbidden by the law.

The only hint that clerical privileges might exist comes in a passage denouncing the fact that distinguished offices within the clergy are reserved for the nobility: "Even the least favored among the privileged find abundant resources everywhere. A throng of chapters for both sexes, of military orders with no object or with an unjust and dangerous object, offer them prebends, commands, pensions and always decorations. And as if our fathers had not committed enough errors already, ardent efforts are now being made to augment the number of these brilliant stipends of uselessness" (*EP* 21–22). This is followed by a note denouncing "a bizarre contradiction in the conduct of the government. It supports, on the one hand, outrageous declamations against the properties devoted to the Church, which at least exempt the national treasury from paying for that part of public functions, and it attempts at the same time to devote as much as it can of these properties, and others besides, to the class of functionless privileged persons" (*EP* 22).

Here, and generally in the *Essay on Privileges,* the term "privileged persons" (*privilégiés*) is utilized as a synonym for "nobles." The implication of this usage in the passages just cited is that only those ecclesiastics who were born nobles could be considered privileged. Sieyes does not speak of chapters, prebends, commands, pensions, and decorations as according privileges but as the resources of the privileged. The notion that the clergy cannot be considered to be privileged in itself is fortified by the argument that exercise of worship is a public function, with the implication (developed at greater length in *What Is the Third Estate?*) that the clergy is a profession rather than a privileged order. The only hint that ecclesiastics might be considered privileged occurs in the very last words of the footnote. To characterize the nobles as "the class of functionless privileged persons" subtly implies the existence of another class of privileged persons with functions. But this phantom class—the clergy?—is not named. As in the footnotes of *What Is the Third Estate?* the privileges of the clergy are subtly effaced from the text, attributed by insinuation to the nobility, but never denied outright.

But if Sieyes never speaks overtly of the privileges of the clergy and says nothing at all about other non-noble privileges, what did he mean when he said that he would examine "all privileges at once" and that "all privileges" are "unjust, odious and contradictory to the supreme purpose of all political societies"? It actually appears that he simply meant all the privileges of the nobility. In the autumn of 1788, it was common to be opposed to the pecuniary privileges of the nobility (their exemption from the *taille*) and also to their political privileges (their right to a representation separate from and equal in power to that of the Third Estate in the Estates-General). But it was also very common to declare at the same time that "distinctions, prerogatives, precedences and honorific rights" of the nobility or its "just prerogatives" (to cite Alexandre de Lameth and Duval d'Esprémesnil, authors of two celebrated pamphlets) should be preserved.[5] Sieyes, however, was violently hostile to such privileges.

In fact, all of the *Essay on Privileges,* after the first three pages of formal definitions and reasoned denunciations of privilege in general, is an attack against the honorific privileges of the nobility—generally considered to be either valuable or anodyne but actually, according to Sieyes, the most dangerous and vicious of all. The passage in which Sieyes makes this point is worth quoting at some length.

> As for myself, I will say frankly that I find [honorific privileges] yet another vice, and that this vice seems to me the worst of all. They tend to degrade the great body of citizens, and it certainly is no small evil to degrade men. It is not easy to conceive how we could consent to humiliate twenty-five million seven hundred thousand men, in order to honor ridiculously three hundred thousand. Surely this is not in conformity with the general interest.

Even honorific privileges granted for the best of reasons are contrary to the public interest.

5. [Alexandre de Lameth], *Lettre à M. le comte de ***, Auteur d'un ouvrage intitulé le bons sens* (n.p., n.d.), p. 18; [Duval d'Esprémesnil], *Réflexions d'un magistrat sur la question du nombre et celle de l'opinion par ordre ou par tête* (n.p., 1788), p. 4.

The most favorable title for the concession of an honorific privilege would be to have rendered a great service to the country, that is to say to the nation, which can only be the generality of the citizens. Very well! Compensate a meritorious member of the body; but do not engage in the absurd folly of debasing the body relative to the member. The mass of the citizens is always the most important thing, the thing that must be served. Should the citizens ever be sacrificed to a servant who deserves only a recompense for having served them?

. . . The real distinction is in the service that you have rendered to the Fatherland, to humanity; public regard and consideration never fail to go wherever this sort of merit calls them.

Let the public dispense freely the testimony of its esteem. When, in your philosophical views, you consider this esteem as a moral money, powerful in its effects, you are right; but if you wish the prince to arrogate to himself its distribution, you are confused. . . . Let the natural price flow liberally from the breast of the nation, to acquit its debt. Do not disorder in any way this sublime commerce between services rendered to the peoples by great men and the tribute of consideration offered to great men by the people. It is pure, it is true, it is fertile in happiness and in virtue, so long as it is born from free and natural relations. But once it is seized by the court, it will be corrupted and lost. Public esteem will wander into the poisoned channels of intrigue, of favor, or of criminal complicity. Virtue and genius will lack any recompense, and at the same time, a crowd of insignia and a motley variety of decorations will imperiously command respect and regard for mediocrity, baseness and vice. Finally, honors will smother honor, and souls will be degraded. . . .

By contrast, the esteem that emanates from peoples, necessarily free, is withdrawn the moment it ceases to be merited.

It is the only price always proportional to the soul of the virtuous citizen; the only one capable of inspiring good actions without irritating the thirst of vanity and pride; the only one that can be sought and found without intrigue and baseness. (EP 4–7)

This is a fascinating and complex passage. Sieyes proposes a kind of free market of esteem that, like the free market for goods, encourages men to offer to the public that which the public truly wants. Honorific privileges, even when they are conferred by the prince as a recompense for great public services, are vicious for three reasons. First, they tend to lower the great body of citizens. Second, they disorder the "sublime commerce" between real services and the free esteem of the people, subjecting it instead to the corrupt intrigue of the court. This means that the rewards will go to intriguers rather than to the worthiest servants of the public. And finally, honorific privileges are permanent, whereas the virtues they reward are not necessarily so. They deprive the public of the possibility of effectively withdrawing from its servants a recompense they have ceased to merit.

Honorific privileges therefore harm the public. But they also have disastrous effects on those whom they honor.

> The moment the prince imprints upon a citizen the character of a privileged person, he opens the soul of this citizen to a private interest, and more or less closes it to the inspirations of the common interest. The idea of the fatherland shrinks for him, it comes to be enclosed in the caste into which he has been adopted. All his efforts, hitherto employed fruitfully in the service of the national interest, will turn against the national interest. It was wished to encourage him to do better; the real effect was only to deprave him. . . .
>
> Penetrate for a moment into the new sentiments of a privileged person. He regards himself and his colleagues as forming an order apart, a chosen people within the nation. He thinks he owes first allegiance to those of his caste, and if he continues to be occupied with the others, these are no longer anything but the *others;* they are not his own.

Honorific privileges, thus, alienate their recipients from the people and make them feel that they belong to a superior race.

> Yes, the privileged come really to regard themselves as a different species of men. This opinion, apparently so exaggerated and without any obvious connection to the notion of privilege,

insensibly becomes its natural consequence, and eventually establishes itself in all minds. I ask any frank and honest privileged person, and such no doubt exist: when he sees next to him a man of the people, who has not come to seek protection, does he not feel, most often, an involuntary movement of repulsion, ready to express itself, at the slightest pretext, by a cruel word or a disdainful gesture?

Thus, the feelings of the privileged as individuals are corrupted. But the individual corruption is multiplied and made more dangerous by the concerted action of the privileged as a class.

Vanity, which for an ordinary person is individual and tends to result in isolation, here is quickly transformed into an indomitable *esprit de corps.*

Let a privileged person feel the least difficulty from the class which he disdains. First he will be irritated; he will feel wounded in his prerogative; he will regard himself as being on his terrain, on his property; and soon he will get excited; he will inflame all his fellow privileged persons, and he will eventually form a terrible confederation, ready to sacrifice all for the maintenance, and then for the increase, of his odious prerogative.

Thus the political order is turned upside down, leaving nothing but a detestable aristocratism. (*EP* 9–12)

Honorific privileges are far from benign. They are the source of the nobility's vanity, of their pretensions of caste, and therefore of their antinational esprit de corps. Sieyes's account implies that it is above all the *honorific* privileges of the nobility that make them a foreign body, an enemy of the nation.

As in *What Is the Third Estate?* Sieyes sees *caste,* the heritability of noble privilege, as the core of the problem.

Up to now, I have not distinguished privileges that are hereditary from those obtained by their holders. It is not the case that they are equally noxious, equally dangerous in the social state. If there are ranks in the order of evil and absurdity, it is undoubtedly hereditary privileges that should occupy the first rank, and I will not lower my reason to the point of providing proofs for so palpable a truth. To make a privilege into a transmissible property is to deprive oneself of all the feeble pretexts that might be used to justify the concession of privileges; it is to overturn all principles, all reason. (*EP* 14–15)

Hereditary honorific privilege is particularly vicious because it destroys all incentives for meritorious action. If a man is deemed honorable by the mere fact of his birth, he will have no motive for working to achieve honor. Sieyes notes that there are "two great motives in society: . . . money and honor." Both of these motives make men work, but the love of honor is also valuable because it helps to dampen a too avid pursuit of money. "The desire to merit the esteem of the public . . . is a necessary brake on the passion for riches" (*EP* 18). But for a person who has inherited privileges, all is modified; the love of honor does not serve to balance out the love of money.

As for *honor,* it is assured to him; it is his destined apanage. For other citizens, honor is from the outset the prize of good conduct. But for the privileged, it is sufficient to be born. They do not feel the need of acquiring honor, and they can renounce in advance everything that might merit it.

But the privileged have at least as much desire for money as the rest of the population.

As for *money,* it is true that the privileged feel its need powerfully. They are even more disposed to embrace that ardent passion because the prejudice of their superiority excites them incessantly to force their expenses and because in embracing it they need not fear, like the others, that they will lose all honor, all consideration. . . .

What means remain, then, to the privileged to satisfy this love of money, which dominates them more than other citizens? *Intrigue* and *mendacity.* These two occupations become the particular *industry* of this class of citizens. . . .

They fill the Court, they lay siege to the ministries, they monopolize all grace, all pensions, all benefices. *Intrigue* casts a universal gaze at the Church, the Robe, and the Sword. . . . Thus it is that the State is devoted to principles entirely destructive of all public economy. (*EP* 18–19)

Finally, the nobles, never satisfied with their riches, continually absorb the capital produced by the labor of the unprivileged. This happens by means of

> what they dare to call *misalliances,* a term which does not succeed in discouraging stupid citizens from paying so dearly for getting themselves insulted. As soon as the labor and industry of someone in the common order creates a fortune worthy of envy; as soon as fiscal officers, by easier means, amass treasures: all these riches are sucked up by the privileged. It seems that our unfortunate nation is condemned to labor and impoverish itself unceasingly for the privileged class.
>
> It is in vain that agriculture, manufactures, commerce and all the arts demand a part of the immense capital they have formed, to sustain themselves, to grow, and for the public prosperity. The privileged swallow up both capital and persons; all are destined without return to a privileged sterility. (*EP* 23–24)

Wealthy commoners, seeking powerful protectors for themselves and social advancement for their children, pay fabulous dowries in order to marry their daughters off to nobles, who accept these "misalliances" as a means of replenishing their dwindling fortunes. By this means, Sieyes claims, the wealth accumulated by commoners is siphoned out of productive uses and consigned to "a privileged sterility."

In sum, the honorific privileges of the nobility are the inexhaustible source of nearly all the great problems that beset the French state and society. They result in the degradation of the ordinary people, the extravagance and idleness of the nobles, the ruin of the national economy, the corruption and incompetence of public services, uncontrollable expenses to the state, and the disorder of its constitution.

Such is the argument of the *Essay on Privileges.* It should be evident that it fails to resolve the questions posed by *What Is the Third Estate?* In fact, it redoubles them. The *Essay* begins with general definitions that would apply to all privileges, major and minor, that existed in Old Regime society. By condemning privilege so defined, Sieyes seems to oppose all kinds of privileges. Moreover, his uniform and univocal concept of law, which he uses to condemn privilege, implies that all exceptions to the common law, whether the regulations of a shoemakers' guild or of the pecuniary privileges of the nobility, are unacceptable. But at the same time, in the course of the *Essay,* Sieyes speaks exclusively of the specific privileges of the nobility. Indeed, he is even more obsessed with the privileges of the nobility in the *Essay on Privileges* than in *What Is the Third Estate?* In the *Essay, privilégié* is used quite unambiguously as a synonym of "noble," clerical privileges are never acknowledged, and the nobles are attacked with unparalleled fury. To judge from the principles Sieyes declared in both of the pamphlets, he was against privileges in general. But to judge from the extended discussions of privilege in the texts, he seems to have been thinking only about the privileges of the nobility.

The Question of Privilege in Sieyes's Other Writings

None of Sieyes's other writings can definitively clear up this ambiguity. None is focused directly on the question of privilege, and most date from after the night of 4 August 1789—that is, from a time when the wholesale abolition of privileges had essentially resolved this previously burning question. But several texts treat the question of privilege at least in passing, thereby providing a useful perspective on *What Is the Third Estate?* and the *Essay on Privilege.* There are three in particular, dating from 1789 and 1790, that seem to indicate that Sieyes was hostile to privileges of all sorts.

Two of these texts treat the problem of the territorial division of France and therefore touch on the privileges of the provinces. Sieyes, in his capacity as a member of the Constitutional Committee of the National Assembly, was the leading advocate of abolishing the ancient French provinces and dividing the territory into new and uniform districts called departments, which were in turn divided into cantons and communes. Largely through his efforts, this reform was enacted in the new Constitution of 1791, and Sieyes's scheme has remained the basis of French administration ever since. He authored two pamphlets sketching out and arguing for these changes. The first, *Some Constitutional Ideas, Applicable to the City of Paris,* was published in July 1789,[6] and the second, *Observations on the Report by*

6. Sieyes, *Quelques idées de constitution, applicables à la ville de Paris, en juillet 1789* (Versailles, n.d.). This pamphlet is republished in Dorigny, *Oeuvres de Sieyès.*

the Constitutional Committee Concerning the New Organization of France, in October 1789.[7] In these two pamphlets, and in the reforms themselves, Sieyes appears as a passionate partisan of absolute legal and administrative uniformity and a declared enemy of provincial privileges. In his *Observations,* he put it as follows: "I have long sensed the necessity of submitting the surface of France to a new division. If we let this occasion pass, it will never return, and the provinces will eternally keep their esprit de corps, their privileges, their pretensions, their jealousies. France will never arrive at that political *adunation* so necessary to make it *one* great people regulated by the same laws and under the same administration."[8] In this passage he speaks explicitly of the privileges of the provinces—which shows that he recognized the existence of privileges other than those of the nobility or the clergy—and he demanded their abolition in order to obtain a unified nation in which all citizens would be governed by the same laws. Here he gives specific and practical support to a position he embraced only abstractly and by inference in his two prerevolutionary pamphlets.

The same concern for radical uniformity and for the destruction of privileged bodies is also evident in his pamphlet *Project for a Provisional Decree on the Clergy,* which dates from February 1790.[9] Although he criticized the confiscation of the church's property by the National Assembly, he proposed a radical reform of the status of the clergy. Sieyes's project should not be surprising for those who have carefully read his footnotes in *What Is the Third Estate?* It called for the complete destruction of the clergy as a privileged order. This he saw as in keeping with the revolutionary tenor of the weeks following the night of 4 August. "Everyone," he remarks, "today senses the

7. Sieyes, *Observations sur le rapport du comité de Constitution concernant la nouvelle organisation de la France* (Versailles, n.d.). This pamphlet is republished in Sieyes, *Ecrits politiques,* and Dorigny, *Oeuvres de Sieyès.*
8. Sieyes, "Observations sur le rapport," in *Ecrits politiques,* p. 247. The word "adunation," as Antoine de Baeque points out, was a nearly forgotten term that signified "the act of uniting, of forming a whole out of unconstituted fragments." It had been employed up to the sixteenth century "to designate the grouping of the apostles around Christ" or "the union into the French Crown of adjoining or enclosed duchies and principalities"; Antoine de Baeque, *Le Corps de l'histoire: Metaphores et politique (1770–1800)* (Paris: Calmann-Levy), p. 123. Sieyes used it to designate the combination of individuals into a properly constituted nation.
9. Sieyes, *Projet d'un décret provisoire sur le clergé* (Paris, 1790).

necessity of establishing the unity of society by destroying the orders and all the great Corporations."[10]

Sieyes's proposal envisaged a revolutionary transformation of the church; it was a kind of blueprint for the civil constitution of the clergy, one of the most sweeping and disruptive reforms introduced by the National Assembly.[11] Sieyes proposed that ecclesiastics, like other public functionaries, become salaried employees of the nation. His plan stated that "in the future the clergy will be composed only of bishops, *curés,* and *vicaires,*" and that "all ecclesiastical corporations, whether general or particular, whether regular or secular, will be suppressed." Hence all orders of monks, friars, nuns, and canons would be abolished. Any citizen who wished to engage in the ecclesiastical profession would be required to obtain the authorization of his municipality; this would place a veto over clerical recruitment into the hands of local political authorities. The church would become entirely national, to the point that "any man ordained by a foreign bishop, or outside of France, . . . cannot be employed in the kingdom." The project would also abolish the vow of chastity: "In the future, no person may take the anti-social vow to remain celibate during his entire life." Finally, it would suppress the wearing of ecclesiastical garb except during the performance of ecclesiastical duties: "Any exclusive privilege of dress for an ecclesiastic outside the functions of his profession is abolished. The uniform of a public functionary of any sort, is only necessary during his service. Outside of that, there are only Citizens, and it would be the affectation of a ridiculous pride among a free people to carry into society the pretension of distinguishing oneself from others by an exclusive form of dress."[12]

Sieyes's project for a reformed clergy was extremely radical. Ecclesiastics would be stripped of all privileges and would become citizens like any others. They would, moreover, lose two of the marks that currently distinguished them from other citizens: their obligatory chastity and their particular garb. If Sieyes did not think it wise for the Assembly to confiscate church property as "national lands," he

10. Ibid., p. 5.
11. Timothy Tackett, *Religion, Revolution and Regional Culture in Eighteenth-Century France: The Ecclesiastical Oath of 1791* (Princeton: Princeton University Press, 1986).
12. All of these quotations are from Sieyes, *Projet,* pp. 25–28.

certainly wished to see clerics brought under the control of the nation. The abolition of religious orders of monks, nuns, sisters, and friars was not only a blow against "idle benefices" but, since many of these orders were controlled by their own international hierarchies, also an attempt to create a thoroughly national church. The prohibition of ordination by "a foreign bishop" and the requirement that candidates for ordination be sanctioned by municipalities would effectively end papal authority in France, creating a national, rather than a Roman Catholic, church. In Sieyes's project, the clergy would become a branch of the national administration, manned not by a privileged body of clerics but by individual citizens who had chosen the clerical profession, just as others had chosen the profession of highway inspector or customs official.

All three of these pamphlets written between the summer of 1789 and the winter of 1790 indicate that Sieyes was thoroughly opposed not only to the privileges of the nobility but to privileges of all sorts, and that he was more than willing to demolish totally the privileges of his own order, the clergy. The contradiction initially identified in *What Is the Third Estate?* therefore remains, and indeed is heightened: Sieyes not only opposed privileges in general in the abstract, but he also attacked non-noble privileges in detail in his legislative proposals for reform of the clergy and reorganization of territorial administration. He cared passionately about establishing a genuinely privilege-free state in which all citizens, without exception, were subject only to a uniform common law and administration. Yet in his political pamphlets from the end of 1788 and the beginning of 1789, he was concerned exclusively, almost obsessively, with the privileges of the nobility. How can we explain the absence of concern about non-noble privileges in the texts of *What Is the Third Estate?* and the *Essay on Privileges?*

A Rhetorical Strategy?

One possibility is that Sieyes's ambiguity about the meaning of privilege in *What Is the Third Estate?* and the *Essay on Privileges* was a fully conscious rhetorical strategy. From the point of view of formal rhetoric, one could say that in these texts Sieyes speaks of privilege in a metonymic fashion. By denouncing privilege in general and in the abstract but giving as concrete examples only the privileges of the nobility, he made one kind of privilege—to be sure, the most resented and spectacular variety—stand for the entire complex tapestry of Old Regime privileges. If this metonymic strategy was conscious, it was a brilliant stroke. After all, many of the comfortable and cultivated bourgeois to whom Sieyes was making his appeal in *What Is the Third Estate?* were themselves beneficiaries of privileges—including, in some cases, an exemption from the *taille*—as members of municipalities, administrative bodies, professions, academies, or guilds, and sometimes even as proprietors of seigneuries.[13] A forthright campaign explicitly attacking the entire range of existing privileges might well have cooled, rather than heated, the revolutionary ardor of the crucial upper layer of the Third Estate. But by piquing wounded bourgeois pride and speaking of privilege as if it were exclusively an arm of civil war directed against the Third Estate by the nobility, Sieyes induced a social category that was in fact rather well treated by Old Regime society to adhere to a project of destruction that in the end would annihilate its own privileges as well as those of the nobility. This is, after all, more or less what happened on the night of 4 August. A session that began as an assault on the privileges of the nobility ended with the collapse of the entire structure of privileges. It turned out to be impossible to destroy the privileges of the nobility without also destroying the principle of privilege itself and therefore a social order composed of privileged bodies.

It is this metonymical strategy—which caused one's own privileges to be forgotten in a rage against the privileges of the nobility—that I call a rhetoric of amnesia. But was Sieyes's rhetoric of amnesia conscious? It is of course impossible, as Derrida and his followers have pointed out, to determine definitively an author's intentions from the traces left in his or her text. But some of Sieyes's actions make it seem extremely improbable that his metonymic rhetoric was consciously intended to dupe his compatriots into a wholesale abolition of privilege. Most telling was his own response to the night of 4 August. Seemingly the culmination of Sieyes's revolutionary proj-

13. On bourgeois privileges, see Bossinga, *The Politics of Privilege* and "City and State."

ect, the decrees voted on the night of 4 August and promulgated on 11 August actually marked the end of his predominant influence over the Assembly. Sieyes was not in the chamber on the night of 4 August, so he was certainly not among the deputies whose backroom preparations launched these events. On 10 August he denounced the Assembly's plan to abolish the tithe without compensation. A few days after, he published a pamphlet against the plan to appropriate the lands of the church for the benefit of the nation. His defense of the interests of the church provoked accusations that he placed his private interests as a cleric above the interests of the nation. It seemed to many deputies that the archenemy of privilege wished to call off the attack when the privileges of his own order came under threat. At the very point when it appeared that his revolutionary program had succeeded, Sieyes found himself in acrimonious disagreement with the majority of the Assembly. He took considerable offense at what he regarded as abusive treatment at the hands of the majority, and he henceforward adopted a much more hesitant and moderate tone in his speeches and writings. The night of 4 August was a turning point in his revolutionary career. Until 4 August he had been a guiding spirit of the radical or "patriot" faction of the Assembly. Afterwards, although he continued to be an influential deputy, he became a somewhat withdrawn and distinctly moderate presence. The radical momentum of the Revolution passed definitively into other hands.

Sieyes's new tone of moderation is evident in his pamphlet *Summary Observations on Ecclesiastical Property*, which was published in August 1789 and included both a spirited defense of ecclesiastical property and the text of the remarks about the tithe which he had delivered to the Assembly on 10 August.[14] "Such reforms should not be brusque, and no moment could be more ill-chosen for suddenly throwing into the midst of the Public great changes that disturb an infinite multitude of relations all at once, and which are likely to excite the interests of some against the interests of others."[15] In his speech of 10 August he mentioned "the irregular movement which

14. Sieyes, *Observations sommaires sur les biens ecclésiastiques, du 10 août 1789* (Versailles, n.d.). This work is reprinted in Dorigny, *Oeuvres de Sieyès,* and in Sieyes, *Ecrits politiques.* My citations refer to the original.
15. Sieyes, *Observations sommaires,* p. 7.

has, recently, seized the Assembly, this movement that our enemies applaud with smiles, and that could lead us to our ruin. . . . We ourselves are astonished at the rapidity of our march, almost frightened by the extremity to which unthinking sentiments could lead us."[16] Rather than applauding the vigor of the assembly's assault against privileges on the night of 4 August, he became frightened and began to counsel prudence and moderation.

As late as February 1790, by which time the initial shock of the night of 4 August had long since passed, he still warned in his project for reform of the clergy that the deputies to the Assembly must not begin "by wounding, by irritating men who are called to cooperate with you. Because it is with Priests, with Nobles, that you must make your Constitution, do not have the imprudence to attack them, to insult them, in advance."[17] These are odd words from the pen that wrote *What Is the Third Estate?* and the *Essay on Privileges,* from an author who owed his political fame to his bitter and intrepid assault against the nobility! It is also clear that in February 1790 he still believed himself to be the victim of anticlerical calumnies and prejudices. He accused the majority of the Assembly of wishing to appropriate the church's property because they were animated by hatred of priests: "Will you suffer little hateful passions to lay siege to your soul, and thereby succeed in soiling with immorality and injustice the most beautiful of revolutions? Will you resign your role as Legislators to show yourselves as, what? *anti-Priests!* Can't you forget for an instant that animosity against the Clergy, whose existence I can hardly contest, since in your midst I have the trifling privilege of having been its solitary victim?"[18]

The reasoning of his tract of 10 August also shows serious hesitations about the radical act of destruction undertaken by the Assembly on 4 August. Sieyes was struggling against two of the Assembly's radical actions: the appropriation of church property as "national lands" (*biens nationaux*) and the abolition of the tithe without indemnity. As for ecclesiastical properties, he claimed that these were legitimate properties of the clergy and could not simply be appropri-

16. Ibid., pp. 42, 44.
17. Sieyes, *Projet,* p. 5.
18. Ibid., pp. 14–15.

ated: "The most elementary idea of property is that a property belongs to someone to whom it has been given, or who has acquired it. Ecclesiastical property was not given to the nation, but to the clergy." The clergy, Sieyes goes on, is "a moral and political body" (*corps moral et politique*), and "in its capacity as a moral and political body, it is capable of possession." Thus, "as long as the body of the clergy has not been suppressed, it is the sole proprietor of its property; you cannot seize the property of either bodies or individuals." And if it should be protested that the clergy "is not a physical body, but only a collection of individuals . . . [i]s the nation anything else? Why do you wish to render it a proprietor, when you refuse this possibility to the clergy? I do not know if your new legislation will be practicable, but it certainly has not, up to now, been that of France or of any other country in the world."[19]

This argumentation shows how completely Sieyes had been passed by on the night of 4 August. As late as 10 August he still failed to recognize what the Assembly had accomplished in that fateful session. What the night of 4 August had achieved was precisely the annihilation of the moral and political bodies of the Old Regime— not only the clergy but the nobility, the provinces, the municipalities, the bodies of magistrates, and so on—to leave only one surviving moral body: the nation. If the nation was capable of being a proprietor after 4 August, it is precisely because it was the sole moral and political body that existed under the embryonic new constitution, from which all privileged bodies had been swept away. By abolishing the tithe, appropriating ecclesiastical property, and suppressing the ecclesiastical exemption from the *taille,* the Assembly had already served notice that it intended to suppress the clergy as a privileged body and therefore to make ecclesiastics into citizens who differed from others only in that they performed a particular public service. To judge from the footnotes of *What Is the Third Estate?* this appears to be precisely what Sieyes wanted. Yet in August 1789 he was not ready to accept the abolition of the clergy as a body or even to recognize that such an abolition had taken place.

In short, far from having conspired to bring about the wholesale abolition of privileges by the Assembly, Sieyes was surprised, con-

19. Sieyes, *Observations sommaires,* pp. 1–3.

fused, and even a little dazed by the actions of the night of 4 August. The radical actions of the Assembly had momentarily rendered him a moderate, perhaps even a conservative. Thus he protested against the "new legislation" of the Assembly by citing the fact that this legislation "has not, up to now, been that of France or of any other country in the world." This argument, based on history and precedent, is nothing short of bizarre coming from the author of *What Is the Third Estate?* who consistently belittled such reasoning in his great pamphlet. For Sieyes, the night of 4 August came as a shock. It took him several weeks to recover his equilibrium, to recognize that the reforms of 4 August had the altogether desirable goal of "establishing the unity of the nation on the ruins of the orders and all the great corporations," as he himself eventually put it in February 1790. Even though the abolition of privileges on 4 August had been a logical consequence—and in part a historical outcome—of his great pamphlet, Sieyes seems to have neither projected nor wished for such an event, and he even failed to recognize it when it happened.

If, as seems to be the case, the metonymic rhetoric of amnesia employed by Sieyes was not a conscious strategy intended to accelerate the general abolition of privileges, how is it to be explained? It appears that in spite of the rhetorical mastery he displayed in *What Is the Third Estate?* Sieyes was as capable of lapses and confusion as the rest of us mortals. During the growing debate about the role of the Third Estate that took place between the summer of 1788 and the summer of 1789, Sieyes had probably made a mental elision between the privileges of the nobility and privileges in general. According to this hypothesis, even though he defined privilege in general and inclusive terms, to himself, as well as to his readers, he represented privilege exclusively as the odious and unmerited advantages of the nobility. Thus, he had never really thought out the unsettling consequences that the abolition of privileges might have for the interests and social relations of persons in all classes of society. Even though he was an unusually astute politician, even though he detested privileges and the very principle of privilege, and even though he wished to see the establishment of a rational society where all citizens of a nation would be subject to the same laws, he had never imagined the terrifying revolution that would be necessary for the achievement of his ideal.

But it was precisely this partial amnesia, this lack of reflection about the troubling consequences of the abolition of privileges, that gave Sieyes and the political classes of the Third Estate the ardor and energy necessary to throw themselves into the assault. Amnesia about non-noble privileges was an important condition for the successful radicalization of the upper stratum of the Third Estate and therefore of the French Revolution as a whole. The susceptibility of Sieyes's readers to his breathtaking radicalism depended on a selective amnesia that blinded them to their own substantial interest in maintaining a privileged corporate society and filled them with righteous envy of a class whose interests and sentiments were often not far from their own. The rhetoric of *What Is the Third Estate?* brilliantly combined both the blindness and the envy. But this combination seems not to have been the consequence of an ingenious rhetorical strategy on the part of Sieyes. Sieyes appears to have been passing on to his readers his own envy and blindness.

The Genealogy of Amnesia

If the rhetoric of amnesia in *What Is the Third Estate?* was the product of Sieyes's own amnesia, where did this affliction come from? I would propose three origins, two having to do with Sieyes's biography and one with the discursive context in which he wrote. All are instances of the interpenetration of social and textual realities. There are two aspects of Sieyes's personal experiences and social location that could have motivated a metonymic illusion about privilege. First, although all his biographers are agreed that Sieyes totally lacked a religious vocation, it is nevertheless true that he was a member of the clergy and was therefore inclined to view the clergy's interests with a certain sympathy. Such sympathy is apparent in several of the writings examined in this chapter. Sympathy for his own order could easily have rendered a philosophical cleric like Sieyes little disposed to see the institutional structures and practices of the clergy as privileges. His texts seem to indicate that he had rethought the clergy as a public profession charged with a useful service, projecting what was in reality a proposal for a radical reform of the clergy onto the screen of an Old Regime privileged order. And he seems to have suppressed uncomfortable facts that tainted his order. Thus, for example, when he claimed that ecclesiastical properties were devoted to the support of worship, education, and poor relief, he took no account of the disproportionate share of clerical property that belonged not to the secular clergy who were actually occupied with these useful functions but to "idle" orders of monks. His metonymic discussion of privileges in *What Is the Third Estate?* and the *Essay on Privileges*—the rhetorical reduction of privilege in general to the privileges of the nobility—could easily have been a consequence of his psychological attachment to the interests of his own order, which was thereby rhetorically absolved of the taint of privilege.

It is also likely that Sieyes's violent hatred of the privileges of the nobility arose from his experience as the son of a minor municipal officer from the small provincial city of Fréjus attempting to make a career in the church on the basis of his talents. In spite of his evident gifts, Sieyes had to struggle long and hard to attain his position as a canon of Chartres. He saw plenty of mediocre nobles rise past him to become bishops. Moreover, he succeeded in advancing as far as he did not only by his own considerable merits but because he became the loyal protégé of nobly born bishops. Acting the part of a protégé caused Sieyes considerable pain and humiliation, but it was absolutely necessary to the success of his career. Sieyes had experienced himself the bitter humiliations of a bourgeois attempting to advance himself in the institutional hierarchy of Old Regime France. The resentment that infuses the text of *What Is the Third Estate?* was more than a brilliant rhetorical stroke: it was also the expression of his own long-simmering feelings.

Far from a deliberate strategy, then, the metonymic figuration of privileges in *What Is the Third Estate?* may be read as the product of his experience as an ambitious but frustrated young bourgeois who had carved out a career in the Old Regime church. Little disposed to see the position he had obtained at the cost of great personal sacrifices as soiled by privilege, and obsessed by the flagrant and unmerited advantages of ecclesiastics of noble extraction, Sieyes had concentrated all his rage on the privileges of the nobility, thereby obscuring the fact that privilege was at the same time the constituent principle of the entire social order in Old Regime France. Consequently, he failed to recognize that the destruction of privilege implied the destruction of advantages enjoyed by nearly all the elements of the

Third Estate who were wealthy and educated enough to take an interest in public affairs. Sieyes's personal experiences provided him with precisely the emotional ammunition necessary to mobilize the simmering resentments of the prerevolutionary bourgeoisie and to direct them toward an assault on noble privileges. But the assault succeeded beyond his dreams, annihilating on the night of 4 August an entire range of Old Regime privileges, including those of the clergy, whose disappearance Sieyes had not seriously thought through. If this interpretation is right, Sieyes, no less than his readers, was the dupe of the rhetoric he employed so brilliantly in *What Is the Third Estate?*

But if the rhetoric Sieyes deployed against the privileges of the nobility was amnesiac for reasons of his personal biography, it also participated in a kind of collective amnesia. After all, Sieyes's rhetoric was embraced ardently by large numbers of "patriot" readers and frequently echoed in subsequent political discourse. Sieyes's attack on the nobility apparently touched a sensitive nerve among his bourgeois readers. Without this powerful collective response, *What Is the Third Estate?* would be only a historical curiosity. Moreover, Sieyes's amnesiac rhetoric was not an isolated example in the political culture of the late Old Regime. In fact, one might maintain that Enlightenment discourse paradoxically fostered a general amnesia about privileges. Until fairly recently, scholars had regarded Enlightenment thought as ferociously critical and corrosive, with Voltaire's "*Ecraser l'infâme!*" as its motto and the French Revolution and Jacobinism as natural consequences. But over the past thirty years the diligent work of historians has shown that the visages of the Enlightenment were often far milder. It has shown that Enlightenment ideas could be adapted with surprising ease to the defense of certain entrenched interests in Old Regime society. Thus, for example, the political ideas of Montesquieu could easily be used in the defense of noble, provincial, and parlementary privilege, and the rationalism of the Enlightenment was very favorable to the development of the administrative centralization being undertaken by the royal bureaucracy. Above all, it is by now evident that a language of utility became increasingly dominant in nearly all spheres of public discourse in the final years of the Old Regime.

It is the generalization of utilitarian rhetoric that is especially interesting here. Utilitarian rhetoric has always been particularly plastic, capable of being used in defense of almost any interest or institution. In the discursive climate that had developed in the 1780s, a climate permeated by Enlightenment language and notions, privileged bodies, even the nobility, tended to define and defend their interests in utilitarian terms instead of by citing their venerable privileges. Two examples will suffice to illustrate this practice. The first is the "Ségur law," normally taken as an incontestable proof of the strength of the "aristocratic reaction" in the final decades of the Old Regime. The law required that no one be admitted into the officer corps of the French army unless he could prove "four quarterings" (that is, four generations) of noble ancestry, thereby excluding not only commoners, but even nobles whose families' titles were not sufficiently ancient. But, as two classic articles by David Bien have demonstrated, the justification offered for this seemingly archreactionary law was not the traditional privileges of the nobles of the sword, but the utility of such nobles to the state. It was argued that only families with venerable military traditions could be counted on to produce officers with the courage, devotion, and commitment to hard work that were necessary for success in this demanding service.[20]

Or one may take the Assembly of Notables of 1787, which was dominated by the highest nobility. The Assembly has usually been treated as an arm of the privileged orders, whose defense of the pecuniary privileges of the nobility and the clergy necessitated the fatal convocation of the Estates-General and thereby inadvertently launched the revolution. But a recent article by Vivian Gruder has demonstrated that the great nobles in the Assembly justified their resistance to the reforms demanded by the royal ministers not by insisting on their venerable privileges, but by presenting themselves as the natural guardians of national interests, and above all of the interests of agriculture. Rather than appearing in the guise of privileged seigneurs, they presented themselves as enlightened agrarian proprietors of a markedly physiocratic bent who resisted new forms of

20. David D. Bien, "La Réaction aristocratique avant 1789: l'exemple de l'armée," *Annales: Economies, Sociétés, Civilisations* 29 (1974):23–48 and 505–34; and Bien, "The Army in the French Enlightenment: Reform, Reaction and Revolution," *Past and Present* 85 (1979):68–98.

taxation of the land in order to protect the general prosperity of the nation.[21]

These two examples seem to demonstrate that even the most privileged of the nobles could think about and justify their social relations in purely utilitarian terms. Although nobles of course chose utilitarian rhetoric in part because they believed that such a form of argument would best advance their interests, thinking about themselves in this way was not purely cynical; after all, the nobles of the sword did have distinguished military traditions and the great noble landowners were deeply concerned about the productivity of their estates. In a perfect example of how social interests shape discourse while discursive forms simultaneously shape the social, the nobles' wholesale adoption of the utilitarian rhetoric that so dominated public discourse surely changed the way they conceived of themselves and of their position in society. It tended to suppress from the nobles' discourse the fact that their social relations—indeed, the social relations of all categories in Old Regime society—were constituted and defined by privileges. Here the way that Sieyes thought about the Old Regime clergy as public functionaries is entirely symptomatic of a much broader cultural current. It was almost exactly the same phenomenon as Old Regime nobles thinking of themselves as great agrarian proprietors. It emphasized the useful functions of a social category and obscured the fact that the category was also a privileged class.

The selective amnesia of Sieyes and his readers was, in other words, but one example of a much broader social amnesia that resulted from the spread of the utilitarian language of the Enlightenment in Old Regime public discourse. The more the language of utility dominated public discourse, the more the realities of a society of privileged estates and bodies disappeared from view. And it was in this context of general amnesia that Sieyes's metonymic rhetoric so powerfully seized the public imagination in the spring and summer of 1789.

Most studies of the spread of Enlightenment ideas have tended to

21. Vivian R. Gruder, "A Mutation in Elite Political Culture: The French Notables and the Defense of Property and Participation, 1787," *Journal of Modern History* 56 (1984):598–634.

argue that the increasingly wholesale use of Enlightenment language to defend all kinds of vested interests meant that these ideas were far more anodyne, far less revolutionary in their consequences than had previously been thought. Yet the argument I have been advancing here suggests that the very process that made Enlightenment language increasingly banal may paradoxically have heightened rather than diminished its revolutionary consequences. If the language of the philosophes lost much of its explicitly critical bite when it was adapted to the defense of all sorts of Old Regime interests and institutions, the increasingly general use of this language habituated its users to thinking in terms that made them misunderstand and ignore the corporative and privileged aspect of their society. And this made them capable of countenancing what was in fact the destruction of their own privileges without realizing exactly what they were doing. The revolutionary consequences of the Enlightenment may have been produced less by a reasoned critique that convinced the public that institutions contrary to reason should be abolished than by a systematic misrecognition that made the public feel that such institutions hardly existed any more, so that abolishing them would require only the suppression of a handful of flagrant abuses rather than the traumatic dismantling of an entire social order. Without the general amnesia induced by the domestication of utilitarian language and the specific amnesia induced by Sieyes's metonymic rhetoric about noble privilege, it would be hard to explain the extraordinary dynamics of the night of 4 August, whose results so largely surpassed the initial intentions of its authors. The fourth of August, in other words, was a kind of rapturous awakening from an amnesiac trance. But the abbé Sieyes, absent from the session of 4 August and more deeply committed than most to his rhetoric of amnesia, remained semisomnambulant for several weeks after what appeared to be the victory of his own program. However desirable the wholesale abolition of privilege may have seemed to him in retrospect, it was an unanticipated consequence of *What Is the Third Estate?* and not the fulfillment of a conscious plan.

5

WHAT IS THE CITIZEN? THE DENIAL OF

POLITICAL EQUALITY

A T THE BEGINNING OF THE FIRST CHAPTER OF *WHAT IS the Third Estate?* Sieyes established that productive work was an essential criterion of citizenship. This principle—derived, as we have seen, from political economy—is the foundation of the radically democratic rhetoric of the pamphlet. It excluded the idle nobility from the nation by fiat, and it implied that all who contributed to the nation's productive work—whether in agriculture, industry, commerce, or services—should participate in its governance. The opening pages of *What Is the Third Estate?* powerfully insinuate a commonality among the abused producers of the Third Estate, who are united not only positively, by the fact that they work, but negatively, by their common oppression at the hands of a class of idlers. In the rest of the pamphlet, this implied equation of work with citizenship serves as an assumed foundation of the argument, underlying denunciations of the nobility, elaborations of the rights of the nation, analyses of contemporary political issues, and discussions of political strategy.

Although Sieyes never develops at length the definition of citizenship implied in his opening chapter, the egalitarian implications of these early passages are certainly echoed elsewhere. The rhetoric of political democracy is perhaps clearest in chapter 5, where he elaborates "What Ought to Have Been Done." His answer, of course, is that rather than convoking the Estates-General, which was vitiated by its division into three orders, the crown should have convoked an extraordinary assembly, chosen by the nation as a whole without distinction of orders, which could then decide on the nature of the constitution. Here Sieyes's language seems unambiguously democratic. The French nation that should choose its representatives is made up of the whole of the people. "Where," he asks, "do we find the nation? Where it is; in the forty thousand parishes which embrace all the territory, all the inhabitants, and all that pertains to the public good" (187). Moreover, he seems to avow an unequivocal right of the majority to decide: "A political society can only be the totality of its associates. . . . Hence a nation has never been able to decree that the rights inherent in the common will, that is to say, the plurality, can be ceded to the minority. . . . Individual wills are the only elements of the common will. One can neither deprive the greatest number of the right to play their part, nor decree that ten wills are worth only one while ten others are worth thirty" (188–89). Sieyes makes it clear that the nation must choose its representatives by majority vote, with each citizen casting one vote. And the same principle must govern the work of the extraordinary assembly; once they have assembled and debated the issues, they also must make decisions by majority vote.

What Is the Third Estate? employs a rhetoric of political equality. Although it does not deny that there are significant differences of wealth and status among the citizens of the nation, it implies that these differences should not be reflected in citizens' political rights and duties. Unlike the current aristocratic constitution of the kingdom, which grants a monopoly of political power to the nobility, a proper constitution would assure political power to the nation as a whole—that is, to all who perform society's useful work. And *What Is the Third Estate?* specifies that this political power should be exercised by a majority vote of all the nation's citizens. A reader of the pamphlet would surely assume that Sieyes was an advocate of political equality and universal citizenship.

Did Useful Work Imply Citizenship?

But a closer reading of the pamphlet reveals a few passages that qualify or undermine this overall rhetoric of political equality. At only one juncture in the argument of *What Is the Third Estate?* did Sieyes discuss in any detail the question of how various citizenship rights might be defined. These reflections on the mechanics of citizenship occur in chapter 3, where Sieyes argues that the Third Estate should only be represented by genuine members of their own order, rather than by *gens de robe,* the ennobled legal magistrates who had served as their representatives in 1614, the last time the Estates-General had met. These discussions of citizenship rights strongly temper the expansively democratic implications contained in the opening pages of his pamphlet.

Sieyes argues that the Third Estate should be represented only by genuine members of its order, and that it should not be allowed to choose nobles or clergy as representatives even if it wishes to. To the argument that this would limit the liberty of the Third to choose its representatives, Sieyes responds:

> In no circumstances can any liberty or right be without limits. In all countries, the law prescribes certain qualifications without which one can be neither an elector nor eligible for election. For example, the law must decide the age under which one is incompetent to represent one's fellow citizens. Thus women are everywhere, rightly or wrongly, excluded from such mandates. It is unquestionable that vagabonds and beggars cannot be charged with the political confidence of nations. Would a servant, or any person under the domination of a master, or a nonnaturalised foreigner, be permitted to serve as a representative of the nation? Political liberty, thus, has its limits, just as civil liberty has. (139)

In this passage, Sieyes sets forth criteria of eligibility by listing the categories of persons excluded. The exclusions are substantial, as even the most casual perusal of this passage indicates. Foreigners, children, and women are ineligible, although Sieyes's remark that women are "rightly or wrongly" excluded implies that he was skeptical of the justice of this particular exclusion. In his *Observations on the Report by the Constitutional Committee concerning the New Organization of France* in October 1789, Sieyes was more explicit.

> In the present state of mores, opinions, and human institutions, we see women called to wear the crown; and, by a bizarre contradiction, they are nowhere permitted to count among active

Citizens, as if wise policy should not always tend to increase more and more the proportional number of true Citizens, or as if it were impossible for a woman ever to be of the least utility to the commonwealth. According to a prejudice which permits not even the slightest doubt in this regard, we are therefore forced to cut out at least half of the total population.[1]

But Sieyes showed no compunction about the exclusion of certain categories of adult French males: vagabonds, beggars, and servants, who, between them, made up a far from negligible fraction of the Third Estate.

However, none of these exclusions were arbitrary, and none seriously undermined the equation of useful work with citizenship. Indeed, the exclusion of beggars and vagabonds arose precisely from the principle that those who did not work should not be citizens. From the standpoint of useful work, beggars, vagabonds, and the nobility belonged in the same category: all were idlers. The exclusion of foreigners was justifiable even though they might perform work useful to the nation, on the grounds that they owed allegiance to a different nation. But what about women, children, and servants? Since women and minors commonly performed useful labor, their exclusion was not, on the face of it, entirely compatible with Sieyes's implied equation of citizenship with useful work. In fact, in the very passage in chapter 1 where he establishes the identity of useful work and citizenship, Sieyes explicitly mentions the utility of domestic service. Yet Sieyes could easily argue that excluding domestic servants, women, and children from citizenship rights did not actually contradict his earlier remarks, since these categories were excluded by a distinct but equally valid principle, which Sieyes makes explicit

1. Sieyes, *Observations sur le rapport,* pp. 19–20. Although Sieyes was the only major political figure to attack publicly the exclusion of women from political rights at this point in the Revolution, he submitted to the majority view in this and his other constitutional writings. A year later his political ally Condorcet argued at greater length for women's political rights. Marie-Jean-Antoine-Nicolas Caritat de Condorcet, "Sur l'admission des femmes au droit de cité," *Journal de la Société de 1789* 5 (3 July 1790): 139–44. It was, however, only female political activists who made women's political rights a major focus of their efforts. For an account of their activities, see Darlene Gay Levy, Harriet Branson Applewhite, and Mary Durham Johnson, *Women in Revolutionary Paris, 1789–1795* (Urbana: University of Illinois Press, 1979).

in his discussion of servants. All of them, in the current state of civil society, were "under the domination of a master"—that is, of the adult male head of the household. According to the patriarchal logic that predominated in eighteenth-century Europe, their wills were not independent but were extensions of the wills of their (adult male) masters. If they were denied citizenship rights, it was because from a patriarchal perspective they and their labor were actually represented through the persons of their masters. The more precise definition of the citizen hence would seem to be threefold: (1) a French national (2) who is the head of a household and (3) performs useful work.

However, a few pages later in *What Is the Third Estate?* there is a passage that seems to contradict even this more precise and restricted definition, a passage that seems blatantly incompatible with the principle that labor implies citizenship and idleness implies exclusion. In this passage, Sieyes is once again arguing that members of the Third must be represented by genuine members of their order. According to Sieyes, members of the privileged orders had argued that the Third should be allowed to elect noble representatives because

> the Third did not have enough members who were sufficiently intelligent, courageous, etc. to represent it, and . . . it was necessary to turn to the enlightenment of the nobility. . . . This strange assertion deserves no response. Consider the *available* classes [*classes disponibles*] of the Third Estate; and like everyone else, I call available those classes where a sort of affluence [*une sorte d'aisance*] enables men to receive a liberal education, to train their minds to take an interest in public affairs. Such classes have no interest other than that of the rest of the people. Judge whether they do not contain enough citizens who are educated, honest and worthy in all respects to represent the nation properly. (143–44)

This passage is revealing in more than one way. A twentieth-century democratic sensibility would probably find most curious Sieyes's assertion that the affluent and cultivated classes of the Third Estate had "no interest other than that of the rest of the people." Was he not aware that these classes possessed large amounts of property and that it was in their interest to protect these properties against the propertyless members of the Third? It appears that Sieyes decided to explain himself on this subject, because in the second and third editions of *What Is the Third Estate?* he added a footnote at the end of the immediately preceding paragraph in which he spelled out what he meant by "interest."

> An aristocrat who wishes to make jokes about what he calls the pretension of the Third Estate, always affects to confound this order with his saddler, his shoemaker, etc. . . . When, on the contrary, they wish to sow division within the Third, they know full well how to distinguish the various classes of the people; they excite, they stir up one class against another, the inhabitants of the cities against those of the countryside. They seek to set the poor against the rich. . . . But all in vain, for it is neither the difference of professions, nor that of wealth, nor that of enlightenment that divides men, it is that of interests. In the current question, there are only two, those of the privileged and those of the nonprivileged; all the classes of the Third Estate are linked by a common interest against the oppression visited on them by the privileged.[2] (143)

"In the current question," that is to say the question of the political rights of the Third Estate, the interests of the rich and poor of the Third were identical—because, according to Sieyes, neither the rich nor the poor of the Third Estate had any privileges to defend. In this respect, at least, they were equally oppressed by the privileged classes. But this footnote is not entirely clear about the question of interest. The words "in the current question" seem to imply that there could be other questions in which their interests might not be identical.

Yet even in other contexts the fact that some classes had property and others did not would not necessarily, according to Sieyes, give them opposing interests. According to Sieyes's strongly Lockean conception of property, the origin of all properties was the ownership of one's person. As Sieyes put it in his *Reasoned Exposition of the Rights*

2. This is the text of the third edition; the second edition differs in a few insignificant particulars.

of Man and Citizen in July 1789, from this "primitive right" of property in the person "flow property in *actions* and in *labor*. . . . The property of exterior objects, or real property, is similarly merely a consequence and an extension of personal property."[3] Hence, all citizens are equally proprietors, whether or not they own "real property," and therefore are equally interested in the defense of property. Between those who possess different varieties of property, for example property in labor and in land, relations are not those of a conflict of interest. As he said in his *Essay on Privileges,* "all relations of citizen to citizen are free relations. One gives his time or his goods, another renders in exchange his money; here there is no subordination, but a continual exchange" (*EP* 16–17). Even in relations between rich and poor, it seems, there are no opposing interests. It would therefore be reasonable to conclude, at least on the basis of Sieyes's published works, that from his point of view the affluent classes had no interests opposed to those of the poor.[4]

In any case, the assertion that the rich had the same interests as the poor did not contradict Sieyes's equation of work and citizenship. But the claim that the "available classes" were the natural representatives of the nation contradicted this notion profoundly. What did Sieyes mean when he wrote that certain classes of the Third Estate were "available" [*disponible*] to represent the people? To be available, men have to receive a liberal education, cultivate their reason, and interest themselves in public affairs, which implies that they must have "some sort of affluence" [*une sorte d'aisance*]. But what, precisely, did "*aisance*" mean in 1789? Here is the definition in the *Dictionnaire de Trévoux* of 1771: "*Aisance.* The comforts of life. One says in familiar speech that a man is in *aisance,* that he lives in *aisance;* in order to say that he is rich, that he has what he needs."[5]

To be available, then, one has to be rich. But how do riches make a man "available"? Here it is helpful to consult Turgot, from whom Sieyes borrowed the rather uncommon term "available classes." In his

3. Sieyes, *Préliminaire de la constitution françoise: Reconnoissance et exposition raisonnée des droits de l'homme et du citoyen* (Versailles, 1789), p. 26.
4. Such a conclusion is far less certain when one also considers his unpublished writings, as will be seen shortly.
5. *Dictionnaire de Trévoux,* 5 vols. (Paris, 1771).

Reflections on the Formation and Distribution of Wealth, Turgot spoke of the "available class" as those (adult male) proprietors who, because they had sufficient revenues to furnish their personal needs, were capable of devoting all their efforts to the general needs of society.[6] Wealth, consequently, served not only to procure a liberal education, but also to furnish the leisure which alone permitted a man to concern himself with the public interest, rather than with his family's personal subsistence. As Sieyes himself implied, it was quite conventional at the end of the eighteenth century to say that the leisured should govern. (*"Like everyone else,* I call available those classes where some sort of affluence . . ."). Traditional political philosophy at least since Aristotle had seen leisure as necessary for the rational pursuit of public affairs; that consideration, in fact, had always been a major justification for leaving politics to an aristocracy.

At this point the deep contradiction in Sieyes's argument becomes evident. On the one hand, he claims that the Third Estate is the entire nation because its members do all the useful work of society and that the nobility is alien to the nation because of its idleness. But he then presents as the natural representatives of the people as a whole those classes of the Third Estate whose wealth frees them from the daily press of labor and gives them sufficient leisure to concern themselves with public affairs. Sieyes argues, in effect, that a leisured class is the natural representative of useful labor. The implications of Sieyes's brief remarks on the "available classes" are therefore troubling. The passage retains a certain ambiguity, since it is far from clear how much wealth and leisure are implied by "some sort of affluence." Read expansively, this passage could be seen as canceling out the entire first two chapters of the pamphlet—those in which Sieyes proved that the nobles were not part of the nation—and inverting Sieyes's social metaphysics by quietly restoring the right of the idle to rule over the industrious. It reveals not only an instability in Sieyes's text but an instability in the Revolution itself. It gives us a glimpse into a chasm that reaches to the core of the "bourgeois" revolutionary project.

6. Anne-Robert-Jacques Turgot, Baron de l'Aulne, "Réflexions sur la formation et la distribution des richesses," in *Ecrits économiques,* pref. Bernard Cazes (Paris: Calmann-Lévy, 1970), p. 130.

Two Nations?

But can Sieyes's discussion of the "available classes" really bear such a heavy interpretive weight? It occurs in only one brief passage in a long pamphlet that elsewhere clearly implies an identity between work and citizenship and explicitly states that the aristocracy's idleness excludes it from citizenship. Perhaps Sieyes's observations on the "available classes" are only a momentary aberration in his thought, or perhaps I have read more into them than is actually there.

But I think not. The ideas Sieyes expressed about the "available classes" in this brief passage of *What Is the Third Estate?* are consistent with many of the notes about political economy found in Sieyes' personal papers. We saw in chapter 3 that Sieyes's discussions of the division of labor in his papers always presented the major types of labor—agriculture, industry, commerce, intellectual labor, and so on—as equally productive and therefore equally necessary for the happiness of society. However, when he spoke not of these divisions, which one might call *horizontal,* but rather of *vertical* divisions of labor, his accent was altogether different.

This dimension of Sieyes's thinking is perhaps most strikingly revealed in a particularly bizarre note from his papers. It is entitled "Slaves. For another species that would have fewer needs and be less capable of exciting human compassion."

> Because a large nation is necessarily composed of *two peoples,* the producers and the human instruments of production, the intelligent and the workers who have only passive force, educated citizens and auxiliaries to whom is granted neither the time nor the means of receiving an education; would it not be desirable, especially in countries that are too warm or too cold, that there be a species between men and animals, a species capable of serving man for consumption and production?
>
> We have the great and the small orangutan, or the gorilla and the chimpanzee and the ape, three species of monkeys that breed perfectly with ours and with negroes, species very susceptible to domestication and to improvement. The crossing of these races would furnish: 1. a strong race (six to eight feet tall) for hard labor whether in the country or the city, the gorillas; 2. a middle-sized race (three to four feet tall) for domestic details,

the chimpanzees; finally 3. a small race (from twelve to fifteen inches) for petty services and amusement. 4. The negroes would command, train, and answer for them. . . . Thenceforth the citizens, the heads of production, would be the whites, the *auxiliary* instruments of labor would be the negroes, and the new races of anthropomorphic monkeys would be your *slaves*. . . . However extraordinary, however immoral this idea may appear at the first glance, I have meditated it for a long time, and you will find no other means, in a large nation especially in very warm and very cold countries, to reconcile the directors of work with the simple instruments of labor.[7]

This note is fascinating, complex, and troubling. It begins with the premise that a great nation is *necessarily* composed of *two peoples*. Rather than grouping together all kinds of useful human activities as labors that support society, Sieyes very clearly distinguishes those who do manual labor from those whose intelligence governs the labor of others. The second people, the manual laborers, are only "auxiliaries." They are spoken of as machines or tools—"human instruments" who contribute only a "passive force" to production. By contrast, the first people is composed of intelligent and educated persons who are the real "producers"—a title he refuses to "workers." Sieyes does not deny that workers are useful, but only because one would not deny that a machine or a draft horse was useful. Their utility is, in his terms, purely passive, derived from the intelligence of the directors of work. Like all other instruments, the workers produce only because they are directed by a superior intelligence. According to this note, at least, production is not the effect of those who perform the painful manual tasks, but of those who administer or govern labor. The opening lines of this note stand in stark contradiction to the claims of *What Is the Third Estate?* Here Sieyes explicitly denies the central premise of his great pamphlet: that the Third Estate, which is also the French nation, is one people united by

7. "Esclaves. D'une espèce qui ait moins de besoins et moins propre exciter la compassion humaine," in Sieyes, *Ecrits politiques,* p. 75, and AN, 284 AP 3, dossier 1.2. This dossier is entitled simply "Varia" by Sieyes, although Fortoul has marked it "Sort of collection of moral reflections. During the revolution." I can see no internal evidence that either this note or others in the dossier may have been composed during the Revolution rather than earlier.

work. Rather, the Third Estate, the working nation, is made up of "two peoples" who are not united but *divided* by their labor.

What Sieyes offers as a solution to the troubling duality of the working nation is a rather shocking fantasy: the production of new species of "anthropomorphic monkeys" to accomplish the "passive labors," to be supervised by "negroes." This bizarre utopia would return humankind to the conditions of the antique polis of Sparta, where all manual labor would be done by slaves regarded as members of inferior species, and all the whites would be "directors of work"— which would give them the time and the means to be educated and to become active and intelligent citizens. Manual production would no longer be carried out by two white peoples, but by *five* peoples, alternately called "races" or "species": whites, blacks, and three types of anthropomorphic monkeys. It is notable that Sieyes cites as the advantage of this arrangement not that it would increase the supply of labor and hence of material goods. The advantage is more moral than material: the inferior species would have "fewer needs" and above all would be "less capable of exciting human compassion." They could be exploited, in other words, with a clear conscience. The exploitable inferior species seem to include, for Sieyes, blacks as well as anthropomorphic monkeys. Without discussing the question, he places Africans in a position intermediate between whites and mon-keys, and the fact that they would be mere "auxiliary instruments of labor" under the guidance of the white citizen "heads of production" apparently causes him no moral anxiety.[8]

Like most utopias (remember that utopia means "nowhere"), this one is displaced outside Europe, to "countries that are too warm or too cold." Its displacement, however, is tentative: the new species would be desirable "in a large nation . . . *especially* in countries that are too warm or too cold" (emphasis added) but presumably not *exclusively* in such intemperate countries. Although he mentions countries that are "too cold"—possibly Russia?—the displacement

---

8. The one echo of this fantasy about inferior species that I can find in Sieyes's published writings appears in a footnote to the *Essai sur les privilèges,* p. 8. But there the desire for inferior species is imputed to the aristocracy: "You do not aspire to the esteem or the love of your fellow men; you respond only to the irritations of a hostile vanity against men whose equality wounds you. At the bottom of your heart, you reproach nature for not having consigned your fellow citizens to inferior species destined uniquely to serve you."

seems to be above all to Europe's tropical colonies in the New World. This is suggested by the mention of very warm countries, and also by the fact that "negroes" appear, quite unannounced, in the second paragraph as species capable of interbreeding with monkeys and as the trainers and commanders of the resulting intermediate species. The existence of New World tropical colonies, with their plantations and slave labor, certainly provided a novel space for thinking about work and work relations.

But it seems unlikely that Sieyes was actually concerned primarily with productive relations in the colonies. In the first place, except for Brazil and the southern colonies of British North America, few of the colonies constituted anything like "large nations." The most prominent colonies that used African slaves in the eighteenth century were sugar-producing islands in the Caribbean, which ranged from Saint-Domingue (Haiti), Jamaica, and Cuba at the large end to such diminutive but very productive islands as Martinique or Guadeloupe. Moreover, there is little evidence elsewhere in Sieyes's writings or private papers that he had any special interest in the colonies; the only sign of interest is that he once spoke in a debate on colonial affairs in the National Assembly, supporting the citizen rights of free men of color.[9] Rather, his reflections were focused on Europe, and especially on France—the preeminent large nation of eighteenth-century Europe, bigger in population than any of its rivals and larger in territory than any European country except hopelessly backward Russia. As we shall see, the concern expressed in this note about the division of large countries into two nations—the producers and the human instruments of production—was a frequent, almost obsessive theme of Sieyes's reflections on the political economy of his own country. I believe that the specification of very hot and very cold countries was precisely a displacement, a way of distancing an all too disturbing fantasy that arose out of specifically European anxieties.

Lurking behind the bizarre fantasy of this note is a tragic vision of the human condition, a vision that arises directly from Sieyes's understanding of political economy. If one believes, as Sieyes seems to have done, that great nations are necessarily composed of intelligent, educated producers on one side and passive human instru-

9. *Le Moniteur,* 12 May 1791.

ments on the other, the only way of escaping from the anguish caused by compassion for the fate of one's suffering fellow humans is through the fantasy of creating new slave races whose exploitation would not excite the same sympathies. Thus Sieyes excuses this apparently "extraordinary" and "immoral" idea by the fact that he can find no "other means, in a large nation . . . , to reconcile the directors of work with the simple instruments of labor." It is easy to see why he would have "meditated" this idea "for a long time"; it is only through the meditation of this utopian fantasy that he could resolve the anguishing contradiction between the natural equality of all men and the crushing inequality that he believed to be necessitated by the conditions of productive labor in modern countries.

It must be stressed that this view of the nature of productive labor was a matter of Sieyes's "belief," since such a view could not have been derived from a "realistic" observation of his society. It was, in fact, an almost delusionary picture of France or Europe in the late eighteenth century. In both industry and agriculture, the scale of enterprise in Sieyes's Europe was almost universally tiny, usually corresponding to a single household. The model of a passive mass of laborers moved by the intelligence of directors of enterprises bore no relation to the actual structures of productive activity. With rare exceptions, the rich in late-eighteenth-century France were either rentiers, who were more interested in the revenues yielded by their property than in the details of the organization of production, or merchants of one sort or another, whose relations with the actual producers of goods were essentially commercial. The commercial nature of business was characteristic not only of *négociants,* or wholesale merchants, who dominated the economies of the great trading cities, but also of the businessmen who dominated the most important industries—for example, textile production. It was not the educated classes but peasants, workers, and artisans who had the technical knowledge necessary for the production of wealth in eighteenth-century France. [10]

10. See, e.g., William M. Reddy, *The Rise of Market Culture: The Textile Trade and French Society, 1750–1900* (Cambridge: Cambridge University Press, 1984), esp. part 1, "A World Without Entrepreneurs, 1750–1815," pp. 19–86; and Ernest Labrousse et al., *Histoire économique et sociale de la France,* vol. 2, *Des Dernier temps de l'âge seigneurial aux préludes de l'âge industriel (1660–1789)* (Paris: Presses Universitaires de France, 1970).

Sieyes's view of relations of production seems to anticipate the nineteenth- or twentieth-century factory as characterized—perhaps caricatured would be a better word—by Dickens, Marx, Engels, and a host of other observers; it certainly did not fit the small industries and small farms of his own day. His conception of "two peoples" divided by work was entirely imaginary. It was a theoretical vision, derived from a metaphysical model of the universe, of humans, and of productive activity as machines—as complicated clocks designed and set in motion by the clockmaker God—that Sieyes shared with the Physiocrats, the Scottish political economists, and Enlightenment thinkers more generally. Sieyes was a philosophical ecclesiastic who had little experience of the world of work except in books. He had, to be sure, seen enough of his society to know that there were major differences of culture and education between the rich and the poor of eighteenth-century France. But onto this palpable difference in general culture between the rich and the poor Sieyes superimposed an analogous but in fact utterly imaginary difference between their roles in production—a difference between the enlightened directors of production and the benighted and passive workers.[11] The fact that the knowledge necessary for production was possessed by uneducated and unenlightened classes—peasants, workers, and artisans— so contradicted his theoretical framework as to be invisible to him.

Laboring Machines

This vision of workers reduced to machines, crushed by mindless labor, is not limited to this single bizarre note. It is found quite commonly in Sieyes's notes and occasionally even in his published writings. We saw in chapter 3 that Sieyes said in his "Speech on the Royal Veto" that "the greatest part of mankind" were "laboring machines,"[12] and that he had described the poor in one of his notes as

11. Sieyes's view of workers as passive beings directed by the intelligence of their superiors was shared by other Enlightenment thinkers. For an interpretation of the illustrations of labor in the *Encyclopédie*, see William H. Sewell, Jr., "Visions of Labor: Illustrations of the Mechanical Arts before, in, and after Diderot's *Encyclopédie*," in *Work in France: Representation, Meaning, Organization, and Practice*, ed. Steven Laurence Kaplan and Cynthia J. Koepp (Ithaca: Cornell University Press, 1986), pp. 258–86.

12. Sieyes, *Dire*, p. 14.

"this immense crowd of biped instruments, without liberty, without morality, without intellectuality."[13]

How Sieyes responded to this perception that humans were degraded to the level of biped instruments fluctuated greatly in the notes in his private papers. Sometimes his tone was of worry and compassion; this was true, for example, in a note entitled "Moderate Labor."

> When I say that the legislator should moderate the labor of the last classes of society, I do not deceive you; I do not wish to diminish the mass of real happiness. I know that expenses lead to happiness, but I also know that expenses when they pass natural limits are felicific only by comparison; what would a few more silk ribbons on the clothing of the rich do for happiness, if at the same time the rich could participate in a diminution of silk ribbons by reducing forced labors? A few false pleasures among a small number should not be more respected than the essential rights of the great number. I fear that by sacrificing to a unity of goals, one immolates the happiness of the instruments which lead to this end. It is the general advantage of citizens that is the great end to which all particular ends should be subordinated.[14]

Here Sieyes admits the fear that immoderate luxuries of the rich—which he designates as "false pleasures" (*jouissance factice*)—are paid for by "forced labors," and therefore by suffering, on the part of the poor. In this note Sieyes seems to recognize a direct opposition between the interests of the rich and those of the poor.

This example and others indicate that Sieyes was sometimes deeply troubled by what he saw as the fate of the majority in the advanced societies of his time—those who were condemned to painful labors.[15] He feared that the undeniable progress of wealth in his era was actually subjecting the poor to ever increasing labor and there-

13. Sieyes, "Grèce. Citoyen—Homme," in *Ecrits politiques*, p. 81.
14. "Travaux modérés," in *Ecrits politiques*, p. 70.
15. Examples include "La division du travail en faisant concourir une infinité de bras au bien-être le plus simple, n'ajoute pas à ce bien-être" [The division of labor, in making an infinity of hands cooperate in the simplest well-being, does not add to that well-being], in *Ecrits politiques*, p. 64; and "Comparaison des différents âges de la société" [Comparison of the different ages of society], in *Ecrits politiques*, p. 73.

fore decreasing their happiness. One can easily see, consequently, how a person who had some sympathy for humanity could meditate on the fantasy of new species of anthropomorphic monkeys that could liberate his fellow humans from a dehumanizing labor.

But Sieyes also had his hard-boiled moments. He was ready, for example, to contemplate instituting a form of temporary slavery, modeled after the English colonial institution of indentured servitude, for the poor of France. In a note simply entitled "Slavery," he suggested that

> the last class, composed of men who have nothing but their hands, might need a legal *slavery* to escape from the *slavery of need*. Why restrain natural liberty? I want to sell my time and my services of all kinds (I do not say my life) for a *year*, two *years*, etc., as is done in English America. The law is silent on this subject, it should only speak to forbid abuses of this dangerous exercise of liberty. Thus one could not engage/enslave oneself for more than five years at most. . . . I see in these assurances of labor given to masters a great means for all enterprises in agriculture and industry.[16]

Here Sieyes is ready to accept as a legitimate consequence of the liberty of exchange the right to extinguish the liberty of a human being for up to five years. And although he remarks that this "exercise of liberty" might be "dangerous" and would therefore have to be regulated by law, one senses that in this note Sieyes was interested more in the "great means" that this institution would supply for enterprises than in the loss of liberty it would imply for the poor—who were in any case already subject to the "slavery of need."

But Sieyes could be yet more callous, as in a note with the long title "Nation. A great nation is necessarily composed of two species of men, citizens and auxiliaries. Of two peoples distinguished by the fact of education." Sieyes annotated the dossier in which this note is found with the words "Estates-General." It therefore probably dates from about the time that Sieyes wrote *What Is the Third Estate?*

---

16. "Esclavage," in *Ecrits politiques,* p. 76, and AN, 284 AP 3, dossier 1.2. Emphasis and ellipses in original.

In vain do we dream of the general good of the human species, it will always be divided into two parts essentially distinguished by the difference of education and labor. If in a small space you wish to retain equality, you condemn the nation to a simplicity of industry and of happiness which could be sustained only with the degradation of the faculties of imagination and will. We would have to roll back the human species. That is not possible. One must return to the distinction between respectable men [*honnêtes hommes*] and instruments of labor. It is no longer equal men who are united, it is the *heads* of production. Union is founded on the perfection of morals, and these morals belong to only a portion of the people; the rest are only admitted into society as auxiliaries.

I do not want to divide my men into Spartiates and Helots, but into citizens and working companions [*compagnons du travail*].[17]

17. "La Nation. Une grande nation est nécessairement composée de deux espèces d'hommes, les citoyens et les auxiliares, de deux peuples distingués par le fait de l'éducation," AN, 284 AP 3, dossier 2.3. This note is written on the overleaf of a folded piece of paper between the first and second sections of another note which is titled "Citoyens, Eligibles, Electeurs" [Citizens, Eligibles, Electors]. Zapperi, in transcribing the note, made the understandable mistake of thinking that the second half of the longer note was a continuation of this one. Hence, the third, fourth, and fifth paragraphs of the note Zapperi reprints on pp. 89 and 90 of Sieyes's *Ecrits politiques*, which I quote at length below, are not properly part of this note at all.

Sieyes's annotation is on the paper forming the dossier, not on the sheet that contains these notes. Even in this case of an annotated dossier, some doubt remains about the precise time at which the notes may have been composed. In the longer of the two notes, Sieyes considers questions of citizenship, eligibility, suffrage, the distinction between active citizens and auxiliaries—questions that were very practical in the summer and fall of 1789, questions about which he reported to the National Assembly in his sketch of a declaration of the rights of man and citizen. The note also includes remarks on the king, which are appended to the portion I quote. There Sieyes remarks that "as a citizen, will he [the king] not be an elector, confounded with all others, in order better to engrave in our minds that he is a citizen, and interested as such in good legislation?" This fragment on the king as a citizen is very close to what Sieyes said in the Assembly in his September 1789 speech on the question of the royal veto over legislation. But there are also reasons to believe that this note probably does not date from the summer or early fall of 1789. First, it was precisely during this time, in July and October of 1789, that Sieyes published two pamphlets—the *Préliminaire de la constitution* and his brochure *Quelques idées de constitution applicables à la ville de Paris* [Some constitutional ideas

Here Sieyes seems to be denying any possibility of equality among the persons who form a modern nation. This possibility has been superseded forever by the progress of human industry. It exists only in the past or in dreams. The truth is that modern nations are composed of two peoples, of "two species of men." Only men of the superior species—"respectable men," the "heads of production"—are citizens. It is only they who have the morality that is perfected in the state of society. Members of the inferior species, made up of "instruments of labor," without education, without morals, are not even admitted into society, except as auxiliaries. They are not citizens but merely "working companions" of the citizens. They are the modern equivalents of the Helots of ancient Sparta.

It is unsettling, to say the least, that this note was apparently written by Sieyes at about the same time as *What Is the Third Estate?* for it seems to contradict the central argument of the great revolutionary pamphlet. If there are "two peoples" in *What Is the Third Estate?* these could only be the true people of the Third Estate, who do all the work of society, and the false, idle, and parasitical people—whom Sieyes called in his pamphlet the "false people" (125)—who make up the nobility. But in this note Sieyes speaks of two people among those who do society's work. The unity of the true, laboring nation that is affirmed in *What Is the Third Estate?* is denied in this note. Moreover, just like the aristocrats whom he denounces with such vehemence in the *Essay on Privileges* and in *What Is the Third Estate?* Sieyes distinguishes the superior men from the inferior in terms of race: they constitute two distinct species. The ideas that Sieyes confides to paper in the beginning of this note totally contradict the central premises of *What Is the Third Estate?*

---

applicable to the city of Paris] (Versailles: Baudouin, n.d.)—which take the most optimistic position of any of his writings about the political capacities of the people, whereas this note is perhaps the most violently pessimistic. Finally, it seems unlikely that Sieyes would be contemplating electoral rules that would seem to give nobles—the most important landowners and possessors of "third names"—an advantage in elections of representatives of the nation. This consideration would indeed seem to place it in 1788, before the composition of the *Essay on Privileges* and *What Is the Third Estate?* Whenever it was written, it seems to show us Sieyes meditating criteria of citizenship for a constitution—most likely for a utopian constitution conceived sometime in 1788 but possibly for a very practical constitution in 1789.

It should therefore not be surprising that Sieyes then goes on to modify what he has said.

> But nature does not pass out mental gifts exclusively to a single race of men. But it would be cruel, ghastly to condemn to an existence as auxiliaries those who feel that they have soul and intelligence. According to these considerations, let us establish the law: that the door to citizenship always be open to any man whom nature or circumstances make truly a citizen, and to allow those whom nature or circumstances have marked with the seal of nullity to fall . . . with the consequence that the nation will rest on a real and essentially stable basis, and that the means of felicity will be proportioned to the value of desires. [18]

On further reflection, Sieyes decides that the two types of humans ought not to be considered two racially distinct species. There will always be children of working companions who will have intelligent souls, and those of citizens who will be "marked with the seal of nullity." Thus the door of citizenship must be open in both directions, and Sieyes concludes, bravely, that this modification will assure stability and felicity in the state. But even with these modifications, which back away from a racial conception of the difference between the "heads of production" and the "working companions," this note indicates the depth of Sieyes's disdain for the great majority of those who do the useful work of society, and his despair over the possibility of raising any but a few rare individuals of this auxiliary class to the level of citizens.

In short, Sieyes's unpublished notes seem to prove incontestably that he had a very low opinion of the majority of his compatriots. He continually spoke of them as instruments of labor, working machines, biped instruments, moral and intellectual nullities, passive beings. His attitude toward this dehumanized mass oscillated considerably, but the oscillations were always between disdain and pity. Never in his notes did he consider that the mass of humans condemned to painful labor might be morally valid citizens, capable of legitimate political judgments. Everything indicates that Sieyes

18. AN, 284 AP 3, dossier 2.3; ellipsis in original.

wished to confer political power only on a restricted minority of the population, on those who were active, moral, educated, well-to-do, and capable. The evidence of Sieyes's notes indicates that we must take very seriously indeed the brief passage in *What Is the Third Estate?* where he seems to deny the right of most of those who "support society" by their labor to govern themselves and instead confers the right to govern on the "available classes," whose wealth relieves them of constant labor.

The Law of Availability?

The note that begins by dividing the nation into two peoples was written on the overleaf of a folded piece of paper containing a longer note reflecting on the appropriate qualifications for citizens. The note is entitled "Citizens, Eligibles, Electors," and it too excludes "working companions" from the title of citizenship.

> To be a citizen, it is necessary to know the relations of human associations, and in particular those of the society of which one is a member. Men who cannot improve themselves, or whom one cannot raise to this knowledge, are only *working companions*. [19]

Here Sieyes speaks not of differences of species but of differences in knowledge and education. However, the distinction between citizens and working companions is equally sharp.

He apparently felt pangs of conscience in so summarily casting most of his compatriots out of the sphere of citizens, for the note continues hesitatingly:

> But can we refuse the quality of citizen to nine-tenths of the nation? . . . Do not put exertions of sentiment in the place of reason. . . . However, we must invite governments to metamorphose human beasts into citizens, to make them participate actively in the benefits of society. [20]

He worries about refusing citizenship to nine-tenths of his compatriots but then chides himself for allowing sentimentality to over-

19. "Citoyens, éligibles, électeurs," AN, 284 AP 3, dossier 2.3.
20. Ibid.; ellipses in original.

come his reason. Still, working companions, here designated "human beasts," should if possible be raised to the quality of citizens by their governments—presumably by means of education.

But after these hesitations, Sieyes continues with the argument he had begun.

> It is evident that there is a great difference between effectual citizens and those who only become so by their *physical utility.* It is evident first, that deputies in the national parliament can only be chosen among the effectual citizens; the difficulty can only be to find the law that designates the necessary qualities for *electors.* That depends on how much one will require for admission to the rank of *citizen.* If one demands as an essential condition a *sufficient moral education,* there is no doubt that every citizen is an elector.[21]

This passage is not very clear. Sieyes is trying at the same time to establish criteria for three potentially distinct political categories: citizens, electors, and eligibles (that is, those eligible for election to public office). It is evident, he says, that those eligible to serve in the parliament must be "effectual citizens." This means that they cannot be the sort of men whose effects depend purely on their "physical utility"; they must be morally or intellectually effectual as well. One might expect that those to be designated as citizens, or to be accorded the right to participate in the election of members of parliament, would be subjected to a somewhat less exacting standard than would those eligible to serve in the parliament. But in this passage Sieyes in effect applies the same standard for all three categories: citizens must have "a sufficient moral education," which would qualify all citizens as electors. And by implication, it is precisely a sufficient moral education that distinguishes the "effectual citizens," who should be eligible to serve in the parliament, from those having only a "physical utility."

Sieyes therefore warns against any effort to extend suffrage downward to all possessors of freehold properties.

> Electors would not be so easy to corrupt if they were all truly citizens. What should one expect from freeholders whose spec-

21. Ibid.

ulations extend only to knowing how to make a living, who have little talent for increasing their fortune, and know only how to use for that sole purpose the political instrument that you have the imprudence to place in their hands? They know nothing of its importance or its use. . . . But, someone will say, do you believe that enlightened citizens cannot have a depraved soul and sell their votes? Without doubt, passions corrupt a portion of men, but ignorance animates passions all the more, leading astray the entire mass of the state.[22]

Men poor and ignorant enough to have no interests beyond making a living cannot be trusted with citizenship rights, even if they are property owners, because rather than using politics to promote the general good they will use it purely to further their selfish interests. Such selfishness and lack of political virtue could, of course, be found even among more educated men, but ignorance—which Sieyes implicitly equates with insufficient wealth—greatly increases the probability of corruption, and enfranchising the ignorant could easily "lead astray the entire mass of the state." It is clear, then, that some degree of affluence or "availability" is a requirement for citizenship, although Sieyes develops no clear criteria for determining the appropriate threshold of wealth and enlightenment.

He is somewhat more concrete, however, in setting forth the standards that should be met by "eligibles"—those capable of standing for election as representatives of the people.

To be *eligible* [for election to the national parliament] a citizen must have obtained a third name; it is also necessary that he possess wealth in the State and a certain quantity of wealth of some kind. This because it is just on the one hand that men charged with representing the nation be drawn from among those who have done it the most honor and are most deserving. In the second place because deputies must be among those who have the greatest interest in good order, and the most to fear from disorder, and are the least susceptible to selling themselves, to debasing themselves. . . .[23]

22. Ibid.; see also Sieyes, *Ecrits politiques,* pp. 89–90; ellipsis in original.
23. Ibid.; see also Sieyes, *Ecrits politiques,* p. 90; ellipsis in original.

He begins by enumerating qualifications that would restrict the suffrage to substantial landed proprietors. To be eligible, a citizen must have acquired a third name. By this I assume that Sieyes means the name of an estate, which is added to the Christian name and surname by means of the particle *de*. All nobles, of course, affected the particle, but it was also used by plenty of commoners who had bought estates—even by many future revolutionaries, such as de Lambeth or Brissot de Warville or even de Robespierre. Eligibility must be restricted to those who possess wealth not only because it implies a higher level of education and enlightenment but because it renders them less susceptible to graft and gives them a more powerful interest in the good order of the state.

These are standard eighteenth-century arguments for a highly restricted franchise; they could as easily have been heard in America or England as in France. Sieyes, in other words, seems to be defining the "available class" in quite conventional terms. But having laid out these criteria, Sieyes again hesitates: "I fear that in establishing the condition of the third name for eligibility, I have totally weakened this spring. The third name should be the effect, the recompense of a representative, of an administrator, of a soldier, or a legist who has served well."[24] An honorary title of the sort conferred by the "third name," Sieyes worries, should be the consequence, not the condition, of public service. Awarding eligibility on the basis of the third name as it is now used—that is, to all who have acquired substantial landed estates—would have the effect of unwinding the spring of virtue that should power the state. Sieyes therefore ends his discussion of eligibility not by declaring clear criteria, but in indecision.

What is particularly striking about this note is Sieyes's difficulty in finding workable criteria for citizenship. From the beginning to the end, he is sure of one thing: that the mass of "working companions" cannot be citizens. But he is far from sure about the positive definitions that should determine the exact threshold of citizenship either in general or for the exercise of particular citizen functions, such as suffrage or standing for election. Sieyes makes it clear in this note that for him the true characteristics of the good citizen are qualities of the soul: intelligence, cultivation, and public virtue. He also as-

24. Ibid.; see also Sieyes, *Ecrits politiques*, p. 90.

sumes that these intellectual or moral characteristics are determined by economic conditions—whether one is an active director of production or a passive instrument, whether one has sufficient wealth to pursue the public good or so little as not to be able to see beyond one's own self-interest, whether one has the means of acquiring an education, and so on. But when it actually comes to specifying criteria, Sieyes is never satisfied. Thus he disputes mere ownership of a freehold property as a criterion. He then posits more exacting property standards as criteria for eligibility to serve in the national parliament, but disputes them as well. Although Sieyes seems to remain convinced that "a law that designates the necessary qualities" can somehow be found, he does not find one in this note.

Sieyes apparently spent a good deal of time attempting to discover what he hopefully called in the title of one of his notes "the law of availability."[25] The object of his search was to discover the appropriate economic criteria for citizenship. Finding these required uncovering the economic mechanisms that generated political availability. In this effort he was clearly influenced by Turgot, from whom he borrowed the concept of "available classes." For Turgot, a good Physiocrat, it was natural that those who possessed land, the sole source of productivity, should also be the nation's political class. As is clear from the note analyzed above, Sieyes's first instinct was to argue, like Turgot, that landed proprietors were the natural representatives of the nation. But neither in this note nor in others was he able to decide conclusively that the right to represent the nation should be given over entirely to the landowner class. This unwillingness to join in Turgot's unproblematic acceptance of government by landlords arose in part from his critical but never fully clarified stance toward physiocracy as a system of political economy.

This stance is manifested in his uncertain relation to the physiocratic concept of the "net product." In physiocratic thought the net product is a surplus, essentially the produce of the soil beyond the expenses in labor and physical products necessary to maintain its productivity. Because a surplus or profit of this sort renders certain classes of the population "available," it should not be surprising that Sieyes discussed the "net product" and such cognate terms as "profit"

25. "La loi de la disponibilité," in Sieyes, *Ecrits politiques*, p. 68.

and "available product" in several of his notes on political economy. But most of these notes are particularly baffling and contradictory.

In some notes, Sieyes seemed to accept the Physiocrats' claims that the net product was produced by land and that its accumulation and use depended on the institution of private property in land—what Sieyes called "the exclusive privilege of land."[26] He observed, for example, that "if landed work [travaux fonciers] were not exclusive, there would surely be much less available product."[27] Such a physio-cratic view also implied that the landed class, which benefited from the "exclusive privilege" of landownership, would have a virtual monopoly on availability for citizenship. But in other notes, and occasionally in other passages of the same notes, Sieyes disputed the claim that the net or available product could be regarded as having any particular link with the land or landed property. Because Sieyes regarded labor, rather than land, as the source of wealth, the available surplus had to be the product of arts and industry as well as of agriculture:

> If the *exclusive privilege* of land makes it possible to remove without danger a net product from primary materials [matierès primaires, a physiocratic term for agricultural produce], it is also certain that the progress of the arts permits the birth of a net product for the state.[28]
>
> The essential product is not limited to the product of land. It is the sum of *all* necessary subsistence. The fruit of *all* labors beyond the essential forms the available product.[29]

Indeed, in one of his notes, entitled "Net Product Relative to the Whole of Society," Sieyes implies that the net product is the result *exclusively* of the perfection of the arts or techniques of work. The net product "increases as much as the instruments with which work is done are improved." Because it is "the product of that part of work beyond what is necessary to produce a just subsistence," the net

26. "Le Produit net vu sous un rapport politique" [Net product viewed from political relations]," in *Ecrits politiques*, p. 57.
27. "A propos du produit net" [Concerning net product], in *Ecrits politiques*, p. 56.
28. "L'Agriculture et l'industrie" [Agriculture and industry], in *Ecrits politiques*, p. 61; emphasis in original.
29. "A propos du produit net" [About the net product], *Ecrits politiques*, p. 56; my emphasis.

product "is the fruit and the recompense of the genius which has perfected labor."[30]

Sieyes's notes on political economy in fact contain a jumble of inconsistent ideas about the "net" or "available" product. His vocabulary was inconsistent as well—for example, opposing net and available products in one note and equating them in another. Consequently, it should not be surprising that he also never developed a consistent argument about precisely what made certain classes available for citizenship. He seems to have had no doubt that some degree of wealth—"a certain affluence," as he put it in *What Is the Third Estate?*—was essential, but he never succeeded in establishing what amount or type of wealth might be required. He followed Turgot and many other eighteenth-century political theorists in accepting land ownership—the exclusive privilege of the land—as the most obvious criterion for citizenship. But he could not follow their lead uncritically. In part this was probably a consequence of his belief that land was not the only source of the "available product"—that labor in arts, manufactures, and services also created net product. But it may also have been due to a usually unstated worry that if the legitimate privilege of private property could give rise to an "available class," so might the illegitimate privileges of the nobility.

Sieyes pondered this possibility explicitly in two successive notes in a notebook labeled "Production." The first is given no individual label, but the second is promisingly entitled "The Law of Availability." The first is basically a meditation on the varying degrees of availability.

> There are no men whose *entire* life belongs to the expenses of reproduction, hence the population of the class of men who are most absorbed by labor could be considered as being of greater interest than animals and working machinery. Besides, in addition to the small *available* portion of their time which makes them *social* beings, they form at least the elements of the public force, and in certain circumstances they can themselves, by turning away from a labor temporarily less pressing than some danger, augment that force in passing.[31]

---

30. "Produit net relativement à la société entière," in *Ecrits politiques,* p. 50.
31. AN, 284 AP 2, dossier 13. This note appears on p. 26 of a notebook, entitled "Production," with numbered pages.

Here Sieyes admits that even the men most absorbed by labor are at least partially available—something that he elsewhere denies by dealing exclusively in such dichotomous oppositions as educated versus ignorant, active versus passive, or citizens versus working companions.

He also observes that the inverse is true of the wealthy: "There are no men whose *entire* life is *available*." Availability, then, is a relative rather than an absolute condition. Indeed, "if there are titles that occasion such abuses, they are socially illegitimate."[32] If a man

> obtains his revenues without any labor, whether he leads an idle life or a useful life, in the first case his life is a theft from the partial availability of other lives; in the second case his availability is still antisocial, even though he makes a good use of it and renders it more useful than if it belonged to others. . . . An entirely available life depends on the net revenue of others; we need instead lives whose availability is only taken from net revenues acquired by non-available time, or *lives that are self-supporting.*[33]

Socially legitimate availability, then, must be a surplus that arises from some useful work, rather than a theft from the useful work of others. Thus it seems that there are legitimate availabilities—those based on a surplus arising from personal labor—and illegitimate availabilities—those stolen from the labor of others.

But in a new note entitled "The Law of Availability," on the page immediately following, Sieyes indicates an exception to this rule. "The exclusive use of the soil," he writes, "is useful to production. This title earns a rent to the proprietor, his costs are little, and his net revenue is considerable." In this case, "his privilege is legitimate." But then he announces certain conditions to this legitimacy. A proprietor who benefits from the exclusive use of the soil must "replace his expenses, administer, repair and even ameliorate his natural fund, otherwise he does not fulfill his duties, he devours a part of his reproductive revenue, he damages future production, and as a consequence all works that this production would have sus-

32. Ibid.
33. Ibid.; emphasis in original.

tained, all the free revenues it would have occasioned; he damages society."[34]

In fact, the only sure means of distinguishing between legitimate and illegitimate availabilities is the criterion of free exchange.

> The circumstances regulating the differences that occur in each work between the reproductive revenue and the net revenue must be left at their liberty; any constraint, any privilege which augments or diminishes their influence, unless it is dictated by enlightened law, is a vexation, a theft made against *supply* in favor of *demand* or against demand in favor of supply.
>
> In general any title that takes from one to give to another, is illegitimate; the availability of one citizen cannot be at the expense of others. It should only be a part of the total price which one earns with one's work, work left to competition according to the laws of order. Perpetual hereditary interests, unnecessary pensions, favors of the court, give only *illegitimate availabilities*. All unnecessary taxes are in the same case. These availabilities are not due to labor, but to ignorance, and to vexation.[35]

He completes the note with a list of four types of availabilities. The first is "availability due to free work, freely appreciated." This is the availability that results directly from work subject to the laws of supply and demand, without any privileges—for example, those of entrepreneurs working in a free market. The second type is an "availability due to useful work, admitted, but privileged." This is the availability of the good landowner, who does useful work, but who benefits from a rent resulting from a "legitimate privilege." The third is an "availability due to work advantaged by useless privileges." Here I presume he means privileges, other than that of exclusive property of the soil, that are accorded to various occupational groups, such as the privileges of the clergy, of magistrates, or of guilds. The fourth type is "an availability accorded to idleness" (that is, that of those who are rich but do nothing), "or even to

34. "La loi de la disponibilité," AN, 284 AP, dossier 13, and Sieyes, *Ecrits politiques*, p. 68.
35. Ibid; emphasis in original.

harmful occupations" (for example, courtiers who engage only in intrigue). This sort of availability derives from the vexatious privileges of the aristocracy.

The final two types of availability are clearly illegitimate; they would disappear if privileges in the usual sense (that is, not including private property in land) were abolished. The first type is clearly legitimate, because it results from "work left to competition according to the laws of order." The troublesome type is the second, availability based on rent, whose legitimacy depends on the beneficiary engaging in useful work, but whose existence does not. The possession of landed property, after all, could be a consequence only of inherited wealth, and it did not necessarily give rise to a service useful to the nation.

This note, like so many others, ends not with the confident announcement of a "law of availability" that could be applied unambiguously in the establishment of a constitution but in another provisional and unstable typology. Sieyes's notes indicate that he tried again and again to establish proper economic criteria for citizenship. "Like everyone else," he wished to designate those appropriate to represent the nation by applying the criterion of property. But he was never able to embrace this criterion with real enthusiasm. He hesitated, I believe, because he knew at some level that a regime of private hereditary property often accorded great properties to idle, stupid, or immoral persons. He feared that the criterion of property had only a mediocre fit with the personal characteristics that he wished to see in representatives of the people—education, moral cultivation, and public virtue.

Here it seems to me highly significant that Sieyes used the word "privilege" to designate the exclusive right to the use of land. We have seen in chapter 4 that it was above all the hereditary character that he detested in the privileges of the nobility. He attempted to demonstrate in the *Essay on Privileges* that the effect of hereditary noble privileges was to render nobles idle, antisocial, beggars, and intriguers. The privilege of private property in land was different from the honorific, political, and pecuniary privileges that he denounced in the *Essay* and in *What Is the Third Estate?* because "the exclusive usage of the land is useful to production." But it was nevertheless true that the fact of inheriting a great landed property could have the same effect on its possessor as that of inheriting a privilege of any kind—that is, it could encourage idleness. Sieyes's employment of the term "privilege" for exclusive property rights in land seems to indicate a resemblance between private property in land, which he quite conventionally regarded as the very basis of society, and the honorific, political, and pecuniary privileges of the aristocracy, which he regarded as society's worst plague. It may have been a dim recognition of this enormous flaw of private property that made Sieyes incapable of finding a satisfactory "law of availability," a clear rule for designating citizens by means of property ownership. The simple fact of availability, of the capacity to satisfy one's needs without constant labor, was not in the end a sufficient guarantee for Sieyes of political capacity. Sieyes's notes indicate that he put a good deal of effort into his search for "the law of availability." But he was not destined to find a law that could satisfy him.

Why No Law Could Be Found

Sieyes's attempt to find sure and exact criteria to designate citizens capable of the exercise of political power was destined to failure by the multiple contradictions of his thought—contradictions he shared with many of his contemporaries. In the numerous notes in which Sieyes attempted to distinguish the capable elite from the incapable mass, he employed three different types of distinctions: of economic activities, of knowledge, and of availability. When Sieyes erected dichotomous contrasts between the elite and the mass, all three criteria seemed to fit together. In part this was the standard consequence of sharply dichotomous thinking: if society was to be divided into two distinct categories, a small elite and a great mass, the elite would of course be superior to the mass in wealth, knowledge, and availability alike. Moreover, according to Sieyes's abstract schema, there were logical links between the three criteria. According to his thinking, economic activity—that is, the direction of work—is the real source of wealth. It is wealth that creates property, and hence the availability that is the necessary condition for the acquisition of knowledge. And finally, it is knowledge that constitutes the superiority of the directors of work over their human instruments and that makes them capable of effectively creating wealth. As an abstract schema, the three criteria fit together perfectly.

But this schema was more than a linguistic or rhetorical network. It was also a means of thinking about a particular social and political world, a world that, like all worlds, resisted abstract schemas. Social relations deviated significantly from Sieyes's abstract sketch of them. This made a perfectly coherent intellectual construct an impossibly clumsy guide to action in the world. The principal deviations from Sieyes's schema were three. First, although a certain affluence or availability was necessary for the acquisition of education and for a more or less total devotion to public affairs, this availability could be used very differently—in a folly of luxurious consumption, in idleness, or in vice. The link between availability on one side and its utilization for education and for public service was only probable and enabling, not necessary. Second, the link between knowledge and economic activity was very weak, at best. As I have already remarked, virtually all active production of wealth was carried out by peasants, workers, artisans, and small manufacturers on their own, without any direction from educated men. The *Encyclopédie* and the philosophes had, of course, declared that all production was in fact applied science, but with very few exceptions the interventions of science in production remained entirely at the level of philosophical speculation. In eighteenth-century economic life the possession of scientific knowledge that might potentially have been applied to production probably had, in the statistical sense of the term, a negative relation to active participation in the creation of wealth. And finally, among the classes who had attained "a certain affluence," those who were most active as directors of work—that is to say, the merchants and manufacturers—were the most "absorbed by work" and as a consequence the least "available." Because the correlations between availability, knowledge, and economic activity were at best mediocre, and at worst negative, all of Sieyes's attempts to find exact criteria of citizen capability ended in frustration. Here social realities impinged powerfully on Sieyes's thought and writing, disrupting the logic of his formulations through failures of reference. In his prerevolutionary notes, Sieyes never succeeded in finding the elusive law of availability. And once he got involved in the legislative work of the Revolution, he gave up the search altogether.

From Economic Criteria to Constitutional Tinkering

One striking thing about Sieyes's writings after *What Is the Third Estate?* is that they avoided by one means or another any pure property criterion for the exercise of the powers of citizenship, even though all of his constitutional schemes, no less than his prerevolutionary notes, had the goal of putting a cultivated and capable elite in power. In his *Reasoned Exposition of the Rights of Man and Citizen,* published by order of the Constitutional Committee of the National Assembly in July 1789, Sieyes insisted on the inevitable inequality of means and consumption: "There exist, it is true, great inequalities of means among men. Nature made the strong and the weak; it gave to some an intelligence that it refused to others. It follows that there will be among them inequality of work, inequality of product, inequality of consumption or enjoyment."[36] Society cannot and should not try to institute an equality of means where nature has refused it. All it can do is to guarantee an equality of natural and civil rights so that the feeble will be "sheltered from the enterprises of the strong."[37] The natural and civil rights of all members of society must therefore be equal. But the same is not true for political rights.

> So far we have only explained *natural and civil rights* of citizens. We still need to recognize *political* rights. The difference between these two sorts of rights consists in the fact that natural rights are those *for* whose maintenance and development society was formed; and political rights, those *by* which society is formed. It would be better, for the clarity of language, to call the first *passive* rights, and the second, *active* rights.
>
> All the inhabitants of a country should enjoy the rights of the *passive* citizen: all have a right to the protection of their person, of their propriety, of their liberty, etc., but not all have the right to take an active part in the formation of public powers; not all are *active* citizens. Women, at least in the current state of things, children, foreigners, those also who contribute nothing to the maintenance of the public establishment, should not actively influence the public weal [*la chose publique*]. All can

36. Sieyes, *Préliminaire*, p. 22.
37. Ibid, p. 25.

enjoy the advantages of society; but only those who contribute to the public establishment, are like true stockholders in the great social enterprise. Only they are true active citizens, the true members of the association.[38]

Here we are witnessing the invention of the distinction between active and passive citizens—a distinction that had a celebrated and troubled history in the French Revolution.[39] One would naturally expect the distinction between active and passive citizens to be linked to the distinctions that Sieyes made in his prerevolutionary notes between directors of work—those who take the active part in production—and the working companions or human instruments— those whom Sieyes regarded as passive. If so, the number of active citizens would have been quite small. But Sieyes gives no explicit rules for determining the boundary, either in his "reasoned exposition" or in the forty-two articles of his projected declaration of the rights of man and citizen. In Article 30, he indicates that the right to act as electors will be limited to certain classes of citizens: "The law can only be the expression of the general will. In a large nation, it should be the work of a body of representatives chosen for a short term, mediately or immediately by all the citizens who have interest and capacity for the public good. These qualities need to be positively and clearly determined by the constitution."[40] But he chose to leave the specification of precise rules, the definition of those who have "interest and capacity for the public good," to the deliberations of the National Assembly.

However, some of Sieyes's other writings from the same period show clearly that he was not thinking of a very elevated level of wealth or capacity as a qualification for being a simple active citizen. In his pamphlet entitled *Some Constitutional Ideas, Applicable to the City of Paris,* also published in July 1789, Sieyes proposed an explicit means of distinguishing active from passive citizens. He proposed the establishment of a "voluntary tribute," a payment to the state

38. Ibid., pp. 36–37; emphasis in original.
39. William H. Sewell, Jr., *"Le citoyen/la citoyenne:* Activity, Passivity, and the Revolutionary Concept of Citizenship," in Lucas, *Political Culture of the French Revolution.*
40. Sieyes, "Préliminaire," p. 48.

made by the citizen in addition to ordinary taxes. The payment of this tribute, he said,

> will be . . . the simplest political means of regulating the number of *active* citizens, according to the zeal and the capacity that the French show for exercising their political rights. . . . I would like . . . every citizen . . . who does not voluntarily pay the sum of three livres, to be considered as wishing to deprive himself or to abstain from the exercise of the rights of the active citizen [i.e., the right to vote]. . . . But to be *eligible* [to stand for election] he must immediately pay twelve livres. These two tributes will carry the names tribute of electors, and tribute of eligibles.[41]

This was, from Sieyes's point of view, a brilliant solution, one that avoided all the problems raised by instituting property qualifications for electors and eligibles. Because the voluntary tribute was a charge beyond the taxes owed by everyone, its payment would be a criterion at once of zeal and of availability. Moreover, the distinction between the tributes of electors and of eligibles established grades of zeal and availability which would be proportional to the difficulty and the gravity of the political tasks potentially facing those who would choose representatives and those who might also be called on to serve as representatives.

But if this solution was ingenious from the point of view of the questions that preoccupied Sieyes, the Committee of the Constitution and the Constituent Assembly preferred distinctions based on payment of varying levels of ordinary taxes. Sieyes continued to contest this decision as late as October 1789, when he wrote his pamphlet *Observations on the Report of the Constitutional Committee on the New Organization of France,* where he noted that "one could make this exercise [of political rights] depend upon a positive condition, which would be a voluntary tribute of a given value. The Constitutional Committee did not dare to propose it to the Assembly; it did not go beyond [requiring payment of] an obligatory, direct contribution having the value of three days of labor."[42]

41. Sieyes, *Quelques idées de constitution,* pp. 19–21.
42. Sieyes, *Observations sur le rapport,* pp. 21–22.

Yet if the Committee, of which Sieyes was a member at this time, did not accept his idea of a voluntary contribution, the provisions it accepted were in other respects quite close to those Sieyes had proposed in his July pamphlet, with a fairly low property tax requirement for active citizens and a much higher threshold for "eligibles"— the celebrated requirement of a "mark of silver" that was denounced by Robespierre and other radical deputies. According to Sieyes, the distinction between active and passive was intended only to ban "the lowliest class . . . the most destitute people," who are "strangers, by their intelligence and by their sentiments, to the interests of the association." These men, "valid in physical force" but "foreign to all social ideas, are not in a condition to take an active part in the public weal." They must be removed "not . . . from legal protection and public assistance, but from the exercise of political rights."[43] He does not mention, but takes for granted, that women and minors would also be incapable of taking an active part in the public weal and could therefore be only passive citizens.

The Committee also accepted, with a few modifications, another of Sieyes's proposals: a system of indirect elections, in which the active citizens would choose electors who would vote for representatives. By this procedure of pyramidal selection, the influence of citizens who lacked talent, knowledge, and wealth was limited strictly to their capacities. As Sieyes put it in his October pamphlet,

> The least available classes of the people, and those most devoid of knowledge of public affairs, are nevertheless quite capable of placing their confidence well. This aptitude cannot be contested, even for the most populous states, when elementary assemblies are reduced simply to naming electors. The little people [le petit peuple], in most countries, may very well not have formed a sufficiently sure idea of the qualities necessary for those who will represent them in the legislature, but they will not be mistaken in designating the most honest men of their district, to make, in superior electoral assemblies, a choice of the greatest importance for the public good.[44]

43. Ibid., p. 21.
44. Ibid., pp. 16–17.

Thus, Sieyes never ceased to be profoundly elitist. He always had a low opinion of the mass of his fellow citizens. But he was also a politician who keenly felt, in the conjuncture of 1789, the political necessity of a broad suffrage. Moreover, he had never been able to convince himself of the value of purely financial criteria of availability. Hence he opted, in the summer and fall of 1789, for a sort of electoral filtering, in which a broad system of suffrage would nevertheless assure the choice of the most capable representatives by the wisely managed play of what he had called in the *Essay on Privileges* "the free market of esteem." The electoral filtering adopted by the National Assembly and put into practice in the Constitution of 1791 was designed to reconcile the political necessity of a broad suffrage with what Sieyes and most of his colleagues in the National Assembly regarded as the no less pressing necessity to assure that only the educated, public-spirited, "available" elite would actually serve as representatives of the people.

Was What Is the Third Estate? *an Aberration?*

What do these investigations of Sieyes's notes and writings tell us about the two contradictory criteria of citizenship that appear in *What Is the Third Estate?* It is clear that Sieyes, in many of his writings, both published and unpublished, was obsessed by the relation between citizens' economic functions and political roles. For this reason, it should not be surprising to find an exclusion of the idle from the nation in the first chapter of *What Is the Third Estate?* nor to find in the third chapter the notion that the available classes should take in hand the destinies of the nation. But the specifics of the proposals made in both of the chapters are rather more surprising.

In the context of Sieyes's later writings, and above all in the context of his prerevolutionary personal notes, the principal argument of *What Is the Third Estate?* about citizenship seems downright aberrant. The clear implication of the first chapter—that all those who work should be citizens and that only the voluntary and hereditary idlers of the aristocratic class should be excluded from citizenship—is found nowhere in his other writings, either published or unpublished. He constantly maintained that the mass of the French people were passive and ignorant human instruments who were absolutely incapable of acting wisely on public issues. It was not until October 1789, after much discussion within the Constitutional Committee, that he was ready to admit that those whom he still disdainfully called "the little people," "the least available classes of the people," "those most devoid of knowledge of public affairs," were capable even of electing more capable men who would vote for them in choosing representatives.

It therefore seems clear that the unity of citizen-workers put in place by Sieyes at the very beginning of *What Is the Third Estate?* reflected not his permanent elitist convictions but rather the necessities of a particular and momentary political polemic. Thus, in *What Is the Third Estate?* he expressed his already well-developed opinion that all types of labor contributed to the creation of wealth, but he suppressed his equally well-developed conviction that most workers were useful only as biped instruments in the hands of wealthy and educated men and consequently were incapable of valid actions in political matters. Suppressing this second conviction made possible the appearance of a political unity among the entire Third Estate, a unity in which he did not believe, but which was a rhetorical necessity in his polemic against the nobility.

Sieyes's remarks on the "available classes" in the third chapter of *What Is the Third Estate?* are far less surprising in view of his other writings; he frequently wrote similar things both before and after *What Is the Third Estate?* What is lacking in the great pamphlet are only the hesitations, the doubts that elsewhere kept Sieyes from pronouncing so clearly in favor of a government by rich rentiers. But Sieyes's normal, indeed permanent opinions were far closer to the sentiments expressed in the brief and obscure passage on the available classes in the third chapter than to those he expressed much more fully and with far greater rhetorical force in the first chapter and elsewhere in the pamphlet. In the context of the pamphlet, the brief passage on the available classes represented only a minor contradiction in an otherwise astonishingly well-made text. But in the context of the entire body of Sieyes's writings and of his actions as a political leader, it is *What Is the Third Estate?* that stands in contradiction to his permanent opinions. Ironically, the work that made the abbé

Sieyes famous, the most influential pamphlet of the most important revolution in modern history, also turns out to have been the most uncharacteristic work of its author's career.

This does not necessarily mean that when he wrote *What Is the Third Estate?* Sieyes was simply cynical. To begin with, it should be noted that Sieyes never said explicitly that those who did society's work should have the right to participate actively in politics. He merely said that the Third Estate did all of society's work and that the nobility, because it did not work, was excluded from the nation. This implied, to be sure, that those who work are members of the nation, but not necessarily that they should all participate actively or equally in its political affairs. He certainly made statements that seemed to imply an equality of political rights—for example, his declaration in chapter 2 that "one is not made free by privileges, but by the rights of the citizen, rights that belong to all" (127). But even here he did not specify what he meant to include as rights of citizen; he may have been thinking of what he would later dub "passive rights" attached to all citizens, rather than the "active rights" limited to those who make an active contribution to the society. Sieyes allowed his readers to believe in a uniformity of political status within the Third Estate, in part by avoiding statements that might imply the impossibility of such a uniformity, but he never explicitly affirmed that such uniformity existed.

Besides, he seems sincerely to have believed that the work of the mass of the population was organized and governed by the educated and cultured classes. It has already been remarked that this conviction on Sieyes's part was entirely philosophical and abstract, and that it was sharply at odds with the actual organization of productive activity in his time. But if Sieyes sincerely held this conviction, it was not contradictory for him to believe that those who incarnated the active soul of national work were also the natural representatives of the productive nation. The contradiction only appears when one recognizes that the "available classes" of late-eighteenth-century France were usually rentiers rather than entrepreneurs. Sieyes never avowed this difficulty, although he more than once came close to recognizing it in his notes. The contradiction within the text of *What Is the Third Estate?* remains real, but it may not have been recognized consciously by Sieyes.

But if Sieyes had illusions that hid from him the contradictions in his own arguments, why did others not recognize them? Once again, it is necessary to consider the readers of the pamphlet, as well as its author. For Sieyes's readers, and possibly for Sieyes himself, I believe that the nonrecognition of this contradiction probably arose at least as much from the common sense of the Old Regime as from Enlightenment philosophical ideas. The notion that the Third Estate produced all the society's wealth was hardly an invention of Sieyes or of other revolutionary pamphleteers. It was a commonplace of traditional aristocratic discourse of the Old Regime. Defenders of the old order—for example, the Parlement of Paris, in its celebrated remonstrances against Turgot's reforms in 1776—designated the production of wealth as the particular service carried out by the Third Estate. The Parlement said of the Third Estate that this "last class of the nation, which cannot render such distinguished service to the state [as that of the clergy or the nobility], fulfills its obligation through taxes, industry and physical labor."[45] As early as the twelfth century, the Latin motto of the society of three Estates had been "Oratores, Bellatores, et Lavoratores"—which means "Prayers, Fighters, and Workers."[46]

To be sure, by designating the Third Estate as those who produced goods by means of labor, the traditional ideology meant not to praise it but to disdain it. In this respect the Enlightenment carried out a major transvaluation of values. Enlightenment discourse, which, as we have seen, became increasingly dominant even among nobles in the late eighteenth century, placed utility above spirituality, which it derided as superstition, and above the sense of honor, which it viewed as the unjustified arrogance of the idle and an offense against the natural equality of men. Hence, when Sieyes wished to demonstrate that the Third Estate was everything and the nobility nothing, everyone was already willing to assume that the Third Estate was the producer of society's wealth. All he had to do was to translate this Old Regime commonplace into the language of the Enlightenment and draw from it new political conclusions. Because Sieyes did not

45. Jules Flammermont, ed., *Remontrances du Parlement de Paris au XVIIIe siècle (1715–1788)* (Paris: Imprimerie Nationale, 1888–1898), 3: 287.
46. Georges Duby, *Les Trois ordres ou l'imaginaire du féodalisme* (Paris: Gallimard, 1978).

deviate in *What Is the Third Estate?* from a centuries-old identification between the Third Estate and productive work, his readers were prepared to assume uncritically that all members of the Third Estate by definition represented such work.

For this reason, the "available classes of the Third Estate" were by definition producers, even if they were actually rich rentiers who did not differ significantly in their economic functions from most nobles. They were, so to speak, "classificatory producers," while nobles who lived in identical economic conditions were "classificatory idlers." Here the fictions of the traditional discourse of the three Estates had already obscured, perhaps in the mind of Sieyes as much as in that of his readers, the broad identity of material interests, of manner of life, and even of philosophical opinions between rich noble proprietors and rich non-noble proprietors toward the end of the eighteenth century. It is a delicious irony that the rhetorical power of a pamphlet that did so much to annihilate the distinction between the three estates depended heavily on traditional rhetorical assumptions that had justified that very distinction.

6

AN UNCONTROLLABLE REVOLUTION

W*HAT IS THE THIRD ESTATE?* DID MUCH TO SET THE tone and direction of the French Revolution in the fateful year of 1789, but its author could hardly control the Revolution's course over the longer run. In his pamphlet, Sieyes succeeded in scripting both the triumph of the National Assembly on 17 June and its radical abolition of privileges on 4 August. He did this by joining a rhetoric of political revolution that pointed toward a seizure of power by the delegates of the Third Estate with a rhetoric of social revolution that inflamed bourgeois resentment against the aristocracy. From August 1789 forward, however, the Revolution veered increasingly out of his control. There was, to be sure, much in the constitutional work of the National Assembly that Sieyes not only supported but influenced. His ideas were significantly reflected in the Declaration of the Rights of Man and Citizen, the administrative reorganization of the country, the civil constitution of the clergy, and the distinction between active and passive citizens that was written into the Constitution of 1791. But in spite of his continuing influence on certain constitutional issues, the political culture of the Revolution developed in directions that Sieyes found antipathetic.

A Failed Bourgeois Vision?

The abbé Sieyes gained his initial fame by expressing in a novel and brilliantly conceived rhetoric the aspirations and resentments of the French bourgeoisie—the diverse class of well-to-do officials, merchants, lawyers, professionals, rentiers, men of letters, and land-owners who made up the politicized segment of the Third Estate. By simultaneously telling them that they were the real leaders of the nation and reminding them of the countless petty humiliations they had suffered at the hands of aristocrats, Sieyes harnessed the energies of the bourgeoisie to a project of political and social revolution—a project that triumphed in the summer of 1789, when the deputies of the Third Estate declared themselves the National Assembly, abolished the privileges of the aristocracy, and laid the foundations of a new social and political order based on the sovereignty of the nation and equality before the law. In *What Is the Third Estate?* Sieyes represented the bourgeoisie to itself as a class of producers, whose useful private and public activities assured the prosperity of the country. It was this quality that set the bourgeoisie off from the nobility, whom Sieyes's rhetoric banished from the nation as a class of idlers and parasites. To judge from the extraordinary reception of the pamphlet, the politically active segments of the French bourgeoisie passionately embraced a self-definition that drew its fundamental terms from a political-economic view of the human condition.

But bourgeois acceptance of the discourse of political economy turned out to be provisional. In the context of a political struggle against the nobility, political economy supplied a perfect argument. The opening chapters of *What Is the Third Estate?* used the language of political economy to transform the Third Estate from the lowliest of the three orders that made up the kingdom into the whole of the nation—and to transform the nobility from superiors deserving deference to parasites and enemies. Political economy provided a language of exclusion that severed the nobility from the body of the nation, thereby avenging the thousands of petty acts by which the nobles had previously excluded the bourgeoisie from its rightful place of honor. But when Sieyes moved from this negative usage of political economy as a language of exclusion to a positive portrayal of the social order as an association for the creation of wealth, he was unable to win general assent for his arguments.

Sieyes had what was perhaps the most thoroughly "bourgeois" vision of any of the great revolutionaries. He broke thoroughly and explicitly not only with the aristocratic view that men of superior breeding and ancient family traditions should govern the state, but with the classical Greek and Roman model of civic simplicity and military virtue. He believed that the modern states of Europe had abandoned such archaic notions and had embraced instead the peaceful pursuit of material well-being. He celebrated the growing complexity of society as the most potent source of prosperity and liberty and fashioned a theory of representative government based on these "modern" trends. He advocated administrative and juridical reforms that would abolish all forms of legal privilege and open to merit all careers in public service. He elaborated a political and social theory that cast the elites of the former Third Estate as the prime movers of economic activity, public reason, and social well-being. And he enunciated a theory of political representation meant to ensure that these elites would maintain a firm grip on state power.

There are reasons to think that this vision should have been widely attractive to the French bourgeoisie. As Colin Jones has recently reminded us, France at the end of the eighteenth century was a highly commercialized society. [1] It had experienced a substantial increase in wealth and trade over the past three-quarters of a century, and its people, particularly its well-to-do urban dwellers, had developed an expanding taste for a whole range of consumer goods: clocks, books, coffee, sugar, chocolate, furniture, cutlery, glassware, textiles, and minor luxuries of all kinds. Manufactures, commerce, and public and private services had all expanded impressively, opening ever greater opportunities for those with the requisite wealth or education to make profitable employment of their capital and talent. Sieyes's political and social vision would seem to have been perfectly calculated to win an enduring endorsement from the bourgeoisie of late-eighteenth-century France.

In fact, the new constitutional order elaborated between the summer of 1789 and the summer of 1791 seems on the whole to have been consonant with Sieyes's views. The Assembly dismantled privileges and venal offices, decreed that careers in public service were open to talent, abolished guilds, established a unified market, made the first steps toward a new uniform legal code, replaced the provinces with uniform departments, made priests into public function-

1. Colin Jones, "Bourgeois Revolution Revivified: 1789 and Social Change," in *Rewriting the French Revolution,* ed. Colin Lucas (Oxford: Oxford University Press, 1991), pp. 69–118.

aries, and established an electoral system that distinguished between active and passive citizens and assured that only members of what Sieyes called the available classes could be elected to the Legislative Assembly. It is true that many of Sieyes's pet projects were rejected: the National Assembly chose another's draft of the Declaration of the Rights of Man and Citizen, seized the lands of the church over his protests, overwhelmingly rejected his position on the royal veto, modified his scheme for the establishment of geometrically uniform departments, and never seriously considered the establishment of tributes of electors and eligibles. Nevertheless, the constitutional and legislative work of the National Assembly not only was consistent with the general outlines of Sieyes's vision but was profoundly influenced by many of his specific proposals.

It was only in the following years, when France was wracked by war on the frontiers, the overthrow of the monarchy, and the onset of violent civil strife, that the revolution diverged sharply from Sieyes's "bourgeois" ideals. This was in part, as Soboul (and before him Mathiez) insisted, a consequence of the alliance between the Jacobin faction in the National Convention and the Parisian *sans-culottes,* who campaigned openly for direct democracy and for the reimposition of controls on the economy.[2] But only in part. The bourgeois deputies associated with the Jacobin factions diverged from Sieyes's vision not only by reimposing economic controls but by passionately embracing classical Greek and Roman notions of virtue. The values of classical republicanism had been prevalent in French and European political culture well before 1789 and had constituted a major theme in political debate during the early years of the Revolution.[3] But it was only from 1792 forward that the passion for classical republicanism became hegemonic in the political culture of the French Revolution. This passion was hardly imposed on the Jacobins by the *sans-culottes;* it was, rather, a specialty of the classically educated bourgeois Jac-

2. Soboul, *Les Sans-Culottes parisiens;* Albert Mathiez, *La Vie chère et le mouvement social sous la terreur* (Paris: Payot, 1927).
3. See, e.g., Baker, *Inventing the French Revolution,* esp. "A Script for the French Revolution: The Political Consciousness of the Abbé Mably," chap. 4, pp. 86–106, and "A Classical Republican in Eighteenth-Century Bordeaux: Guillaume-Joseph Saige," chap. 6, pp. 128–52; and J. G. A. Pocock, *The Machiavellian Moment* (Princeton: Princeton University Press, 1975).

obins. As the storms engulfing the Republic intensified in 1792 and 1793, left-wing orators and publicists styled themselves tribunes and invoked Solon, Pericles, Brutus, Cato, the Gracchi, and Caesar; they imagined their Republic as a modern replica of Roman history. This classicizing mode, moreover, outlasted the Terror and even the Republic: Napoleon, after all, made himself a modern Caesar, replacing the Republic with an Empire in 1804 and administering its provinces with prefects.

Karl Marx, in *The Eighteenth Brumaire of Louis Bonaparte*, wrote astutely about the revolutionaries' obsession with Rome, which he saw as a mask hiding from them their tawdry bourgeois objectives— "releasing and setting up modern *bourgeois* society," which would be "wholly absorbed in the production of wealth and in the peaceful struggle of competition." The "classically austere traditions of the Roman republic," he went on, provided the revolutionaries with "the self-deceptions that they needed in order to conceal from themselves the bourgeois limitations of the content of their struggles and to keep their passion at the height of the great historical tragedy."[4] Although I think Marx's interpretation gets at some of the attraction of the classical model, it cannot be accepted whole. During the relative calm of 1789 to 1791, the revolutionaries needed no self-deception to mask their establishment of the legal conditions for capitalist enterprise. They promulgated revolutionary transformations of the nation's administrative, constitutional, and juridical structures under the banner of enlightened reason, efficiency, and natural law, without significant recourse to Roman and Greek masks.

But when the affairs of the Revolution grew desperate, when the very survival of the Revolution was threatened by external war and internal revolts and the legislature was faced with the awful task of trying and executing the king for treason, the language of political economy—indeed, the language of Enlightenment rationalism more generally—no longer sufficed. Political economy, whose leading advocate in the French Revolution was Sieyes, lacked a heroic vision. Political economy had been developed to explain the peaceful arts of production and exchange; it extolled efficiency, self-interest, and the

---

4. Karl Marx, *The Eighteenth Brumaire of Louis Bonaparte* (New York: International Publishers, n.d.), p. 14.

rational division of labor, rather than virtue, solidarity, and selfless sacrifice for the common good. It assumed a bland linear narrative of gradual and anonymous improvement rather than a perilous narrative of danger, heroism, tragedy, and triumph. Political economy provided a plausible language for thinking about juridical and constitutional relations among citizens—not about fateful decisions or struggles to the death. Classical antiquity, by contrast, offered a host of heroes and tragic plots—and, given the dominance of the classics in contemporary education, heroes and plots intimately familiar to the revolutionary politicians. Faced with genuinely herculean tasks and historic decisions, it is not surprising that revolutionary actors identified themselves and their times with Greek and Roman history. Although I do not agree with Marx that the bourgeois revolutionary leadership needed classical draping to conceal from themselves their establishment of a social and juridical order consistent with a capitalist economy, their classical obsessions did serve to "keep their passion at the height of the great historical tragedy" during the most desperate moments of the Revolution.

Marx saw the recourse to classical models as the choice of an imaginary but heroic vision over a humdrum but accurate recognition of the Revolution's real tasks, which were to erect a state apparatus and legal system appropriate to a rising "bourgeois" social and economic order. Yet it is far from obvious that Sieyes's political-economic view of the Revolution and its tasks was any more realistic than the revolution's Roman drapery. Because capitalism and political economy triumphed in the nineteenth century, we tend to credit the eighteenth-century inventors of political economy with a realism far in advance of the aims of their contemporaries, who were steeped in classical rhetoric, utopian longings, or aristocratic fantasies and failed to see with steely clarity the actual historical trends of their time. But this assumption is dangerously anachronistic. Political economy was a visionary enterprise, not the product of painstaking empirical investigations into the workings of the economy. Adam Smith, for example, was an absent-minded professor whose lack of touch with the daily world was legendary; his distracted unconcern for quotidian problems casts some doubt on the assumption that his system was especially realistic. Moreover, the highly deductive, logical, and closed character of his doctrine bears the marks of a totalizing philosophical vision, not of a down-to-earth empiricism.

Whatever we may think about Smith, Sieyes is certainly an odd candidate for the mantle of "worldly philosopher."[5] After all, he had been a sickly and scholarly child who spent his entire youth in the seminary of Saint-Sulpice and lived out his prerevolutionary adult years in the clergy. In the seminary he rebelled against ecclesiastical discipline not by indulging in the fleshly pleasures of Paris but by reading incessantly in the texts of the philosophes and scribbling reams of notes. Throughout his life he remained an aloof intellectual, a spinner of systems and ideal constitutions. He was taciturn and solitary; his friends were few and his favorite occupation was reading. He had no firsthand experience of day-to-day economic life and little empirical curiosity about commercial and industrial matters. His view of political economy was drawn entirely from the texts of economic philosophers, both the French Physiocrats and the Scottish political economists. We have seen that some of his ideas about his country's economy were absurdly inaccurate. He imagined that a small intellectual elite organized and set in motion French economic activity, when both entrepreneurship and technical knowledge were actually the province of artisans and peasants—whom Sieyes dismissed as ignorant and passive working machines. His cognitive map of the French economy was logical, but it was also delusionary. Sieyes was nothing if not a visionary, and he was at his most visionary, not his most realistic, when he thought about economic questions.

The French bourgeoisie at large and the bourgeois political activists who manned the revolutionary legislative bodies may therefore be excused for failing to recognize themselves consistently in the mirror held up to them by Sieyes. He certainly shared important motivations and worries with his bourgeois contemporaries. Both his

5. I take the expression from Robert L. Heilbroner's *The Worldly Philosophers: The Lives, Times and Ideas of the Great Economic Thinkers* (New York: Simon and Schuster, 1961). Heilbroner's discussion of Smith seems to me quite contradictory. On the one hand he paints a portrait of the philosopher as an extraordinary eccentric oblivious to the surrounding world and given to fits of abstraction; on the other, he portrays Smith's theory as an accurate representation of the eighteenth-century English economy as it really was. Heilbroner never asks how so removed a philosopher achieved such a mimetic representation of the real world (pp. 28–57).

resentment against the aristocracy and his profound antipathy toward urban and rural laboring people struck responsive chords. The National Assembly did abolish the privileges of the nobility and adopt Sieyes's distinction between active and passive citizens and a pyramidal system of electoral filtering. But neither the National Assembly, nor the Convention, nor any other of the revolutionary legislative bodies embraced his ideas about representation and division of labor. Like all political actors everywhere, they had a choice not between an imaginary and a real political project, but between alternative imaginative constructions of the social and political world. It should not be surprising that the French revolutionaries eventually preferred a Romanizing vision, which drew on images familiar since their school days, to the novel and idiosyncratic political-economic vision of the abbé Sieyes.

Nor should it be a surprise that the French bourgeoisie of the Old Regime, dominated as it was by rent-taking property owners, professionals, and state officials, was ultimately unmoved by a social and political vision based on the primacy of production. Sieyes may have contributed much to the launching of a bourgeois revolution, a revolution spearheaded by the well-to-do elite of the Third Estate. But this bourgeoisie was not the entrepreneurial class imagined by either Marx or Sieyes, and its identity as producers was neither deep nor lasting. This self-definition faded after 4 August 1789, when the privileges of the aristocracy were annihilated. From that point forward, a rhetoric that excluded idlers from members of the nation not only lost much of its utility for the bourgeoisie but might even have proved dangerous to the bourgeois rentiers who made up the most "available" of "the available classes." The politicized elements of the bourgeoisie accepted Sieyes's productivist vision only provisionally, as a language of exclusion that served them in a particular political and social struggle, not as a fundamental and enduring identity.

Limiting the People/Limiting Representatives

We have seen that in spite of the violently democratic rhetoric of *What Is the Third Estate?* Sieyes profoundly distrusted the people and was an advocate of government by expert representatives who would deliberate rationally and choose the wisest course on the people's behalf. In his political imagination, ordinary people were far too "absorbed" by the production and exchange of goods to concern themselves with politics. But the French Revolution proved this judgment to be wishful thinking. The storming of the Bastille on 14 July 1789, the widespread peasant insurrections of that July and August, and the popular insurrection of the "October days," in which the Parisian National Guard forced the king to change his residence from Versailles to Paris, showed that many of the "little people" were not only passionately involved in politics but ready to act on their own behalf rather than respectfully waiting for action by their representatives. Sieyes never reconciled himself to this recurring popular activism, even though the crowds and the political clubs often justified their actions as defensive measures against aristocrats and denounced their enemies in language that echoed *What Is the Third Estate?* When other revolutionary politicians sought to influence the popular movement—for example, by participating in the debates of the Jacobin club, which admitted the public to the galleries—Sieyes restricted his political activity to the committees and debates of the National Assembly. After all, according to his theory of representation, the Assembly already had full authority to decide on behalf of the people and should use its own reason to deliberate about the nation's problems and enact a constitution and laws. Further consultation of the people's will, such as that supposedly taking place among the Jacobins, was not only unnecessary but potentially dangerous.

Even within the Assembly, and after 1792 within the National Convention, Sieyes was frequently out of step. He might be able to convince his fellow legislators to adopt specific reforms—clearly he had an important influence within the Constitutional Committee in 1789 and 1790—but he could not persuade them of his fundamental views about the "representative order" in state and society. If ordinary people failed to conform to his notion that they were too absorbed with production and consumption to care about politics, his fellow representatives refused to understand that they were the specialized deputies of a modern European country, whose very existence as deputies arose from the division of labor and who were commissioned to will on the nation's behalf without continuously consulting the people—or those who usurped the legislators' rightful functions by claiming to speak for the people. Sieyes attempted more than once to convince the legislators of what seemed to him this evident truth— for example, in his speech on the royal veto or the Constitution of the Year III, or in his pamphlet "On the New Organization of France." But his arguments fell on deaf ears. Not only did men and women of the popular classes continue to express their will directly even when they had legitimate representatives to make political decisions, but the representatives themselves misunderstood the basis of their own authority. Under these circumstances, it is no wonder that Sieyes became increasingly alienated from the majority in the revolutionary legislatures, or that his fellow deputies increasingly viewed him as something of a brilliant crank.

Although Sieyes continued to argue for the principle of representation, the constitutional proposals he made later in his career betray an increasing distrust of the judgment of representatives. In *What Is the Third Estate?* he confidently assumed that a single, unified body— the elected deputies of the Third Estate—should assume full power to represent the people. He also opposed the Anglophiles in the National Assembly, who wished to break up legislative power by imitating the bicameral legislature of the English. But the Terror made him rethink the wisdom of undivided legislative power, which he felt had contributed to the tyranny of the Convention's Committee of Public Safety. He became a convinced convert to the doctrine of the separation and balance of powers. In his speech on the proposed Constitution of the Year III, Sieyes called for dividing legislative authority among four different bodies. He proposed establishing a Tribunate, numbering three representatives for each of the nation's eighty-three departments, which was to watch over the needs of the people and propose to the legislature any law it judged useful.[6] There would also be a Government of seven members, which was to execute the law but which would also have the power of proposing legislation. The proposals made by the Tribunate and Government would be pronounced upon by a very large Legislature, composed of nine members from each department. The Legislature would have no right to propose legislation on its own—only to accept or turn

6. By using the Roman term Tribunate, Sieyes himself partook of the classicizing fashion of contemporary politics.

down proposals made by the Government or the Tribunate. Finally, there would be a Constitutional Jury of about a hundred that would judge claims about the constitutionality of laws adopted by the Legislature.[7]

Although the Convention brushed aside Sieyes's proposals, the constitution it adopted in the year III did establish a bicameral legislature and a five-member Directory to serve as a government. Sieyes, however, regarded the new constitution as a monstrosity. He got his chance to forge a basic law more to his liking in 1799, when he joined with Napoleon Bonaparte in a coup d'état against the Directory. The Constitution of the Year VII, which followed the coup, was written primarily by Sieyes, although it included important emendations by Bonaparte. This constitution took extraordinary measures both to blunt the impact of popular participation and to limit the will of the representatives by carefully separating their functions.[8] As in Sieyes's proposals of the Year III, lawmaking power was divided among four authorities, now called the Tribunate, the Legislative Body, the Conservative Senate, and the Government. Once again, the Legislative Body was essentially mute, empowered only to enact or reject laws proposed to it by the Tribunate or Government. The Conservative Senate served as a "constitutional jury," deciding upon the constitutionality of laws appealed to it by the Government or Tribunate. But the Senate, whose members served life terms and were ineligible for any other office, also chose all the other major public officials—the legislators, tribunes, consuls, senators, and judges—from the "national list," the product of a three-stage process of electoral filtering that simultaneously extended the suffrage to all adult males and deprived the populace of any real choice of representatives. Rather than voting directly for representatives or for electors who would vote on their behalf, the citizens of each commune merely selected one-tenth of their number as the communal list, from whose members the communal officials were to be chosen by the government. The members of the communal list

7. Sieyes, *Opinion de Sieyes*, pp. 22–23.
8. This constitution is available in Jacques Godechot, ed., *Les Constitutions de la France depuis 1789* (Paris: Garnier-Flammarion, 1970), pp. 151–62. Godechot discusses the political and historical context of its composition on pp. 143–50.

then chose a tenth of their number, who made up a departmental list from which departmental officials could be chosen. The members of the departmental lists, finally, chose a tenth of their numbers to form the national list, from which the Senate chose national officials. This system effectively removed popular participation from politics.

The Senate, to which the constitution gave the real powers of election of national officials, was to be chosen by cooptation. Sieyes and Roger Ducos, one of his co-conspirators, were named to the Senate by the constitution. Together with the Second and Third Consuls Cambacérès and Lebrun, they were to name a majority of the sixty senators, who would then choose the remaining thirty. Under the Constitution of the Year VII, Sieyes seemed to have gained a position of enormous influence. But real authority immediately gravitated to Napoleon, who was named First Consul and saw to it that the constitution gave him broad governmental powers. Sieyes's complicated, fine-tuned constitutional mechanism soon proved to be largely irrelevant to the government of the country, as the First Consul and his ministers exercised power with little interference on the part of the various legislative bodies. Two years later, in 1802, Napoleon had himself named Consul for Life and imposed a new constitution; in 1804 the republic was officially transformed into an empire, and Napoleon became emperor of France.

The history of Sieyes's constitutional proposals is a measure of his growing disillusionment. In *What Is the Third Estate?* he assumed that the representatives of the Third Estate, who had been chosen by an extremely wide suffrage, would be competent to guide the destinies of the people. But his proposals for pyramidal suffrage requirements for the new constitution, which were made in the summer of 1789, indicate that he preferred to entrust the power to elect legislators to a moral, economic, and social elite. Once a legislative body was elected, however, Sieyes wished to entrust to it full powers of government. By 1795, his distrust of the people extended to the supposedly rational elite they had chosen as their governors, and he tried to divide powers into four distinct bodies, none of which would be able to establish a tyranny over the state. Finally, in 1799, he supported a military coup that purged the legislature, placed himself in the Senate with the power to nominate the rest of that body, divided legislative power so minutely that it effectively ceased to exist, and removed the people's right to choose their own representatives even indirectly. By 1799 he clearly had lost all faith in the wisdom of representatives and made one last doomed attempt to repair the deficiency of their reason by imposing the perfect mechanism to produce wise law even from untrustworthy representatives. Within a few months even this last project had failed, and France became an enlightened dictatorship ruled by a general-emperor. Napoleon eventually rewarded Sieyes by naming him a count of the empire. It was, hence, from the ironic elevation of a new but powerless aristocracy that an aging Sieyes contemplated the ruins of his schemes.

It is this Sieyes, the brilliant but disillusioned would-be architect of human happiness, whom the painter David captured in the portrait reproduced on the cover of this book. The portrait was actually made in Brussels, where they were both exiled as regicides by the restored Bourbons after 1815. Although Sieyes, by the time of the sitting, was nearly seventy, the portrait depicts him as a member of the National Convention, when he was still in his forties.[9] But David retrospectively endowed Sieyes with the knowledge he gained from the experiences of subsequent years. David's Sieyes looks out at the viewer with a rueful and weary expression that he doubtless wore as an aged exile in Brussels. This was the wise but defeated visionary, a man who had both opened and closed the French Revolution, but who had learned through bitter experience that his genius could not contain its powerful dynamics.

9. Bredin, *Sieyès*, p. 524.

EPILOGUE: THE PARADOXICAL HISTORY OF

SIEYES'S RHETORICAL DEVICES

ABOOK ON THE RHETORIC OF *WHAT IS THE THIRD ES-tate?* can hardly end on such a negative note. It is true that Sieyes failed to institute the sort of bourgeois revolution he had hoped for: the French revolutionaries did not establish a "representative order" devoted to the peaceful pursuit of material comfort and led by specialized elites. So far as we can reconstruct Sieyes's political intentions, they were largely unfulfilled. But the failure— or, more precisely, the only partial success—of Sieyes's intentional projects hardly exhausts the effects of his political rhetoric. For if his positive rhetoric of division of labor and representation was ignored, the exclusionary rhetoric of anti-aristocratic social revolution was taken up very widely and sustained, in varying forms, over a long period. The literary devices that characterized Sieyes's rhetoric of social revolution quickly became standard elements in a revolutionary rhetorical lexicon. His language, it seems fair to say, had much more enduring and powerful effects on French political culture than did his intentions. The effects, however, were ironic: Sieyes's rhetoric was soon used primarily against the very classes he had meant to empower and the very political positions he had meant to support.

Consider the fate of the terms "aristocrat" and "privilege." Sieyes, as we have seen, established a fundamental opposition between aristocrat and nation, one that excluded the aristocracy from membership in the nation. The use of the term "aristocrat" as a means of exclusion was one of the most distinctive rhetorical developments of French revolutionary political language. "Aristocrat" turned out to be an extraordinarily labile term in the revolutionary lexicon. Its initial use to designate former nobles was quickly surpassed; any and all enemies of the nation, which in practice meant one's political opponents, were branded aristocrats. Whatever misfortune befell the Revolution—everything from food shortages to resistance to new laws to military defeats—was consequently attributed darkly to an "aristocratic plot." This usage is exemplified by the rhetoric of Robespierre, who denounced as aristocrats not only his enemies on the right, who were calling for a relaxation of the Terror, but also his enemies on the left, who were calling for renewed attacks on the church and the rich and engaging in what he regarded as an excess of democratic zeal: "And so the aristocracy establishes itself in popular societies; counter-revolutionary pride hides its plots and its daggers beneath rags; fanaticism smashes its own altars; . . . the nobility, overwhelmed with memories, tenderly embraces equality in order to smother it."[1]

Although Sieyes certainly played an important role in establishing the aristocrat as the supreme enemy of the people, anti-aristocratic rhetoric was very widespread in political writing and speech as early as 1788; one can hardly attribute to *What Is the Third Estate?* the subsequent inflation of the term "aristocrat" to cover all political enemies. But the specific anti-aristocratic rhetorical devices that Sieyes developed in his pamphlet also proved extremely labile and expansive. *What Is the Third Estate?* was distinctive because Sieyes used political economy to define aristocrats: in his usage, aristocrats made themselves enemies of the nation by their legal privileges and by their idleness. He established a basic equivalence of aristocracy, idleness, and privilege and set this triad in opposition to the working nation. These identities and oppositions were taken up by the *sans-culottes* in 1792 and 1793. But the *sans-culotte* movement, which was supported above all by the petite bourgeoisie and the poorer classes of

1. Maximilien Robespierre, "Sur les principes de morale politique qui doivent guider la Convention nationale dans l'administration intérieur de la République," in *Oeuvres de Maximilien Robespierre,* ed. Marc Bouloiseau and Albert Soboul (Paris: Presses Universitaires de France, 1967), 10:361. An English translation is Maximilien Robespierre, "Report on the Principles of Political Morality," in *The Ninth of Thermidor: The Fall of Robespierre,* ed. Richard T. Bienvenu (Oxford: Oxford University Press, 1969), p. 43.

Paris, redefined the social referents of the terms. For the *sans-culottes*, only the poor people who worked with their hands to produce subsistence were members of the nation; the rich, by contrast, were by definition aristocrats and idlers—and enemies of the nation.[2] The *sans-culottes* also groped toward a redefinition of privilege as wealth. Thus, a *sans-culotte* petition of 1793 could say: "It is an evident verity that the Nation is *sans-culotte* and that the small number of those who have all the riches in their hands are not the nation; that they are nothing but Privileged Persons, who are reaching the end of their privileges."[3] The *sans-culottes* excluded from the nation the most wealthy and leisured of the bourgeoisie, the "available classes" that Sieyes envisaged as the natural leaders of France.

This same set of linguistic identities and oppositions was subsequently taken up by French socialist writers of the 1820s, 1830s, and 1840s, but once again with changed definitions of the key terms. In socialist discourse, the aristocrat/nation dichotomy separated bourgeois, who owned the means of production, from proletarians, who, having no property, had to work for wages. According to socialist discourse, the "bourgeois aristocracy" of the nineteenth century was not productive; it lived on the labor of the proletariat. And its idleness stemmed from a privilege—ownership of property, which was protected by bourgeois legal codes.[4] By shifting the definition of the privileged aristocratic idler—from the nobility to the rich to owners of the means of production—later French revolutionaries transformed Sieyes's language from a justification to a denunciation of bourgeois social and political hegemony.

Just as *sans-culottes* and socialists continued to use Sieyes's distinction between producers and idlers, they also continued to employ his literary devices to illustrate the distinction. Thus, the *sans-culottes* could brand the rich as "vampires of the *Patrie*,"[5] and socialists routinely denounced bourgeois as "parasites." One literary device that became particularly prominent in socialist discourse was Sieyes's thought experiment of imagining a sudden disappearance of the

2. Albert Soboul, *The Parisian Sans-Culottes*, pp. 22–23.
3. Walter Markov and Albert Soboul, *Die Sansculotten von Paris: Dokumenten zur Geschichte der Volksbewegung, 1793–1794* (Berlin, 1957), 176.
4. William H. Sewell, Jr., *Work and Revolution in France*, esp. pp. 199–201.
5. Markov and Soboul, *Die Sansculotten*, p. 176.

aristocracy. It will be remembered that Sieyes had written, "If the privileged order were removed, the nation would not be something less but something more," and later, "How fortunate it would be for the nation if so desirable a secession could be perpetuated!" The most celebrated socialist use of this device was by Saint-Simon in his famous parable in "The Organizer." There he asks his reader to suppose that France has suddenly lost her three thousand best scientists, artists, businessmen, craftsmen, and manufacturers. These men, he goes on,

> are, above all Frenchmen, the most useful to their country, contribute most to its glory, increasing its civilization and prosperity. The nation would become a lifeless corpse as soon as it lost them. It would immediately fall into a position of inferiority compared with the nations which it now rivals, and would continue to be inferior until this loss had been replaced, until it had grown another head. It would require at least a generation for France to repair this misfortune.

Saint-Simon then goes on to compare what would happen if instead France were

> to lose in the same day Monsieur the King's brother, Monseigneur le duc d'Angoulême, Monseigneur le duc de Berry, Monseigneur le duc d'Orléans, [and] Monseigneur le duc de Bourbon. . . . Suppose that France loses at the same time all the great officers of the royal households, all the ministers . . . all the councillors of state, all the chief magistrates, marshals, cardinals, archbishops, bishops, vicars-general, and canons, all the prefects and sub-prefects, all the civil servants and judges, and, in addition, ten thousand of the richest proprietors who live in the style of nobles.
>
> This mischance would certainly distress the French, because they are kindhearted. . . . But this loss of thirty-thousand individuals, considered to be the most important in the State, would only grieve them for purely sentimental reasons.[6]

6. Henri de Saint-Simon, *Social Organization, the Science of the Man and Other Writings*, ed. and trans. Felix Markham (New York: Harper and Row, 1964), 72–73.

Saint-Simon uses this example to demonstrate that it is *industriels* (probably best translated as "producers"), not the dignitaries of contemporary French state and society, who are genuinely valuable to the country.

As usual, this same device was also susceptible to an even more radical usage. As socialism developed in the 1840s, workers increasingly claimed the mantle of usefulness for themselves alone, reducing capitalists and great industrialists from the status of producers to that of parasites no better than landowning aristocrats. During the Revolution of 1848, a manifesto of the delegates to the Luxembourg Commission used a new and radicalized version of Sieyes's and Saint-Simon's thought experiment.

> The people, that multitude of producers whose appanage is misery, the people has only existed until today in order to procure for its exploiters, the enjoyments which it, the pariah of society, has never known.
>
> Yes, it is by its labor that the people makes the bourgeois, the proprietors, the capitalists; yes, it is the people that makes all the happy ones of the earth. . . .
>
> Suppress the producer, and you will annihilate in a single blow the bourgeois, the proprietors, the capitalists, and you will drive the State to bankruptcy.
>
> Hence, the State is the people, the producer. . . . Is it not sovereign, the producer of all riches?[7]

Another device that was taken up in the revolutionary tradition was the rhetorical question that Sieyes used as his title. For example, St. Simon's *Catéchisme des industriels* began with the question "Qu'est-ce qu'un industriel?" [What is a producer?], and Proudhon titled his most celebrated work *Qu'est-ce que la propriété?* [What is property?].[8] The young Marx and Engels, much impressed by Proudhon's book, made the connection clear. In *The Holy Family,* they wrote that "Proudhon's work: *What Is Property?* has, for the modern national

---

7. Alain Faure and Jacques Rancière, *La Parole ouvrière, 1830–1851* (Paris: Union Générale d'Editions, 1979), 305–6.

8. Henri de Saint-Simon, "Catéchisme des industriels," in *Oeuvres de Saint-Simon et d'Enfantin* (Paris, 1875), 37:3; Pierre-Joseph Proudhon, *Qu'est-ce que la propriété? Ou, recherches sur le principe du droit et du gouvernement* (Paris: Garnier-Flammarion, 1960).

economy, the same importance as the work of Sieyes: *What Is the Third Estate?*"9

Sieyes's rhetoric may also have served as a basis for a socialist theory of history. I suspect that Marx assimilated what one might call the metahistorical trope underlying his concept of social revolution from *What Is the Third Estate?* His understanding of the "bourgeois revolution," of which the French Revolution was always the paradigm, seems closely parallel to Sieyes's formulation. For Marx, the feudal aristocracy on the eve of the Revolution had become nothing but a fetter on capitalist development. And the Revolution was the political victory of a bourgeoisie that had already attained real economic superiority. Likewise, the proletarian revolution will succeed when the bourgeoisie has become "nothing" except a fetter on production and the proletariat will have become "everything"—but, to quote Sieyes rather than Marx, "an everything that is fettered and oppressed." The notion that a social revolution is the final dislodging from power of a class that has already become only a shadow was prefigured in the rhetoric of *What Is the Third Estate?* This metahistorical trope has had a deep influence not only on the thinking of revolutionaries but on historical thought as well. It served as an underlying paradigm for the classical Marxist histories of the French Revolution, including those of Georges Lefebvre and Albert Soboul. By unearthing the connection between the metahistorical tropes of Sieyes and twentieth-century historians, we have come full circle historiographically. If Sieyes appeared to Georges Lefebvre as the incarnation of the bourgeois revolution, this was largely because his own conception of the bourgeois revolution, which was inspired by Marx, was itself borrowed from *What Is the Third Estate?*

A history of Sieyes's rhetorical devices indicates something of the generative power of his rhetoric of social revolution. The metaphysical division of human society into producers and idlers, which Sieyes used to motivate a moderate and "bourgeois" French Revolution, turned out to have further revolutionary potentialities he never dreamed of. Sieyes's key terms, "nation," "aristocrat," and "idleness," are of course ambiguous: neither their relations with other terms nor

9. Karl Marx and Friedrich Engels, *The Holy Family or Critique of Critical Critique* (Moscow: Foreign Languages Publishing House, 1956), p. 46. This passage is cited by Roberto Zapperi in his preface to Sieyes, *Qu'est-ce que le tiers état?*, p. 89.

their social referents were ever securely fixed. They were from the beginning terms of assault and exclusion, part of a powerful revolutionary rhetorical figuration that, once invented, could be seized by others than its inventors. Sieyes's intention in the winter of 1788–89, as far as we can reconstruct it, seems to have been to abolish the privileges of the nobility and to establish a leisured and cultured bourgeoisie in power. But the rhetorical means he devised for this end proved to have a life of their own. They escaped his control as early as 4 August 1789 and developed for decades thereafter in ways that he surely would have found distressing. Sieyes, the enigmatic revolutionary whose schemes for representative constitutions were consistently ignored, was also the unlikely progenitor of a tradition of social revolution. This ironic outcome is emblematic at once of the profound ambivalence of the rhetoric of *What Is the Third Estate?* and of the simultaneous power and uncontrollability of all inventive political language.

BIBLIOGRAPHY

Baczko, Bronislaw. "Le Contract social des français: Sieyès et Rousseau." In *The Political Culture of the Old Regime,* edited by Keith Michael Baker. Vol. 1 of *The French Revolution and the Creation of Modern Political Culture.* Oxford: Pergamon Press, 1987–89.

Baker, Keith Michael. *Condorcet: From Natural Philosophy to Social Mathematics.* Chicago: University of Chicago Press, 1975.

———. *Inventing the French Revolution: Essays on French Political Culture in the Eighteenth Century.* Cambridge: Cambridge University Press, 1990.

———. "Sieyès." In *A Critical Dictionary of the French Revolution,* edited by François Furet and Mona Ozouf, translated by Arthur Goldhammer. Cambridge: Harvard University Press, 1989.

———. ed. *The Political Culture of the Old Regime.* Vol. 1 of *The French Revolution and the Creation of Modern Political Culture.* Oxford: Pergamon Press, 1987–89.

Bastid, Paul. *Sieyès et sa pensée.* New revised and augmented edition. Paris: Hachette, 1970.

Benrekassa, Georges. "Crise de l'ancien régime, crise des idéologies: Une année dans la vie de Sieyès." *Annales: Economies, Sociétés, Civilisations* 44 (1989): 25–46.

Besterman, Theodore, ed. *Voltaire's Correspondence.* 107 vols. Geneva: Les Délices, 1953–65.

Bien, David D. "The Army in the French Enlightenment: Reform, Reaction and Revolution." *Past and Present* 85 (1979): 68–98.

———. "Manufacturing Nobles: The Chancelleries in France to 1789." *Journal of Modern History* 61 (1989): 445–86.

———. "La Réaction aristocratique avant 1789: l'exemple de l'armée." *Annales: Economies, Sociétés, Civilisations* 29 (1974): 23–48, 505–34.

Bossenga, Gail. "City and State: An Urban Perspective on the Origins of the French Revolution." In *The Political Culture of the Old Regime,* edited by Keith Michael Baker. Vol. 1 of *The French Revolution and the Creation of Modern Political Culture.* Oxford: Pergamon Press, 1987–89.

———. *The Politics of Privilege: Old Regime and Revolution in Lille.* Cambridge: Cambridge University Press, 1991.

Bredin, Jean-Denis. *Sieyès, La clé de la révolution française.* Paris: Editions de Fallois, 1988.

Calvet, Henri. "Sieys ou Sieyes." *Annales historiques de la Révolution française* 10 (1933): 538.

Chartier, Roger. *The Cultural Origins of the French Revolution.* Durham, N.C.: Duke University Press, 1991.

Clapham, J. H. *The Abbé Sieyès: An Essay in the Politics of the French Revolution.* London: P. S. King and Son, 1912.

Clavreul, Colette. "L'Influence de la théorie d'Emmanuel Sieyès sur les origines de la représentation en droit public." Thèse de doctorat d'Etat, Université de Paris, 1986.

————. "Sieyès, Emmanuel Joseph, 1748–1836, 'Qu'est-ce que le Tiers Etat'." In *Dictionnaire des oeuvres politiques,* edited by François Châtelet, Olivier Duhamel, and Evelyne Piser. Paris: Presses Universitaires de France, 1986.

————. "Sieyès et la genèse de la représéntation moderne." *Droits: Revue française de théorie juridique* 6 (1986): 45–56.

Cobban, Alfred. *The Social Interpretation of the French Revolution.* Cambridge: Cambridge University Press, 1964.

Condorcet, Marie-Jean-Antoine-Nicolas Caritat de. "Sur l'admission des femmes au droit de cité." *Journal de la Société de 1789* 5 (3 July 1790): 139–44.

Darnton, Robert. *The Business of Enlightenment: A Publishing History of the Encyclopédie.* Cambridge: Harvard University Press, 1979.

————. *The Literary Underground of the Old Regime.* Cambridge: Harvard University Press, 1982.

de Baeque, Antoine. *Le Corps de l'histoire: Métaphores et politique (1770–1800).* Paris: Calmann-Lévy, 1993.

Derrida, Jacques. *Of Grammatology.* Baltimore: Johns Hopkins University Press, 1974.

d'Esprémesnil, Duval. *Réflexions d'un magistrat sur la question du nombre et celle de l'opinion par ordre ou par tête.* N.p., 1788.

Le Dictionnaire de Trévoux. 5 vols. Paris, 1771.

Dorigny, Marcel. "La Formation de la pensée économique de Sieyès d'après ses manuscrits (1770–1789)." *Annales Historiques de la Révolution française* 6 (1988): 17–34.

————. *Oeuvres de Sieyès.* 3 vols. Paris: EDHIS, 1989.

Duby, Georges. *Les Trois ordres ou l'imaginaire du féodalisme.* Paris: Gallimard, 1978.

Eisenstein, Elizabeth. "Who Intervened in 1788? A Commentary on *The Coming of the French Revolution.*" *American Historical Review* 70 (1965): 77–103.

Faure, Alain, and Jacques Rancière. *La Parole ouvrière, 1830–1851.* Paris: Union Générale d'Editions, 1979.

Ferguson, Adam. *An Essay on the History of Civil Society, 1767.* Edited by Duncan Forbes. Edinburgh: University of Edinburgh Press, 1966.

Flammermont, Jules, ed. *Remontrances du Parlement de Paris au XVIIIe siècle (1715–1788).* 3 vols. Paris: Imprimerie Nationale, 1888–98.

Forsythe, Murray. *Reason and Revolution: The Political Thought of the Abbé Sieyes.* Leicester: Leicester University Press, 1987.

Furet, François. "Le Catéchisme révolutionaire." *Annales: Economies, Sociétés, Civilisations* 26 (1971): 255–89.

————. *Interpreting the French Revolution,* translated by Elborg Forster. Cambridge: Cambridge University Press, 1981.

————. *Penser la Révolution française*. Paris: Gallimard, 1978.

Furet, François, and Mona Ozouf, eds. *The Transformation of Political Culture*. Vol. 3 of *The French Revolution and the Creation of Modern Political Culture*. Oxford: Pergamon Press, 1987–89.

————. eds. *A Critical Dictionary of the French Revolution*. Translated by Arthur Goldhammer. Cambridge, Mass.: Harvard University Press, 1989.

Furet, François, and Denis Richet. *La Révolution française*. 2 vols. Paris: Hachette, 1965–66.

Garrett, Mitchell B. *The Estates General of 1789: The Problems of Composition and Organization*. New York: Appleton-Century, 1935.

Gauchet, Marcel. "Rights of Man." In *A Critical Dictionary of the French Revolution*, edited by François Furet and Mona Ozouf, translated by Arthur Goldhammer. Cambridge: Harvard University Press, 1989.

Godechot, Jacques, ed. *Les Constitutions de la France depuis 1789*. Paris: Garnier-Flammarion, 1970.

Gruder, Vivian R. "A Mutation in Elite Political Culture: The French Notables and the Defense of Property and Participation, 1787." *Journal of Modern History* 56 (1984): 598–634.

Guilhaumou, Jacques. "Sieyes, lecteur critique de l'article 'Evidence' de l'*Encyclopédie* (1773)." *Recherches sur Diderot et sur l'Encyclopédie* 14 (1993): 125–44.

Halévi, Ran. "La Révolution constituante: les ambiguités politiques." In *Political Culture of the French Revolution*, edited by Colin Lucas. Vol. 2 of *The French Revolution and the Creation of Modern Political Culture*. Oxford: Pergamon Press, 1987–89.

Heilbroner, Robert L. *The Worldly Philosophers: The Lives, Times and Ideas of the Great Economic Thinkers*. New York: Simon and Schuster, 1961.

Hunt, Lynn. *The Family Romance of the French Revolution*. Berkeley: University of California Press, 1992.

————. "The National Assembly." In *The Political Culture of the Old Regime*, edited by Keith Michael Baker. Vol. 1 of *The French Revolution and the Creation of Modern Political Culture*. Oxford: Pergamon Press, 1987–89.

————. *Politics, Culture, and Class in the French Revolution*. Berkeley and Los Angeles: University of California Press, 1984.

Jameson, Fredric. *The Political Unconscious: Narrative as a Socially Symbolic Act*. Ithaca: Cornell University Press, 1981.

Jaume, Lucien. "Citoyenneté et souveraineté: le poids de l'absolutisme." In *The Political Culture of the Old Regime*, edited by Keith Michael Baker. Vol. 1 of *The French Revolution and the Creation of Modern Political Culture*. Oxford: Pergamon Press, 1987–89.

Jones, Colin. "Bourgeois Revolution Revivified: 1789 and Social Change." In *Rewriting the French Revolution*, edited by Colin Lucas. Oxford: Oxford University Press, 1991.

Kaplan, Steven L. *Adieu 89*. Paris: Fayard, 1993.

Labrousse, Ernest, et al. *Des dernier temps de l'âge seigneurial aux préludes de l'âge industriel (1660–1789)*. Vol. 2 of *Histoire économique et social de la France*. Paris: Presses Universitaires de France, 1970.

LaCapra, Dominick. *History and Criticism*. Ithaca: Cornell University Press, 1985.

————. *History, Politics, and the Novel*. Ithaca: Cornell University Press, 1987.

————. *Rethinking Intellectual History: Texts, Contexts, Language.* Ithaca: Cornell University Press, 1983.

————. *Soundings in Critical Theory.* Ithaca: Cornell University Press, 1987.

Lameth, Alexandre de. *Lettre à M. le comte de ***, Auteur d'un ouvrage intitulé le bons sens.* N.p., n.d.

Lefebvre, Georges. *The Coming of the French Revolution.* Translated by R. R. Palmer. Princeton: Princeton University Press, 1947.

————. *The French Revolution.* Translated by John Hall Stewart and James Friguglietti. 2 vols. London: Routledge and Kegan Paul, 1962–64.

————. *La Grande Peur de 1789.* Paris, 1932.

————. *The Great Fear.* Translated by Joan White, introduction by George Rudé. New York: Vintage Books, 1973.

————. *Les Paysans du nord pendant la Révolution française.* Lille, 1924. Reprinted Bari: Laterza, 1959.

————. *Quatre-vingt neuf.* Paris, 1939.

————. *Questions agraire au temps de la Terreur.* Strasbourg, 1932.

————. *La Révolution française.* Paris: Presses Universitaires de France, 1951.

————. "Sieyès." *Etudes sur la révolution française.* 2d. edition. Introduction by Albert Soboul. Paris: Presses Universitaires de France, 1963.

Levy, Darlene Gay, Harriet Branson Applewhite, and Mary Durham Johnson, *Women in Revolutionary Paris, 1789–1795.* Urbana: University of Illinois Press, 1979.

Locke, John. *Two Treatises of Government.* 2d. edition. Edited by Peter Laslett. Cambridge: Cambridge University Press, 1967.

Lucas, Colin. *Political Culture of the French Revolution.* Vol. 2 of *The French Revolution and the Creation of Modern Political Culture.* Oxford: Pergamon Press, 1987–89.

Maiz, Ramon. "Nation and Representation: E. J. Sieyes and the Theory of the State of the French Revolution." Working paper no. 18, Institut de Ciències Politiques i Socials, Barcelona.

Markov, Walter, and Albert Soboul. *Die Sansculotten von Paris: Dokumenten zur Geschichte der Volksbewegung, 1793–1794.* Berlin, 1957.

Marquant, Robert. *Les Archives Sieyès.* Paris: S.E.V.P.E.N., 1970.

Marx, Karl. *The Eighteenth Brumaire of Louis Bonaparte.* New York: International Publishers, n.d.

Marx, Karl, and Friedrich Engels. *The Holy Family or Critique of Critical Critique.* Moscow: Foreign Languages Publishing House, 1956.

Mathiez, Albert. "L'Orthographe du nom Sieys." *Annales historiques de la Révolution française* 2 (1925): 487, 583.

————. "Sieys ou Sieyes." *Annales révolutionnaire* 1 (1908): 346–47.

————. *La Vie chère et le mouvement social sous la terreur.* Paris: Payot, 1927.

Mazauric, Claude. *Sur la Révolution française.* Paris: Editions Sociales, 1970.

Mousnier, Roland. "Les Concepts d'ordres, d'états, de fidélité et de monarchie absolue en France de la fin du XVe siècle à la fin du XVIIIe siècle." *Revue historique* 502 (April–June 1972): 289–312.

Neton, Albéric. *Sieyès, d'après des documents inédits.* Paris: Perrin, 1901.

Notice sur la vie de Sieyes, membre de la première Assemblée Nationale et de la Convention. Paris, 1795.

Orr, Linda. *Headless History: Nineteenth-Century French Historiography of the Revolution.* Ithaca: Cornell University Press, 1990.

——. *Jules Michelet: Nature, History, Language.* Ithaca: Cornell University Press, 1976.

Pasquino, Pasquale. "Citoyenneté, égalité et liberté chez J.-J. Rousseau et E. Sieyès." *Cahiers Bernard Lazare* 121–22 (1988–89): 150–61.

——. "Le Concept de nation et les fondements du droit public de la Révolution: Sieyès." In *L'Héritage de la Révolution française,* edited by François Furet. Paris: Hachette, 1989.

——. "Emmanuel Sieyès, Benjamin Constant et le 'Gouvernement des Modernes': contribution à l'histoire du concept de représentation politique." *Revue française de science politique* 37 (1987): 214–29.

Pocock, J. G. A. *The Machiavellian Moment.* Princeton: Princeton University Press, 1975.

Proudhon, Pierre-Joseph. *Qu'est-ce que la propriété? Ou, recherches sur le principe du droit et du gouvernement.* Paris: Garnier-Flammarion, 1960.

Reddy, William M. *The Rise of Market Culture: The Textile Trade and French Society, 1750–1900.* Cambridge: Cambridge University Press, 1984.

Le Robert: Dictionnaire de la langue française. Paris, 1985.

Robespierre, Maximilien. "Report on the Principles of Political Morality." In *The Ninth of Thermidor: The Fall of Robespierre,* edited by Richard T. Bienvenu. Oxford: Oxford University Press, 1969.

——. "Sur les principes de morale politique qui doivent guider la Convention nationale dans l'administration intérieur de la République." In *Oeuvres de Maximilien Robespierre,* edited by Marc Bouloiseau and Albert Soboul. Paris: Presses Universitaires de France, 1967.

Roche, Daniel. *Le Siècle des lumières en province: Académies et académiciens provinciaux.* Paris and The Hague: Mouton, 1978.

Rousseau, Jean-Jacques. *The Social Contract.* Translated and with an introduction by Maurice Cranston. Harmondsworth, England: Penguin Books, 1968.

Ryan, Michael. *Marxism and Deconstruction: A Critical Articulation.* Baltimore: Johns Hopkins University Press, 1982.

Saint-Simon, Henri de. "Catéchisme des industriels." In *Oeuvres de Saint-Simon et d'Enfantin,* vol. 37. Paris, 1875.

——. *Social Organization, the Science of the Man and Other Writings.* Edited by Felix Markham. New York: Harper and Row, 1964.

Sewell, William H., Jr. "The Abbé Sieyès and the Rhetoric of Revolution." *The Consortium on Revolutionary Europe, Proceedings, 1984* (1986): 1–14.

——. "Le citoyen/la citoyenne: Activity, Passivity and the Revolutionary Concept of Citizenship." In *Political Culture of the French Revolution,* edited by Colin Lucas. Vol. 2 of *The French Revolution and the Creation of Modern Political Culture.* Oxford: Pergamon Press, 1987–89.

——. "Etat, Corps and Ordre: Some Notes on the Social Vocabulary of the French Old Regime." In *Sozialgeschichte Heute: Festschrift für Hans Rosenberg zum 70. Geburtstag,* edited by Hans-Ulrich Wehler. Göttingen, 1974.

——. "Visions of Labor: Illustrations of the Mechanical Arts before, in, and after Diderot's *Encyclopédie.*" In *Work in France: Representation, Meaning, Organization, and Practice,* edited by Steven Laurence Kaplan and Cynthia J. Koepp. Ithaca: Cornell University Press, 1986.

——. *Work and Revolution in France: The Language of Labor from the Old Regime to 1848.* Cambridge: Cambridge University Press, 1980.

Sieyès, Emmanuel-Joseph. "Des Intérêts de la Liberté dans l'état social et dans le système représentatif." *Journal d'Instruction Sociale* 2 (8 June 1793): 33–48.
———. *Dire de l'Abbé Sieyes sur la question du veto royal*. Paris: Baudouin, 1789.
———. *Ecrits politiques*. Edited by Roberto Zapperi. Paris: Editions des Archives Contemporaines, 1985.
———. *Essai sur les privilèges*. N. p., 1788.
———. *Observations sommaires sur les biens ecclésiastiques, du 10 août 1789*. Versailles: Baudoin, 1789.
———. *Observations sur le rapport du comité de Constitution, concernant la nouvelle organisation de la France*. Versailles: Baudoin, 1789.
———. *Oeuvres de Sieyès*. Edited by Marcel Dorigny. 3 vols. Paris: EDHIS, 1989.
———. *Opinion de Sieyes sur les attributions et l'organisation du Jury Constitutionnaire proposé le 2 thermidor, prononcé à la Convention le 18 du même mois, l'an 3 de la République*. Paris: Imprimerie nationale, 1795.
———. *Opinion de Sieyes, sur plusieurs articles des titres IV et V du projet de constitution, prononcé à la Convention le 9 thermidor de l'an troisième de la République*. Paris: Imprimerie nationale, 1795.
———. *Préliminaire de la constitution françoise: Reconnaissance et exposition raisonnée des droits de l'homme et du citoyen*. Paris: Baudoin, 1789.
———. *Projet d'un décret provisoire sur le clergé*. Paris: Imprimerie nationale, 1790.
———. *Quelques idées de constitution, applicables à la ville de Paris, en juillet 1789*. Versailles: Baudoin, n.d.
———. *Qu'est-ce que le Tiers état?* Critical edition with notes and introduction by Roberto Zapperi. Geneva: Librairie Droz, 1970.
———. *Qu'est-ce que le Tiers état?* Preface by Jean-Denis Bredin. Paris: Flammarion, 1988.
———. *Qu'est-ce que le Tiers état? précédé de l'Essai sur les privilèges*. Critical edition by Edme Champion. Paris, 1888. New edition with a preface by Jean Tulard. Paris: Presses Universitaires de France, 1982.
———. *Vues sur les moyens d'exécution dont les représentans de la France pourront disposer en 1789*. N. p., 1788.
———. *What Is the Third Estate?* Translated by M. Blondel, edited by S. E. Finer, introduction by Peter Campbell. London: Pall Mall Press, 1963.
Skinner, Quentin. "Meaning and Understanding in the History of Ideas." *History and Theory* 7 (1969): 3–53.
———. "Some Problems in the Analysis of Political Thought and Action." *Political Theory* 2 (1974): 277–303.
Smith, Adam. *The Wealth of Nations*. Introduction by Andrew Skinner. Harmondsworth: Penguin Books, 1982.
Soboul, Albert. *The French Revolution 1787–1799: From the Storming of the Bastille to Napoleon*. Translated by Alan Forrest and Colin Jones. London: NLB, 1974.
———. *The Parisian Sans-Culottes and the French Revolution, 1793–1794*. Translated by Gwynne Lewis. Oxford: Oxford University Press, 1964.
———. *Précis d'histoire de la Révolution française*. Paris: Editions Sociales, 1970.
———. *Les Sans-Culottes parisiens en l'an II: Mouvement populaire et gouvernement révolutionnaire, 2 juin 1793–9 thermidor an II*. Paris: Librairie Clavreuil, 1962.
Spiegel, Gabrielle M., "History, Historicism, and the Social Logic of the Text in the Middle Ages." *Speculum* 65 (1990): 59–86.

Spivak, Gayatri Chakravorty. *In Other Worlds: Essays in Cultural Politics*. New York: Routledge, 1988.

Tackett, Timothy. *Religion, Revolution, and Regional Culture in Eighteenth-Century France: The Ecclesiastical Oath of 1791*. Princeton: Princeton University Press, 1986.

Taylor, George V. "Noncapitalist Wealth and the French Revolution." *American Historical Review* 71 (1967): 469–96.

Teissier, Octave. *Documents inédits: La Jeunesse de l'abbé Sieyès*. Marseille, 1879.

Turgot, Anne-Robert-Jacques, Baron de l'Aulne, "Réflexions sur la formation et la distribution des richesses." In *Ecrits économiques*, preface by Bernard Cazes. Paris: Calmann-Levy, 1970.

Index

William H. Sewell, Jr., is Professor of Political Science
and History at the University of Chicago. He is also the
author of *Work and Revolution in France: The Language of
Labor from the Old Regime to 1848,* winner of the Herbert
Baxter Adams Prize, and *Structure and Mobility: The Men
and Women of Marseille, 1820–1870.*

Library of Congress Cataloging-in-Publication Data
Sewell, William Hamilton, 1940–
A rhetoric of bourgeois revolution : the Abbé Sieyes and
What is the Third Estate? / William H. Sewell.
p.   cm. — (Bicentennial reflections on the French
Revolution)
Includes bibliographical references.
ISBN 0-8223-1528-9. — ISBN 0-8223-1538-6 (paper)
1. Sieyès, Emmanuel Joseph, comte, 1748–1836. Qu'est-
ce que le Tiers-Etat? 2. France. Etats généraux. Tiers
Etat. 3. Social classes—France—History—18th
century. 4. France—History—Revolution, 1789–
1799. 5. France—Politics and government—1789–
1799. I. Title. II. Series.
JN2413.S5S48 1994
305.5'0944—dc20   94-16703 CIP